THE ACCOUNTING SAMPLER

An Introduction

THE ACCOUNTING SAMPLER
An Introduction

THOMAS J. BURNS

The Ohio State University

HARVEY S. HENDRICKSON

State University of New York at Buffalo

McGRAW-HILL BOOK COMPANY

*New York St. Louis San Francisco
Toronto London Sydney*

Dedicated to
Carl L. Nelson
The George O. May
Professor of Financial Accounting
Columbia University

THE ACCOUNTING SAMPLER: An Introduction

Library of Congress Catalog Card Number 67-12617

1 2 3 4 5 6 7 8 9 0 V B 7 3 2 1 0 6 9 8 7

Preface

ONE NEED NOT conduct an extensive survey of periodicals to discover that there are numerous unresolved controversies and unsolved problems in the field of accounting. Yet, an examination of elementary accounting textbooks would reveal that little attention is being devoted to these issues. This follows from the historical tendency of introductory courses, especially those at the undergraduate level, to be designed as the first in a series of accounting courses with an underlying assumption that the students who enroll in them will enroll in a second series and so on. Writers of textbooks for elementary courses tend to ignore these contemporary controversies on the grounds then that these issues will be considered in more advanced texts. Since most students in introductory accounting courses do not take additional courses, the result is that most students will never be exposed to what are some of the most significant and exciting aspects of accounting. Even those students who do go on to more advanced courses would find preliminary discussion of these issues an excellent preparation for such courses.

This collection of accounting articles, consequently, has been selected to *supplement* (but not serve as a substitute for) the first accounting textbook at either the graduate or undergraduate level. Articles have been chosen which present introductions to current controversies and unsolved problems where the coverage in most textbooks was inadequate or unrealistic.

It has been the personal experience of both editors that the use of these materials in introductory accounting classes can stimulate student interest and, thus, markedly increase the breadth, depth and realism of their understanding and their appreciation for accounting.

Accordingly, the first section was developed to provide insight into the environment of accounting. Granted that courses designed to introduce students to business no longer flourish, there is still a need to provide a better background for the study of accountancy than the perfunctory treatment that prevails in most textbooks. Support for this position is contained in both the Gordon-Howell and Pierson studies which stressed the necessity of giving more attention to the environment of business when considering approaches to analyzing it. In this section, we have reprinted the longest piece in the collection—the six-year-old *Fortune* articles that precisely and vividly convey the nature and ramification of contemporary accounting. We also include a short article by a Dutch accountant which effectively emphasizes the *economic* essence of accounting, a relationship that is neglected despite the need for understanding its importance.

The next section contains an assortment which should flesh out the financial accounting model as presented in most texts. A considerable portion of this material deals with revenues and expenses or the rudiments of the income statement; some emphasis too, is placed upon the nature of position statements. Both categories of materials extend the usual coverage of these topics.

The concluding article, "What Is a Balance Sheet?", is followed by a rejoinder, "What Is an Asset?", which is the first article in the third section. This section on valuation in accounting includes two short pieces by a Canadian on the problems of valuation and a sophisticated but easily understood article on depreciation. Two interesting newspaper articles conclude this section—one on the net worth of the major presidential candidates in the 1964 election and the other on the valuation of a professional basketball team.

The fourth section is concerned with the problems of managerial planning and control. Following a table in which costs are classified in various ways, there is an article on direct costing. The next article reconciles the economists' and accountants' approaches to costing and pricing which neither accounting nor economics textbooks attempt to do. We conclude this section with a resume of how accounting would become more useful to management. Although several articles in other sections have some emphasis on managerial accounting, we have deliberately refrained from selecting further articles on these topics since most elementary courses continue to stress financial accounting rather than managerial accounting subjects.

The next section on financial statements and analysis includes short essays on cash flow, stock dividends, extraordinary items and stock splits, as well as Dun & Bradstreet's industry ratios. The major focus here is on various views of annual reports including the opinion of a labor union leader. The section concludes with a brief essay on the important problem of knowing for whom and from whose viewpoint you are accounting. Next is a section on the "principles" of accounting beginning with a historical summary of the progress to date followed by a possible solution to these problems and concluding with a newspaper article calling for reform in this area.

The final section, entitled "The New Accounting," is concerned with the numerous developments in present-day accounting. The first two articles report how both CPAs and company accountants are expanding their duties. Following these is a short article outlining some of the effects of computers on the accounting process. The concluding article forecasts the future of the accounting profession.

Many of the articles in this collection could be read very profitably by students without subsequent class discussion. The editors have tried to provide a blend of both old and new materials. Many distinguished accounting scholars are represented; at the same time, there are included a number of pieces by non-accountants which, we believe, provide desired breadth and sometimes depth. Most of the leading accounting and business periodicals are represented and there is, we feel, an appropriate international and historical flavor to the collection. Several universities should be especially commended for the aid their faculties provided us, particularly the understanding that accounting courses even at the elementary level should not be "textbook" courses. These include: notably, the University of Minnesota, Stanford University, and of course, the State University of New York at Buffalo and The Ohio State University. Special mention should be made of the assistance furnished by Mr. Daniel L. Jensen and Professor Paul E. Fertig of The Ohio State University faculty. We are especially indebted to Dean James S. Schindler of the School of Business Administration, State University of New York at Buffalo, for his preliminary suggestions which prompted us to do this book.

This book is dedicated to our Ph.D. advisor at the University of Minnesota, currently the first George O. May Professor of Accounting at Columbia University, and a contributor of one of the articles to this collection. As a teacher, advisor, and friend, he has had a profound influence on our lives. Whatever our contributions may be to this book, the most worthwhile aspects can be traced to the influence of Professor Carl L. Nelson.

Thomas J. Burns
Harvey S. Hendrickson

Contents

The Accounting Environment

Meditations of a Student
(After Reading "The Raven")

ONCE at seven-thirty p.m., weary as the tired b.m.
Over many a punk and rotten volume of accounting lore,
There I nodded, nearly snoring, for it was so awful boring,
Sitting there so long a-poring, poring over books of yore.
" 'Tis a waste of time," I muttered, "poring over books of yore,
  Waste of time, and nothing more."

Soon a sound my ears was paining, 'twas the voice of one complaining,
Little knowledge they were gaining and it made the prof. feel sore.
"You will never get your M.A.s, if you waste your youthful heydays,
You will never be C.P.A.s, if you do not study more,
Small returns you'll get on pay-days, if you do not study more
  You'll be dubs and nothing more."

"Is it true that all the rest-er you misfits have not read Kester,
A. Lowes Dickinson, McKenzie, Finney, Jenkinson, and Ror-
em, Van Cleave, or even Pixley, and the famous L. R. Dicksee?

From *The Accounting Review,* vol. VI, no. 4 (December, 1931), p. 307. Reprinted by permission of the publisher.

All you loafers make me sick, See! for these writers I adore,
Great and famous are these writers, writers whom I do adore,
    You'll get D's, and nothing more."

"Mr. Smith, if you've read Paton, what is it, that he is great on?
What's the curious, quaint, and novel great hypostasis he stands for?
Is it not found in the saying that the balance sheet's arraying
Only two groups is displaying, only two, not three or four,
Only Equities and Assets, that makes two, not three or four?"
    Smith said "Yeah," and nothing more.

Then they came to study Canning, rather more than they were
    planning,
Mr. Brown grew thin and pallid, swamped by philosophic lore.
Long they pondered on the saying, "That there may be a prepaying
Of one's rent, there's no gainsaying, but not interest," so he swore.
" 'Tis not interest but an offset to a debt," he roundly swore,
    "Just an offset, nothing more."

Profit, Profit, thing of evil, Profit still, though from the Devil,
By the Heaven that bends above us, and the Science I adore,
Tell this soul, in search of knowledge, if you learned it when in college,
Harvard School, or Business College, what's its meaning, I implore!
Has it any earthly meaning, tell me, tell me, I implore
    Tell me that, if nothing more?

Then methought the class grew denser, Esquerre they could not censor;
Could not even think the thoughts that they had often thought before.
Cried the prof., "I swear by Heaven, you're unfit for Commerce 7
Minds of dough, you need the leaven, given you in Commerce 4 *
Little kindergarten lessons, taught to you in Commerce 4,
    You are fit for nothing more."

Is there any rhyme or reason, any truth that we can seize on,
Since the book that Fra Paciolo wrote in fourteen ninety-four,
Books we've read in great profusion, but they all, without exclusion,
Only add to our confusion, messing up accounting lore,
English, French, Italian, German, only mess accounting lore,
    So does Hatfield, only more.†

---

* An introductory course.

† EDITORS' NOTE: The accountants mentioned were among the best known writers
on accounting thirty-five years ago. The works of several are still widely read today.
Among these is John B. Canning's *The Economics of Accountancy* (The Ronald

QUESTIONS

1. What are the merits of Paton's balance sheet equation? Compare with other versions.

2. Do you agree with Canning's classification of interest? Explain.

Press Company, New York, 1929), an accounting classic. The late Professor Canning taught at Stanford University for many years. Also in this group is Mr. William A. Paton, Professor Emeritus of Accounting and Economics at the University of Michigan. In his long and notable career, the still active Professor Paton has written many influential books beginning with *Accounting Theory* (The Ronald Press Company, New York, 1922). Fra Paciolo, the author of *Summa Arithmetica* (1494), was regarded as "the greatest mathematician of his day." For further details on Paciolo, see page 36.

2

The Auditors Have Arrived

T. A. Wise

IT IS A CURIOUS and noteworthy fact that the tremendous growth of the U.S. accounting profession in the postwar years has taken place almost unnoticed by most Americans. In the same years, other proliferating white-collar types—advertising and public-relations men, union and corporation lawyers, stockbrokers, research scientists—have impinged heavily on the national consciousness; new stories about such men are often in the papers, and their prototypes appear regularly in novels and television dramas. But the rise of the accountants has occurred quietly. To most businessmen, the names of the big accounting firms are familiar, principally because of the way the names recur at the end of published annual reports; but not many businessmen know, or have even heard of, the men portrayed on the following pages, who

Reprinted from the November, 1960, and December, 1960, issues of *Fortune* Magazine by special permission; © 1960 Time, Inc. Mr. Wise is on the staff of *Fortune* Magazine.

are the senior partners of the nation's largest accounting firms. They are among the most powerful men anywhere in business today.

In a way, their anonymity is in keeping with the traditions of the profession, which have always called for a rather aloof public posture. . . . The modern auditor is . . . still unlikely to step out of the shadows very often. One reason for this reticent posture is that an auditor is privy to the secrets of many businessmen, and they naturally feel easier about this relationship if the auditor seems to be a man of reserve and discretion. Moreover, an auditor must preserve his independence in dealing with present or prospective clients. The chiefs of the profession—the leading lights of the Big Eight firms—live very much in a world of their own. Six of the eight have their main offices within a few blocks of one another in New York's Wall Street area; they see a lot of and know a lot about one another. Their firms audit about 80 per cent of all the corporations listed with the Securities and Exchange Commission. But not many line executives know how these eight men operate: how much money they make, how much their firms make, how they have been steadily taking on new functions, how they get new business, and how they have been coping with an extraordinary range of ethical and intellectual problems.

These operations do not constitute all the news about the auditors these days. The profession today is fighting a number of quiet but intense battles to clarify and make consistent the accounting principles used in the U.S. It is a truism in the profession, though it still seems a bit shocking to many businessmen, that two different accountants in possession of the same figures may construct two considerably dissimilar balance sheets. The principal issues in the battles between accountants, and the profession's prospects for resolving them, will be described later.

A few figures and definitions are in order at the outset. When some of the more prestigious members of the profession are asked whether they consider themselves auditors or accountants, they may take a deep breath and reply that they are "independent certified public accountants." On the other hand, the Census Bureau just lumps "accountants and auditors" together (there were 376,459 in the U.S. in 1950). The difference between an accountant and an auditor is a chronic source of confusion, but the operational distinction is a simple one. All accountants assist in the preparation of financial statements according to the principles they believe to be generally accepted by the profession. An audit is an *examination* of such a statement, and an auditor is simply an accountant checking the work of someone else—

often another accountant. The great majority of those listed by the Census Bureau are not recognized as accountants by the profession, and most of them are, realistically, plain bookkeepers, untrained in the many rigorous disciplines, the concepts, and the case lore of modern accountancy, and unrecognized by any state authorities. Just about 108,000 have acquired this recognition: these include the 71,000 certified public accountants in the U.S. (about 11,000 work for the Big Eight) and 37,000 who have "licenses" issued in thirty-one states to do public accounting.

Not all the C.P.A.'s have the same qualifications—these vary from state to state—but all of them have, at least, passed a rigorous examination that is given twice each year and is prepared by the American Institute of Certified Public Accountants. The examination covers accounting practice and theory, auditing, and commercial law; it is given in several installments, each of which begins at the same moment in every state, and all together it usually consumes about nineteen hours, spread over a Wednesday-to-Friday period. Before the examination, the questions are kept under close security; they are delivered in armored trucks to the examination centers and opened in the examination rooms before witnesses.

The C.P.A.'s competition is not limited to other C.P.A.'s. The 37,000 "licensed public accountants" can legally do everything the C.P.A.'s can do, even though many have not passed an examination (they got into business before enactment of the present laws regulating accounting). In nineteen states (including Massachusetts and Pennsylvania) *anyone* can call himself a public accountant—i.e., no license is issued. There are perhaps 15,000 such unlicensed, uncertified public accountants in these states and they too are entitled to do anything a C.P.A. can do.

The growth of the profession has taken place in less than a century. As recently as 1900, there were exactly 243 C.P.A.'s in the U.S., and no more than 1,000 persons employed in all the nation's accounting firms. And the rate of growth is still accelerating: the profession expects to pick up an additional 40,000-odd C.P.A.'s by 1970. Accountants' numbers and influence are increasing in other countries as well as in the U.S.; but the scope and diversity of U.S. capitalism have made this country the modern center of the profession, and the American Institute of Certified Public Accountants is always playing host to droves of visitors from Italy, Japan, Israel, and many other nations who are eager to learn how auditing, and accounting in general, are practiced here.

A Beginning in Breweries

The steadily expanding influence of the auditors derives, in general, from two sources: (1) the increasing complexity of the modern industrial world, and (2) its greater emphasis on *accountability*, meaning the need of one man to refer his actions to judgment by standards he shares with other men. The classical nineteenth-century entrepreneur had little need for an accountant in the modern sense; he was accountable to the law of the land and his own conscience, but beyond that he was the sole judge of whether his performance was meritorious. A very different situation is that of professional managers controlling the property of unknown stockholders, dealing with institutionalized creditors, and entrusted with a host of social tasks from the generation of taxable revenues to the production of essential weapons. Under these circumstances, it becomes a matter of the utmost public importance to know how the management of a public corporation is performing. Accountancy has created several concepts that are useful in evaluating these performances. "Depreciation" is one such concept, "earned surplus" is another, and "net working capital" is a third. Aside from the help such measurements give the public, it is important *within* any top management group to be able to evaluate objectively the performance of subordinates, and accountancy contributes many techniques to the discharge of this responsibility.

The accounting profession in this country can be traced back to about 1880, when some English and Scottish investors began to put their money into U.S. securities. The securities they picked were mostly brewery stocks, which were then regarded in Great Britain as the worthiest of blue chips. The investors who bought heavily into American breweries sent their own auditing firms over here to check on the health of these investments. Two members of the Big Eight, Price, Waterhouse and Peat, Marwick & Mitchell, were originally British firms that got their start in the U.S. this way. Today, of course, they are entirely American-owned but have working relationships with the British partnerships.

By the time of World War I, the ownership of public securities had become fairly widespread, and there was a growing awareness of the need for more uniformity in financial reporting. The nation's first Secretary of Commerce (in the Wilson Administration), William C. Redfield, was a businessman who had been engaged shortly before taking office in an effort to merge several companies. The merger collapsed when he realized that some of the companies involved were substantially overvalued. He discussed the generally chaotic state of financial reporting with officials of the Federal Reserve Board, and persuaded several of them to take the lead in setting down some guidelines for businessmen. In 1917, with the help of the accounting profession, the board produced a memorandum, subsequently published in booklet form, called "Approved Methods for the Preparation of Balance Sheet Statements." This booklet did a lot to systematize financial reporting, and also to make businessmen aware of the need to employ accountants who understand what was required in making reports.

The Moral of McKesson & Robbins

During the 1920's the New York Stock Exchange also boosted the accountant's business by waging a continuous campaign to get corporations to provide more financial information. In 1933, after the crash, the Exchange, with advice from the institute, initiated a whole new series of standards for the treatment of unrealized profit, capital surplus, earned surplus, and other corporate financial items. The standards were incorporated into the accounting principles approved by the American Institute of Certified Public Accountants. That same year the Exchange also began requiring of all listed corporations an audit certificate by an independent C.P.A. Both of these developments did a lot to enhance the prestige and acceptance of the independent accountant.

The sensational revelations of the McKesson & Robbins case in 1939 temporarily impaired the profession's new prestige, but in the end, by showing the need for much more careful auditing practices, the case brought the profession a great deal of new business. When it was first revealed that the head of the drug company had swindled it of millions, principally by carrying fictitious inventories on the books, it was obvious that the profession had to revise completely many of its accepted methods of verification. The SEC investigation showed that the audit of McKesson & Robbins by Price Waterhouse had "conformed . . . to what was generally considered mandatory."

While the case was still warm, the A.I.C.P.A. set up a review committee, which proposed that future audits include direct verification of inventory, by personal inspection of warehouses where that seemed necessary; direct communication between auditor and debtor on a corporation's receivables; and the selection of auditors by directors, with the approval of the stockholders, who, in addition, should be entitled to a description of the scope of the auditor's work, and to read his opinion in a separate section of the annual report.

E.P.T. Gets the Business

The profusion of taxes, and tax complications, have also accelerated the growth of the profession. Many Americans had their first contacts with accountants in the period just after 1913, the year when the first income-tax law was passed. Four years later, in 1917, the government passed its first excess-profits tax. Manufacturers now found that they had to calculate their profits in relation to the capital invested in their firms—a new and burdensome chore for many firms that had never systematically distinguished between, say, maintenance costs and new investment, and now found themselves obliged to reconstruct their books from the ground up. The first E.P.T., like those during World War II and the Korean War, generated a lot of business for the accountants.

Their tax practice is still growing. All of the Big Eight firms have tax departments staffed by anywhere between 100 and 250 specialists. Their clients today include not only corporations and wealthy individuals, but an increasing number of upper-middle-income citizens who find it necessary or convenient to pay $100 or $200 to have their accountancy chores handled by a national firm. No one knows just how many such people there are, but some accountants figure the total market for individuals at about 750,000—this being roughly the number of individuals whose taxable income is over $20,000, and who can expect that the Internal Revenue Service will probably audit their returns.

In building their tax business, the accountants have got into a battle with the legal profession. Back in 1913, lawyers generally shied away from tax work because it was highly technical and involved accounting concepts with which many of them were unfamiliar. But in the 1930's, as the tax rates mounted and tax problems entered increasingly into business and personal decisions, lawyers began to feel that they had let the accountants get too firm a hold on something good. The dispute came to a boil in 1943, when a client in New York balked at paying his accountant a $500 bill on the grounds that, in preparing his tax return, the accountant had given *legal* advice, which he was not professionally qualified to do. The accountant sued. The legal profession sensed an opportunity and the New York County Lawyers Association entered the case on behalf of the defendant. In alarm, the New

York State Society of C.P.A.'s rushed to support the plaintiff. Later, a similar case cropped up in California. In both cases the courts ruled that the accountants were illegally engaging in the practice of law.

Both professional groups felt that the dispute was unseemly. In 1957 they agreed not to engage in any more court contests on such disputes, but instead to refer any cases that came up to a special mediating committee made up of representatives of both professions. However, neither profession has yielded an inch on its own asserted right to practice in the field of taxes.

Accounting to Royal Little

In the postwar years the rise of the accountants has been accelerated by three rather special phenomena: a vast wave of corporate mergers; the need for better accounting on the financial affairs of labor unions, pension and welfare funds, foundations, and other institutions; and the push of the big auditing firms into a vast, sprawling area they call "general management services."

The first two of these new phenomena are well known. During the 1950's the number of mergers involving manufacturing companies, for example, rose from about 300 to about 500 a year. Furthermore, mergers that do not come off—that bog down over some disagreement—also represent a substantial volume of accounting business. Royal Little of Textron, Inc., has had his auditor, Arthur Young & Co., do preliminary investigations of over 100 companies during the past five years alone; only twenty-five of the companies were eventually merged into Textron.

It seems likely that the market for noncorporate accounting services will continue to be expanded. The 1959 disclosure law requires labor unions to file financial statements with the Department of Labor but does not require these to be audited unless the Secretary requests an audit. Over 50,000 unions are affected, and most of them have by now filed their statements—mostly unaudited. The value of such statements is questioned in many quarters, and eventually, it seems likely, auditing of these statements will become widespread. Auditing of the nation's 150,000 welfare and pension funds has improved considerably since the passage, in 1958, of a law which required that the funds' administrators account to the Secretary of Labor for all contributions, salaries, and fees, the rates given insurance carriers, and a variety of other data on investments and loans. Finally, there is a mounting pressure to get better audits of charitable and philanthropic funds. It was intensified by the scandal earlier this year over the finances of the

Sister Elizabeth Kenny Foundation. When this foundation's finances were first audited back in 1951, Arthur Andersen & Co. refused to certify the financial statement attached to the report because the executives did not want to disclose that it had cost $975,000 to collect $1,240,000. It later turned out that these executives had prevented the Andersen audit from reaching the foundation's board of directors. And eight more years passed before the public learned what was happening to the money it had contributed to the foundation.

Bread and Toll Booths

The "management service" business has burgeoned in the accounting profession during the past few years. Many accountants find it confusing and hard to justify, but others consider it a logical and lucrative extension of what they have been doing in the financial field all along.

In effect, the auditors are going into competition with the management consultants. The independent auditor called upon to examine a corporation's financial records often becomes aware of the full range of problems facing the company—sometimes more acutely aware than management itself. Moreover, many auditors are real experts in some fields—e.g., a man who has spent twenty years auditing department stores often knows more about merchandising than some of his clients—and it was probably inevitable that such auditors, observing the surge of business to professional management-consultant firms, would feel a desire to sell their own expertise too. Moreover, many clients of auditors were requesting their help in developing systems to keep track of affairs and of records that were growing increasingly complex.

Some of the big auditing firms have committed themselves wholeheartedly to the management-services field. Ernst & Ernst, Peat, Marwick, and Price Waterhouse have staffs of 250 in their management-service divisions, and offer clients literally any management service they want. Ernst & Ernst, for example, will tackle any assignment in labor negotiations, personnel selection (it has its own staff psychologists available for consulting), new-product planning, and factory design and layout. Recently E. & E. took on the job of working out a control system for the New York State Thruway: it determined the number of men needed to man the toll booths at the heavy traffic periods, and it set up a record system to check the number of tickets sold. Arthur Young helped Becton, Dickinson & Co., the medical-supply firm, to determine the market for a disposable surgical needle it had developed, the price the needle should sell for, and the way it should be promoted. But many big auditing firms will handle only a few kinds of management chores. Recently a bakery firm asked Lybrand, Ross to help it solve the problem of determining the optimum number of loaves to bake—i.e., so that it would not always have large amounts unsold and wasted on rainy days, and run short on sunny days. Lybrand, Ross considered the job to be primarily mathematical, and since the firm has its own research department, which is well able to apply mathematical techniques to inventory sampling and other accounting problems, it felt that it could take on the job.

An accounting firm's revenues are derived, of course, from renting out the services of its staff. Junior accountants in the big firms earn perhaps $5,500 a year, and senior accountants perhaps $7,500 to $12,500. These are the firm's "production workers" and, at the same time, its physical assets, and an idle junior or senior accountant is viewed with the same dismay a manufacturing company might view an idle plant. In general, a big firm feels that it can be profitable if its juniors and seniors are working for customers 75 per cent of the time. At this rate they would ordinarily generate revenues about two times their salaries, which would comfortably cover their own costs to the firm, and also the salaries of their superiors: the "managers" ($12,500 to $20,000), who run the offices, and the senior partners ($25,000 and up), who handle any large questions that arise with clients and in general devote most of their time to what might be called "diplomacy" —e.g., persuading clients that furniture cannot be written off in two years, or making recommendations on some other phase of the client's business, or pitching for new business.

This pitch is hampered by several kinds of restrictions. Not only is advertising unethical, but any competitive bidding is frowned on, and so is contacting a prospect without the knowledge of its incumbent auditing firm. Free-for-all competition is permissible only when a new company, which has never had an auditing firm, comes into the daylight. Then a direct approach can be made.

The elaborate procedures that surround the getting of new business can be seen in a switch in auditing firms recently made by Allied Stores, one of the nation's largest department-store chains. Several months ago, Allied broke the bad news to the firm of Touche, Ross, Bailey & Smart, that it was going to look for a new auditor. It then invited Ernst & Ernst and Arthur Andersen to visit its executive offices and make "presentations" for the account. Both auditing firms had meetings with several Allied executives in order to learn some of the particular requirements of the corporation. (As a matter of professional courtesy, Touche, Ross was kept notified of all these meetings.) Then the two firms sent delegations to Allied's offices on Fifth Avenue in New York and recited their own experience, made some promises about the time that their top men could personally give the account, and volunteered to discuss fees. The Ernst & Ernst delegation consisted of Hassel Tippit, the senior partner, and William Stowe, the head of the New York office, who would be in direct charge of the account, and several staff men; the Arthur Andersen delegation was headed by senior partner Leonard Spacek. The results of these meetings were communicated to a committee of Allied's directors, which had been appointed by the board to make a recommendation.

Ernst & Ernst had several advantages in this competition. It had been Allied's auditor back in the 1940's, and was familiar with the company. It had pioneered the development of the last-in-first-out (LIFO) method of inventory valuation in the retail field. A substantial number of its ninety-five branch offices were near Allied's eighty-five stores, and E. & E. prepared a map that brought home the point forcefully at the presentations. The next day Ernst & Ernst was told it had the job—subject, of course, to the approval of the Allied directors.

Price Cutting by Auditors

As it happened, there was no detailed discussion of fees in these negotiations; Allied simply made it clear that it expected the fees to be in the normal range. But ordinarily such presentations do include some fairly explicit talk about costs and fees. Price competition between auditors can be intense—though price cutting in order to get an account is officially deplored in the profession. Auditing firms generally calculate their fees in relation to the time they expect their personnel to be occupied on an account; but a firm with a high proportion of its junior and senior accountants idle may submit a bid well under "the normal range" just to get them working again. Al Jennings, the senior partner of Lybrand, Ross Bros., & Montgomery, recalled recently that his firm had lost a big account to another of the Big Eight, which put in a "loss-leader" bid—after it had managed to wangle an invitation to make a presentation. Firms often submit such bids in the hope that after they get a foot in the door, they can gradually expand the volume of their work and their fees.

Another large influence on the bids that auditors submit, and on their costs in handling an account, is the extent of the client's own internal controls. A sizable number of large corporations have recently been building up their internal auditing staffs, in order to maintain consistent surveillance and control over their systems and procedures, to guard against fraud, etc. This internal auditing cuts down the independent auditor's case load considerably, and huge companies like General Motors and A.T. & T., which have such internal systems, are able to hold down the fees they pay their independent accountants.

In setting his fees, the independent auditor has to make a calculation about the length of time it will take him to familiarize himself with a company. Its sales volume is only a rough guide, but its "complexity"— the number of operations it performs, the number of branches or divisions—matters considerably. Merril Lynch, Pierce, Fenner & Smith, possibly the most complex "service company" in the world, paid Haskins & Sells $164,000 last year.

In general, the auditing firm's work load is heaviest in the first year, when it is just getting to know the corporation, and some auditors expect to lose money on a big account in this year—even with normal fees. The loss should be recovered in the second year, when the work load drops by perhaps 25 per cent. In the third year, the account pulls into the black. An auditor cannot very well submit a loss-leader bid if there is any danger of his losing the account within a few years, and many auditors are chary of bidding for business where there is a tendency to rotate auditors. For many years E. I. du Pont de Nemours & Co. has been the outstanding exponent of rotation philosophy. The company used to change its auditors every three years; recently the time has been lengthened somewhat.

A Question of Rotation

The rotation problem is a delicate subject in the auditing profession. Some corporations have formal policies calling for the rotation of auditors. They believe that their stockholders are entitled to receive fresh and objective views of their financial operations, and that an old, established auditor may begin simply to take the company's practices for granted. Some companies want to be sure that the auditor's loyalty is to his own organization and not to the officials he is supposed to be reporting on, who get to be his friends after a while. Finally, there is the problem that an auditor who has worked a long time on one account may develop a kind of vested interest in not uncovering any frauds or financial irregularities—i.e., any such discovery would reflect on his own handling of the account in the past.

Auditing firms do not have, to any great extent, the problem, usually associated with the advertising business, of the partner who "controls an account" and is able to walk off with it. The rotation of auditors on an account is one obvious deterrent. Even when some partners in auditing firms develop close and friendly relationships with the executives in client firms, it is hard for the client to justify giving them the account, because stability and manpower rather than any special creative talent, are what auditing firms must primarily offer. One exception: in 1947, George Bailey, the partner in charge of the Detroit office of Ernst & Ernst, fell out with A. C. Ernst, and managed to take the Chrysler Corp. and many other clients away from the firm. Chrysler agreed to go with Bailey, but stipulated that he must have a large enough organization to service the account nationwide. Bailey then pulled together the firm of Touche, Niven, Bailey & Smart (now Touche, Ross, Bailey & Smart) today a member of the Big Eight, and still handling Chrysler's business.

How profitable are the big firms? For many big firms, in an average year, about 20 per cent of total revenues can be considered net income—i.e., it is available for distribution to the partners and for working capital. Auditing firms have one substantial expense that most other companies in "service" industries do not have. This is the cost of liability insurance—to protect the firm from any stockholder suit charging negligence in the event that a client suffers a substantial loss traceable to professional incompetence. (If such a charge were proved, the partnership would, of course, be fully liable for the entire amount.) Any of the Big Eight firms is likely to carry as much as $15 million of this insurance. (Coverage in such large amounts is offered only by Lloyds of London.) The auditing firms all prefer not to publicize the existence of this insurance on the ground that anyone contemplating a fraud is likely to be encouraged by the thought that everyone involved is insured.

The Problem of "Bigness"

What sets the Big Eight apart from most other auditing firms is not only their size and influence, but also the fact that they are national —and international—in the scope of their operations. The bulk of public accounting in the U.S. is done by 25,000-odd small, local firms. In between these and the giants are a number of well-known semi-national firms, whose senior partners are also influential in the profession. These include Seidman & Seidman, Scovell Wellington, S. D. Leidsdorf, Main & Co., Horwath & Horwath, and Alexander Grant.

Like the Big Eight, many of these firms are headquartered in New York; however, they characteristically have only a few branch offices and their gross revenues run below $10 million.

The problem of "bigness" agitates the accounting profession as much as it does many manufacturing industries. Virtually any member of the Big Eight or of the semi-national firms will say that the backbone of the profession is the small, local, independent accounting firm. Such firms still are the training grounds for the great majority of independent accountants. These firms have the great bulk of the personal tax business, and most of whatever auditing is done for the more than four million "small business" enterprises in the U.S. But these local firms have never been able to compete effectively with the national and semi-national firms for the business of big clients—e.g., those that generate over $10,000 a year in fees. The local firms face a continuing succession of tragedies as the small and medium-sized companies they have grown up with locally grow too big for them. It often happens that a local company separates from a local auditor when the company makes its first public offering of stock; at such times the underwriters are likely to insist that the prospectus bear the name of a national auditing firm—to ensure that a competent job will be done, and perhaps for reasons of prestige too.

Some small auditing firms have tried to cope with this problem by merging with other small firms. La France, Walker, Jackley & Saville, with sixty-three professional accountants, thirteen partners, and branch offices in seven cities, was formed last year in a merger of nine small firms—none of whom had more than seven professional employees before the merger. But more often the small firms are absorbed into the medium firms and the Big Eight. In July, 1959, for example, Alexander Grant merged four local firms into its organization.

Within the American Institute of Certified Public Accountants, the smaller firms have been pushing for a series of reforms that would help them to maintain their own identities and remain competitive. Many of them would like the institute's ethical code to include a ban on the vast "publishing activities" of big firms. The latter do, in fact, turn out a steady stream of booklets and magazines explaining and analyzing the operations of state tax codes, the functions of management service divisions, the problems arising out of new SEC regulations, etc. There is a vast amount of real scholarship in these publications, but the small firms feel that there is also a vast amount of promotion for their sponsors. The small firms would like the ethical code to ban the continued use of a deceased partner's name in a firm's name—i.e., they want to prevent the Big Eight from continuing to cash in on the immense prestige of some of their founders.

To help the small firms the institute is now sponsoring a professional training program designed for accountants in two-to-five-partner firms. The program includes, for example, training in the application of management services to small business. It also includes, oddly enough, a study of the special economic problems of small accounting firms—which are often considerable, principally because the partners are apt to be young and inexperienced, and trained in handling other companies' accounting problems, not their own.

The Footing Is Electronic

The widespread introduction of electronic data-processing equipment in the accounting profession recently has left some auditors with a feeling that the profession's economics are about to be transformed. E.D.P. equipment has vastly increased the efficiency of many routine operations of the big clients, especially the so-called "posting and footing" operations. (This is what the profession calls routine bookkeeping work, e.g., checking classifications.) The new equipment will increasingly cut down the proportion of junior accountants required by the big firms. Haskins & Sells, for example, used twenty juniors back in 1950 to make a headquarters audit for one of the big farm-equipment firms. In 1960 they used only seven. Seidman & Seidman reports that the ratio of junior accountants to seniors in its firm has declined by 25 per cent in the past two years. One interesting application of the use of E.D.P. by a *small* firm is provided by Young, Skutt & Breitenwischer of Jackson, Michigan. The firm was approached last year by a local manufacturer who had bought a computer and then found he could not really keep it busy. He suggested that the accountants take it off his hands, use it in their own operations, and rent it out to their clients when they were not using it. This scheme has worked out nicely so far.

The Auditing Boom in Washington

The increasing influence of accountants and auditors has not been confined to private business. Accountants are proliferating furiously in the great public bureaucracies as well, and at all levels, from the municipalities to the federal government. Auditors and accountants are the fastest growing of all occupations in the federal government; there are now 16,845. Of the FBI's some 6,000 special agents, over 700 are trained accountants. In the General Accounting Office there are 1,800 professional accountants—over 400 of these are C.P.A.'s, among them the Controller General himself.

The rise of accountants in government, as in private industry, is essentially a reflection of the endless complexity of the modern world. At many levels of government today, accountants are inextricably in-volved in the formation of policy—often because they are the only officials able to make sense of a modern government budget. Abraham Beame, the budget director of the City of New York, completely dominates many policy-making sessions of the city's Board of Estimate, principally because he is apt to be the only official present who knows what is possible within the scope of the city budget. Professor Wallace Sayre of Columbia University, who recently made a detailed study of the workings of the city government, says that Beame is "the single most powerful official in the city." At the national level, U.S. Budget Director Maurice Stans has played an important role in several major policy decisions, including a very controversial decision to cut back the B-70 program to the development of a single prototype. (Actually, Stans argued for a complete cessation of the B-70 program, but the Air Force finally got the President to agree to a prototype program.)

The whole federal system of accounting was overhauled ten years ago, with the passage of the Budget and Accounting Procedures Act of 1950. This called for much more complete disclosure of the govern-ment's financial operations, and authorized the establishment of new accounting and reporting systems for each executive agency of the government. It directed the Bureau of the Budget, the Secretary of the Treasury, and the Controller General, to conduct a joint program for the improvement of cost accounting in the government. Before 1950, federal accounting systems were dominated completely by the General Accounting Office and the Treasury Department, with the emphasis on "allotment accounting," which was designed to keep agencies' expenses and obligations under control. Few attempts were then made to use cost accounting so that agencies could present budgets that systematically related their costs to their proposed operations. The 1950 act required the Executive Department to project its requirements through the Bureau of the Budget. With the Eisenhower Administra-tion's greater emphasis on balancing the budget, the bureau's power and prestige were steadily expanded. The budget director now receives an earlier and more detailed picture of the over-all operations of the executive department than any other individual; and this fact probably made a policy role for him inevitable.

Why Auditors Are Uneasy

Many accountants and auditors, although delighted with the volume of new business and new responsibilities they have acquired during the 1950's, will confess to a kind of uneasiness about their situation. Their uneasiness stems from a feeling that the profession has not yet done a satisfactory job of resolving all the uncertainties and ambiguities as to the proper ethical conduct of auditors in situations where their private interests seem to clash with their clients'. But there is an even larger ambiguity as to what constitutes "generally accepted accounting principles." And many auditors believe that it is an urgent matter to resolve these before the profession is inundated by the load of new business it expects in the 1960's. The ambiguities are more than mere details; they are numerous and fundamental, and many auditors believe that unless they are resolved, the interpretation of many financial statements will come down to an elaborate guessing game.

"The beginning of wisdom," say the Chinese, "is to call things by their right names." The 71,000 certified public accountants in the U.S. are every year becoming more aware that finding the "right" names for business operations may be the most arduous part of the unending search for a more understandable, more rational, more honest, and more efficient business society. When the terms that measure business performance are used inflexibly, business practice may be unduly constricted, but when these terms are used too loosely, business practice may degenerate into confusion and mistrust.

At their convention in Philadelphia last September, the C.P.A.'s labored mightily to find a set of principles that would minimize both dangers. They need such principles as underpinnings for their professional code of ethics and to gain more respect for their professional independence.

One afternoon during the convention, about a thousand of the most distinguished C.P.A.'s in the U.S. gathered in the Rose Garden Room of the Bellevue-Stratford Hotel, to hear what was billed as a debate on the principles of their profession. An uninitiated visitor wandering into the room might have thought at first that they were arguing over some minor, tedious technicalities, and so might have been puzzled by the passions that were manifestly stirred up. The

C.P.A.'s themselves knew that the debate concerned a lot more than technicalities. They knew that they—the members of the American Institute of Certified Public Accountants—were in a position to influence considerably both the financial reports of companies and the business practices to which the reports refer. In recent years the A.I.C.P.A. has, in fact, become a kind of private financial legislature; working within the limits imposed by tax and securities laws, its members advise businessmen as to correct and permissible procedures to be followed in reporting their financial affairs. What now bothers many members of the profession, and what occasioned the debate, is the fact that the limits of permissibility stretch pretty far these days.

The case against flexibility was argued by Leonard Spacek, the senior partner of Arthur Andersen & Co. Spacek is regarded within the profession as something of a rebel. He knew that he was speaking to a predominantly hostile audience, and he made no attempt to conciliate it; peering sternly from the lectern through thick glasses, never smiling, never raising or lowering his voice, he set forth the case for greater uniformity in accounting procedures. His opponent and opening speaker in the debate was Maurice Peloubet, the white-haired senior partner of Pogson, Peloubet & Co., whose benign and avuncular manner contrasted sharply with Spacek's. Peloubet argued forcefully that businessmen *should* have maximum flexibility in handling their financial affairs. In the ensuing question-and-answer period Spacek promised that his fight would continue; he said that eventually he would "tear to shreds" the case for flexibility. His firm had already done a lot to arouse the profession. Currently, for example, he is circulating a booklet citing twenty different issues on which the institute's own position differs from the practice of many of its members, or on which the institute's position is unclear, or on which new financial developments have raised new questions about the institute's position.

"The Truth As It Actually Is"

The problems the profession is concerned about may be suggested, briefly at this point, by citing some figures:

* In the past nine years Texaco has reported earnings some $213 million below what it might have if it had adopted different (but also acceptable) methods of accounting for intangible costs involved in drilling operations.

* The Great Atlantic & Pacific Tea Co.'s balance sheet shows

about $560 million (arbitrarily capitalized at ten times current rent payments) less of debt than it would if the company had followed a policy of owning its stores rather than one of sale and lease-back. Although the company is under a long-term obligation on the stores, these lease commitments do not have to appear on the balance sheet as debt.

* The American Electric Power Co. has been able to increase its stockholders' equity by some $67 million by crediting deferred federal income taxes to a restricted earned surplus.

* In 1958 the Transamerica Corp. increased its assets figure almost fourfold, to $149 million, by reporting its subsidiaries at book value instead of original cost.

The Institute has been aware for several years that it will have to take a position either for continued flexibility in handling financial statements or for uniformity. C.P.A.'s have been zealous in their insistence that their work calls for a high degree of judgment; yet at the same time they have been apprehensive that their judgments, unless tied to some systematic set of principles, will come to seem arbitrary. Some members of the profession talk ambitiously of the "principles" on which accounting practices rest, and of the "postulates" on which the principles rest—as though the whole edifice had been constructed logically, like theorems in geometry. Yet there is no definitive list of principles or postulates, and many of the practices have simply evolved *ad hoc.*

In the debate in Philadelphia, Spacek made it clear that his quest for uniformity was related to a desire to help investors "find the truth as it actually is." Peloubet, by contrast, ridiculed the notion that there is "some sort of absolute truth. . . . This exists nowhere else and will not be found in the practice of accounting"—which merely requires "that the conventions and assumptions on which the accounts are prepared should be clearly stated." Peloubet's view on this matter has generally prevailed within the profession over the years. George O. May, often identified as the dean of the modern U.S. accounting profession (Exhibit 2), remarked many years ago that the "world of business is subject to constant and sometimes violent change and full of uncertainties." He added that the works of accountants "cannot rise higher in the scale of certainty than the events which they reflect."

The effort to cut through all the ambiguities in modern accounting gained momentum at the 1957 convention of the A.I.C.P.A., with a speech by Alvin R. Jennings, the senior partner of Lybrand, Ross

Bros., & Montgomery. Jennings proposed that the profession buttress its theoretical underpinnings, in part by organizing a sizable new research effort. Specifically, he persuaded the members to support a new research division, staffed by both academicians and practitioners, that would codify, analyze, and recommend changes in prevailing accounting practice. Also the organization of an Accounting Principles Board, which would work out an agreed-upon body of doctrine, was an indirect result of his proposals. The board was organized last year and, since Spacek is now on it, will be addressing itself soon to the issues he has raised.

The Ethics of Auditors

The accountants' intensified concern about their principles is related to their consciousness that the importance and status of their profession have been rising rapidly; but that even so it lacks the independence and authority that come from having at its back a systematic body of solid and settled principles. The lawyer serves his client, but he takes his guidance from a body of law and knowledge on which the client's beliefs and wishes have no influence. The accountant occupies a much lower place on the scale of independency. His code will not, of course, allow him to put his name to an outright untruth. But he is sometimes caught in a position where there is no agreement in his profession about the way "the truth" shall be stated— and this makes it harder for him to be independent of his client's demands.

In 1959, for example, the Alaska Juneau Gold Mining Co. pressed its auditor, Arthur Andersen, to permit a revaluation (upward) of certain of the company's properties to offset partially a substantial net reduction in the over-all assets. The Andersen firm did not agree that any properties should be written up, although it conceded that the case was not clear-cut. Alaska Juneau thereupon switched to Arthur Young & Co., whose partners, after careful study, felt there was merit in the management's position. This sequence of events suggests the pressures that auditors are often under, and the range of ethical problems they face in the absence of agreed-upon accounting principles. In Philadelphia this year, the Institute's efforts to clarify its rules about members' independence, and about their ethical obligations in general, consumed more time than, and created as much of a fuss as, the debate over accounting principles.

Some of the ethical prohibitions confronting C.P.A.'s are clear-cut. It is plainly a violation of the code to advertise or solicit new business, or to tell outsiders about clients' business transactions. But other situations are not easy to resolve. Consider two very sticky problems recently faced by auditors:

Not long ago a partner in one of the Big Eight national firms made the arresting discovery that some employees of one corporation he was auditing received payments from a supplier company that he was also auditing. The partner was ethically bound not to reveal this information to the executives of the first corporation (i.e., because it involved confidential information obtained in the course of auditing the supplier company). At the same time, he was bound to protect the first corporation from repetition of the practice. He finally resolved the matter by asking the chief executive officer of this corporation to state the company policy on such payments. When he was told that they were forbidden, he disclosed that the policy was being violated—but left it up to the management to detect and halt these practices.

A partner in another Big Eight firm found, in checking the books of one client, that a high proportion of its assets consisted of receivables from another client—which, the auditor knew, was close to bankruptcy. He could not reveal this fact to the first company; yet he had to insist that larger reserves than usual be set up against possible losses on the receivables. The management of the first company made it clear that they thought his demand unreasonable. This left the auditor in a painful and precarious position, but he stuck to his guns, and eventually management accepted his recommendation.

Independence—But How Much?

The ethical problem that commanded most attention at Philadelphia concerned the "independence issue." This issue involves a lot more than the problem of the client exerting pressure on an auditor who wants to keep an account. The issue also embraces some questions about auditors' impartiality in handling secure accounts.

It is clear that an auditor must not have, or even seem to have, any motive for failing to disclose misleading information in his client's accounts. The SEC has ruled that no auditor can be considered independent if he has a financial interest in a client; and auditors practicing before the commission cannot own shares or serve as directors or officers in corporations whose financial statements they audit in connection with public offerings. The Big Eight firms generally have adopted this principle, as a matter of policy bar their partners and managers from owning stock in or serving as directors of any client corporation. A partner in Price Waterhouse, for example, is barred from investing in about 400 listed companies.

Several leaders of the A.I.C.P.A. have been prodding the Institute to require *all* C.P.A. firms to follow the Big Eight in barring such investments. The Illinois state society has already passed rules forbidding an auditor to express an opinion on the financial statement of a concern in which he has any financial interest or with which he is associated as a director, officer, or promoter. But at the Philadelphia convention the Institute leaders ran into trouble when they tried to get the membership to bar such holdings formally.

Spokesmen for some of the small firms argued that the concept of independence could not be linked mechanically to the absence of such holdings. In some cases, they said, they had been asked to help out young enterprises, often when these were close to bankruptcy. In many such cases, these auditors argued, they had been willing to help the companies conserve cash by taking payment in stock; now it would be unfair to make them dispose of this stock in order to keep the accounts. Furthermore, they contended, only a small proportion of the nation's C.P.A.'s practice before the SEC, and it would be unfair to saddle a majority of the profession with standards that are relevant only for a minority.

The whole debate was intensely embarrassing to the leaders of the Institute. Part of their embarrassment arose from the strong feeling of many members that the Big Eight, and the semi-national firms, too, already have too much influence in the institute—and the more rigorous standards were plainly modeled on Big Eight practice. The dispute accentuated the divided interest of the big and small firms and highlighted the fact that they have different standards of ethics. Supporters of the proposed standards, not anticipating a proxy contest, had done no campaigning or proxy soliciting. The small firms—the one-to-five-man outfits—did solicit proxies against the proposed rule, and apparently they got enough to make its adoption doubtful. As soon as it was doubtful, its proponents grew leery of bringing it to a vote at all; the one thing they did *not* want was a vote showing the Institute membership against stricter standards. After a great deal of parliamentary maneuvering and a certain amount of unparliamentary chaos—at one point five overlapping and contradictory motions were being entertained by the chair—there was a vote to defer the issue until next year, and the session adjourned. (EDITORS' NOTE: This rule was passed and became effective January 1, 1964.)

How to Try a C.P.A.

The conduct of certified public accountants is subject to several different kinds of discipline. Some of it is imposed by state licensing authorities, which, however, have widely varying standards. Some of the discipline is exerted by state C.P.A. societies, whose standards are in principle—but not always in practice—as high as the national organization's. In addition, a C.P.A. who certifies financial statements concerning securities of any listed company must agree to observe the regulations of the SEC. Finally, he may join the American Institute of C.P.A.'s and agree to abide by its code of ethics. (The Institute has about 38,000 of the 71,000 licensed C.P.A.'s in the U.S.) Of all these organizations, the American Institute exerts the tightest discipline.

Some of the state licensing authorities and associations have, in fact, been powerless to require accountants to adhere to their presumed standards. C.P.A.'s who have been expelled from the A.I.C.P.A. often continue to practice undisturbed by the state authorities. One C.P.A. was expelled by the Institute after he pleaded *nolo contendere* in a federal tax-fraud case; he had been charged with allowing his client, a hardware retailer, to manipulate profit figures in such a way that he evaded $125,000 in income taxes over a four-year period. The auditor is still practicing in Pennsylvania.

The Institute has three penalties it may invoke against transgressors. It may admonish, suspend, or expel them. Many of the admonitions are for borderline offenses—e.g., for seeming to violate the rule against self-advertisement by allowing a local bank to tell its depositor that a C.P.A. who is a "tax expert" will be available for consultation at certain hours. Suspensions and expulsions are for more serious offenses, are relatively rare, and cannot be invoked without a trial. In the period from May, 1956, to September, 1960, twenty-one members of the Institute were brought to trial. Eleven were expelled, eight were suspended, and two were acquitted.

The trial procedure is quite formal. First, a fifteen-member Committee on Professional Ethics establishes a prima-facie case that the rules of conduct have been violated. Then the case is handed over to a twenty-one-man trial board. The accused C.P.A. may be, and usually is, represented by counsel. The case is presented by the chairman of the Committee on Professional Ethics, and the whole trial rarely takes longer than a day—usually only two or three hours. It requires a simple majority of the trial board to suspend a member from the Institute, and a two-thirds vote to expel him.

Despite all the parliamentary uproar over "independence," most of the men at Philadelphia were aware that the larger problem facing their profession was the fuzziness about the basic principles of accounting. The Institute's current attempt to clarify these principles is not its first. Indeed, it had a Committee on Accounting Procedure before its new Accounting Principles Board was set up, and the former issued basic opinions for twenty years, beginning in 1939. There are now fifty-one bulletins outlining accepted accounting principles, and some regard them as a sort of catechism of the profession. They do, in fact, constitute the most authoritative written guides to good accounting practice. But accountants have had varying degrees of loyalty to these bulletins, at least one of them having been virtually ignored by the profession. (This stated the preferred method of writing off plant and equipment under the wartime rapid-depreciation laws.) A more recent bulletin, dealing with the procedure to be followed in treating welfare and pension plans, was two years in preparation, went through fifteen drafts, was finally exposed to the profession, then was revised, re-exposed, and then formally issued. It still has not gained complete acceptance.

Can the Accounting Principles Board gain a more widespread acceptance of *its* recommendations? The new board has at least one large advantage over the old committee: its members are aware that the confusions about acceptable practices cannot be ended merely by issuing a lot of specific recommendations—and they are resolved that the board shall clarify first principles first. With the principles clarified, it may be easier to get agreement on practices.

On the other hand, the new board has some new problems. One problem is simply that tax laws and securities regulations are much more complex than they used to be. In the complexity there is at least some room for businessmen to maneuver—to make decisions more freely—and any attempt to codify the handling of related financial data reduces the area of freedom, and will surely meet some resistance. A related difficulty has arisen from the steady shift in emphasis and interest away from the balance sheet and toward the income statement. Investors, security analysts, bankers, and even some creditors have grown more interested in the earnings capacities of companies than in their assets and liabilities. (It is almost forgotten today that until the passage of the Securities Act in 1933 many public corporations did not even issue income statements; the curious investor could deduce the income only from changes in net worth shown on successive balance sheets.) The tremendous premium placed by the stock market today on high earnings capacities suggests that reforms tending to lower some companies' reported earnings will meet with considerable resistance.

Oily Financial Statements

Perhaps the most spectacular example of the flexibility of modern accounting is provided by the disparate handling of the oil industry. At present there are several alternative procedures, all "generally accepted," that may be followed in accounting for the intangible costs of drilling productive wells—at least, in accounting to stockholders. In tax reports to the U.S. Government, almost all oil companies charge off their intangible drilling costs against income in the year the cost is incurred. But in their published reports, oil companies generally follow one of three procedures. The first, which seems to be the most conservative (because it results in lower reported earnings), is used by Amerada Petroleum Corp. Amerada charges all intangible drilling costs against income immediately. ("Tangible" costs, i.e., of equipment, are of course depreciated at varying rates.) Under the Amerada procedure, a company with, say, $200,000 of income and $100,000 of intangible drilling costs would report the balance of $100,000 as taxable income. After paying the 52 per cent corporate income tax, the company would show a net profit of $48,000—exactly in line with its tax return.

The second procedure, perhaps the most liberal, is followed by Standard Oil of New Jersey and many other companies. Jersey does not charge *any* intangible drilling costs against income, at least not at the time the well is drilled. Instead, the intangible costs of productive wells are capitalized; and so they show up on the balance sheet as new assets, and not on the income statement as expenses. Under the Jersey method, therefore, the company with $200,000 of income would report all of this amount. However, companies using this method report to their stockholders only the actual taxes paid to the government— $52,000 in this case—which means that they can report a net profit of $148,000, roughly three times as much as a company using the Amerada method.

Midway between these two extremes, and increasingly popular with accountants, is a reporting procedure followed by Texaco and Shell Oil and others. Like Jersey, these companies immediately put the intangible costs of productive wells on their books as assets; and if they have the same $200,000 of income, they do not deduct these costs from it. But unlike Jersey, these companies suggest in their published reports that they pay taxes on the full amount—i.e., they show a provision of $104,000 for taxes and so report a net of $96,000. Since they actually had to pay only $52,000 in taxes, they take the other $52,000—i.e., the taxes saved—as a reduction of the $100,000 cost of developing the well; and so the net asset that appears on the balance sheet is the $48,000 difference. This asset is charged against income over the useful life of the well—perhaps at the rate of $4,800 a year if the well is presumed to be good for ten years.

In sum, then three different oil companies, each with revenues of $200,000, each with intangible development costs of $100,000, and each actually paying the U.S. Government $52,000 in taxes, might report three considerably different net-income figures to the public: $48,000, $96,000, or $148,000—and all three would be following "generally accepted accounting procedure." Furthermore, *none of the companies would be under any obligation to tell the public which procedure they were following;* they would only be obliged to indicate if and when and how they changed their procedures. Texaco, Shell, and Jersey Standard do not indicate in their annual reports how they account for intangible development costs. (Amerada does make its accounting practice clear.)

The businessman aghast at all this flexibility can be reassured on one point at least: Amerada's procedure results in lower earnings reports, and Jersey's in higher, only in the short run. In the long run, the *ceteris paribus,* the accounting procedure adopted will have little effect on earnings. Eventually, Amerada's reported earnings will be bolstered by revenues from wells it has already written off. And eventually, Jersey's reported income will be depressed by the amortization costs of its wells.

Hot Water in Pools

Investors also have a problem in evaluating the financial data relating to mergers; and the New York Stock Exchange recently asked the American Institute of Certified Public Accountants to straighten out a large, continuing confusion about two different kinds of mergers: purchases and pools. In principle, a merger may take place (a) when one company purchases another, or (b) when two companies pool their interests. In either case, there is likely to be an exchange of stock. The difference is that in a purchase the smaller company becomes a part of the parent; in a "pooling of interests" the companies are simply blended into one, whose assets, liabilities, and net worth are the sum of these pairs of items on the two original balance sheets. Perhaps a half of all big mergers these days are pools.

Why should the distinction be of any interest to investors? Consider some recent examples:

Not long ago C.I.T. Financial Corp. merged with the privately owned Home Finance Service. To swing the merger, C.I.T. had to give stock with a market value of $5,600,000 in exchange for Home Finance stock with a book value of $3,600,000. If the merger had been construed as a purchase, C.I.T.'s assets would have had to reflect an additional $2-million cost, and amortizing this amount might have created a steady drain on reported profits in the years following. Instead, C.I.T. reported a pooling of interests with Home Finance— and so it had no problem.

The Automatic Canteen Co. of America was recently involved in two mergers. In one of them it exchanged 82,500 shares of its own stock for Nationwide Food Service, Inc. In the second merger, six weeks later, Automatic Canteen exchanged 40,970 shares for the stock of the A.B.T. Manufacturing Corp. In this second merger the stock exchanged was about equal in value, and the deal was called an acquisition. But in the first case the Automatic Canteen stock was worth some $2 million more than the book value of the company it merged with; and calling this deal an acquisition might have required a write-off of the differential. The deal was called a pooling.

Here again, the basic problem is that public corporations have considerable latitude in reporting on their earnings and financial position. The A.I.C.P.A. has, to be sure, outlined a number of standards that accountants are supposed to follow in determining whether a merger can be considered a pooling: the Institute says, for example, that the relative sizes of two companies should not be wildly out of line, and specifically suggests that the smaller company's assets should not be less than 5 per cent of the larger company's. Actually, Automatic Canteen acquired Nationwide Food Service in exchange for only 1.6 per cent of its own stock. Yet it would be unfair to suggest that the deal violated accepted accounting procedure. For different C.P.A.'s assign different weights to the several standards, and no one of them is considered controlling.

Pension Rights and Wrongs

Another large accounting problem, also unresolved by the profession, concerns the proper method of reporting on pension funds. Ever since the first great wave of corporate pension plans broke over the profession a decade ago, accountants have been trying to grapple with the two kinds of costs involved in pension planning. One cost, which has created few problems, reflects the pension credits built up by the employees in the current year. The other cost, which *has* created problems, is incurred in amortizing the employees' "past service liability." The main accounting questions were, and still are, how this liability should appear on the balance sheet, and how much of it should be charged against income every year.

Corporate responses to both questions have varied widely. When U.S. Steel inaugurated its pension plan in 1950, the corporation's unamortized past-service liability was estimated at $574 million—an amount equal to half the market value of all the common and preferred stock at the time! In most subsequent years U.S. Steel has made payments for past-service charges. But in 1958 the corporation contended that past-service charges were amortized adequately and that it did not have to make a payment that year. Price Waterhouse had no real grounds for rejecting the company's contention, but insisted on inserting in the annual report a long paragraph spelling out the change that had taken place. The effect of the change, in any case, was to increase the corporation's reported net profit that year from $200 million to $300 million (i.e., the pension cost was reduced by about $100 million). In 1959, U.S. Steel resumed its payments for past-service costs.

The Institute has done little to clarify pension reporting practices. In 1956 it issued a bulletin to the effect that financial statements should at least indicate the present liability, actuarially calculated, of future pension commitments. But the Institute has never got any agreement on the best way to charge for past-service costs, and some sizable corporations do not even make charges for current-service costs. Until this year, for example, American Tobacco has had an unfunded pension plan, and the only pension charges shown in its financial statements were actual payments to retired employees. At the other extreme, the Gillette Co. is one of the few large corporations that have funded substantially all their past-service liability. And in between are a fair number of corporations—e.g., American-Standard—that contribute to pension funds each year only the additional obligation incurred that year—with no contributions for past-service liability.

Accounting and Inflation

In general, many auditors believe, most of the big disagreements in their profession concern proper methods of allocating costs over periods of time. And some auditors believe that the biggest disagreement of all during the next decade will concern what they call "price-level depreciation"—a method of allocating costs over periods of time when prices are fluctuating.

The debate begins with the concept of depreciation itself. Originally, accountants thought of depreciation simply as an amortization of costs incurred in the past. But since World War II a second concept has become more widespread—the "shoebox" concept of depreciation charges as a *reserve* put aside for replacement of worn-out plant and equipment. This new concept brought a new problem with it. In a period when the purchasing power of the dollar has been declining, it obviously requires more dollars to replace worn-out plant and equipment. Some accountants, including Leonard Spacek of Arthur Andersen, contend that present depreciation charges are not realistic. They believe that annual depreciation charges, whether calculated on a straight-line or accelerated basis, should be increased (*or, conceivably, decreased*) as the cost of living changes. Thomas Higgins, the senior partner of Arthur Young & Co., suggests that the profession might get into price-level depreciation by encouraging its corporate clients to publish two sets of figures—one adjusted for prices, the other unadjusted. A strong body of opinion in the A.I.C.P.A. is still against any such change; however, Carman Blough, the Institute's very influential research head, does not believe that inflation has yet been severe enough to distort the meaning of present depreciation figures. Anyway, he argues, why should price-level accounting be limited to depreciation? Blough points out, for example, that no auditor has proposed charging against income any figure for insurance costs higher than the actual costs, even though insurance premiums are sure to rise in an inflationary era. (Higgins is for using price-level reporting on any item that is "material"—which presumably excludes corporate insurance charges.)

While price-level depreciation is not an accepted accounting method in the U.S., it is accepted in Europe, and more U.S. investors are likely to begin encountering the problem as the securities of more foreign corporations are traded in U.S. markets. In 1956, for example, Simca, the French auto company, sold some capital shares in the U.S. In its prospectus, which was passed by the SEC, Simca noted that under French tax law it was permitted to account for the loss in purchasing power of the franc by putting a higher figure on its fixed assets. Simca has continued to depreciate its assets on the basis of the adjusted figures. Philips' Gloeilampenfabrieken, a Dutch electrical manufacturer with many U.S. shareholders, uses price-level depreciation regularly.

One large difficulty about price-level depreciation is that, in a time of rising prices, the additional charges against income might depress earnings. Five years ago, Professor Ralph C. Jones of Yale made a study of this problem for the American Accounting Association (an organization composed primarily of teachers of accounting). One of the companies Jones studied was the New York Telephone Co., a member of the Bell family. His figures show that in 1946–52, New York Telephone reported 50 per cent more income than it would have reported if depreciation charges had been inflated along with the dollar.

The Power to Decide

It is clear that the profession's principal unresolved problems will have to be solved, ultimately, by the A.I.C.P.A. and its new Accounting Principles Board. It is also clear that the actual powers of the Institute and the Board are still undefined: The scope of these powers was tested early last year in a case raised by three subsidiaries of the American Electric Power Co., which sought a court injunction to prevent the Institute from issuing an "interpretation" of one of its prior opinions. Much of the ammunition against the Institute was supplied by Donald C. Cook, an executive vice president of A.E.P., who also happens to be a member of the Institute. Cook and his company argued that the influence of the Institute had already led the SEC to change its approved procedure on the recording of deferred tax payments, and that some state regulatory agencies had followed the SEC's lead. (Cook also happens to be a former chairman of the SEC.) Until the Institute and the SEC acted, A.E.P. had been allowed to carry deferred tax payments on its books in a "restricted earned surplus," which technically forms part of the stockholders' equity. The change had the immediate effect of reducing this equity by $67 million; and Cook contended that the reduction made it harder for the company to borrow money, and obliged it to sell stock instead—which, he also contended, was more expensive in the long run.

The battle between Cook and the Institute is not over yet. The U.S. Supreme Court has upheld the right of the Institute to circulate its opinions. But in Kentucky, at least, A.E.P. is still fighting. Its subsidiary, Kentucky Power, points to a state utility regulation which specifies that deferred taxes *shall* be reflected in restricted earned surplus. The subsidiary is doing some financing now, which brings it into direct conflict with the SEC, and may enable it to take the issue back to the Supreme Court—this time on the question whether the state's rules or the SEC's should be governing.

The Institute's powers are especially ambiguous as they relate to regulated companies—e.g., railroads, airlines, public utilities, whose rates are regulated, and also banks, savings-and-loan companies, insurance companies, and stockbrokers, where regulation is concerned mainly with protecting consumers against fraud. Perhaps because these companies are regulated in so many other ways—to protect passengers, depositors, policyholders, etc.—not much concern has been given to the problems of their *stockholders,* and many such companies are not required to have audited financial statements. It is often hard for investors to make any meaningful evaluation of these companies as business enterprises. Accounting in the banking and insurance fields, for example, shows a preoccupation with the companies' solvency but is weak on their earning power. Fewer than 20 per cent of the nation's 14,000 banks are audited by independent certified public accountants. Robert A. Eden, a savings-and-loan executive who has extensively studied the varying accounting methods in use, said recently, "Two otherwise identical savings banks might report net income differing by thousands or even hundreds of thousands of dollars . . . might differ in total assets over the years by possibly millions of dollars."

Where the Power Ends

If accountants need some clarification of their powers, they also need a greater public awareness of where that power and responsibility end. Many businessmen are surprised to learn that a corporate financial statement is the responsibility of management, not of the auditing firm. The chief executive of a corporation must give his auditors a letter of representation in which he states that, to the best of his knowledge and belief, all the information in the report is true and fairly presented. Technically, and legally, the auditor is responsible only for the honesty of his own opinion certificate, in which he ordinarily says that his investigations have led him to believe that the company's assets, liabilities, and earnings reports are fairly presented.

Not, of course, that the certificate is an unimportant matter. Any qualifications that may be expressed in it are attentively noted by investors these days. Stockholders are questioning auditors more frequently and more intensively at annual meetings, and often demanding to know why corporations changed their auditors. Questions about conflict-of-interest situations, as at Chrysler Corp. (see "Behind the Conflict at Chrysler," FORTUNE, November, 1960), are increasingly directed at the auditors, as well as at management. The selection of independent auditors is more often being submitted for stockholder approval. Some auditors believe that the time may soon come when U.S. stockholders will have the same legal rights as British stockholders, who are entitled, at annual meetings, to have both the old and new auditing firms present when there is any change in auditors. One way or another, it seems likely that auditors in the U.S. will be answering a lot of questions in the next few years.

Exhibit 1   The Father of the Balance Sheet

The father of the accounting profession is an unsung, largely unremembered Franciscan monk, Fra Luca Paciolo, who gave the world double-entry bookkeeping, and was the greatest mathematician of his day (c. 1445–1523). He was also a teacher, a professor of sacred theology, and a friend and associate of some of the great statesmen, painters, musicians, and churchmen of his period, including Leonardo da Vinci, Pope Leo X, and Pope Julius II. Paciolo's exposition of double-entry bookkeeping was acclaimed at the time by Leonardo, and Goethe later described it as "one of the finest discoveries of the human intellect." Oswald Spengler asserted in *The Decline of the West* that Paciolo's work ranked in importance with the discovery of the New World and the theory of the rotation of the earth around the sun.

It was some time in the thirteenth century that merchants in Italy began to keep track of their business affairs by making two entries, one of debit and one of credit. Essential to this innovation was a growing awareness of companies as *continuing* enterprises. Before the innovation, each transaction had simply been viewed separately—some merchants kept journals bound in different colors to record different kinds of transactions—and the concept of "balance" on a single ledger had been unknown. The income statement was also unknown, except as it applied to single transactions; no attempt was made to determine whether a business was operated profitably over a specific period, such as a year or two.

It was Paciolo's contribution to sense the revolutionary implica-tions of these changes. He recorded and classified them, and set forth the necessary elements of a balance sheet in a special supplement to his *Summa Arithmetica*. His outline of the proper use of the journal and general ledger could be used, with only minor alterations, by a bookkeeper today.

He was forty-nine in 1494, when this work was published. Born in Borgo San Sepolcro, a small town in central Italy, he was early appren-ticed to a wealthy merchant family. When he was twenty, he went to Venice to tutor the sons of a rich merchant. Later he studied at the great universities of the day. In 1470 he joined the Franciscan order and be-gan to teach mathematics and also theology. After the *Summa Arith-metica* appeared, he and Leonardo collaborated on a book about science and mathematics, *La Divina Proportione,* with Leonardo doing the illustrations and Paciolo supplying the text. He died around 1523—the exact date is uncertain.

For centuries afterwards, his text on accounting was translated and often plagiarized. A version reached England and Scotland in the Eliza-bethan era, and there found its most hospitable soil, flourishing as Eng-land embarked on its great era of exploration, with joint stock com-panies financing the ventures. Double-entry bookkeeping became much more important in England in the eighteenth century, when the laws on the limited liability of corporations were passed. These laws enabled corporations to acquire sizable assets, and so to plan ahead for periods of years. Balance sheets got to be infinitely more complex—and ac-countants came into their own.

Exhibit 2   Standings of the Teams

The Big Eight partnerships dominate the auditing world, and their senior partners provide that world with most of its leadership and direction. These firms operate in a stately and dignified environment, mostly in the Wall Street area, and the competition among them often seems to be muffled by all the rules about "ethics." Nevertheless, the competition is real and intense.

Unlike advertising agencies and law firms, auditing firms do not consider it unethical to serve clients competing against one another, and several of the Big Eight firms have important specialties in certain in-dustries. Arthur Young & Co. has been strongest in the oil and gas fields. Touche, Ross, Bailey & Smart does auditing for both Macy's and Gim-bels, and for scores of other retail corporations. Arthur Andersen & Co.

originally made its reputation unraveling the snarled affairs of the Insull utility empire, and still maintains a strong position in utilities: today Andersen audits perhaps a third of all U.S. utility companies. (However, it does not have the business of the world's largest utility, the American Telephone & Telegraph Co., which is audited by Lybrand, Ross Bros., & Montgomery.)

One firm that has expanded in almost all possible directions is Peat, Marwick, Mitchell & Co., which has got to be the largest in the profession through an aggressive program of mergers. Its biggest single lift came in 1950, when it absorbed the established old firm of Barrow, Wade, Guthrie & Co. Price Waterhouse has always had a broad client base, and although smaller today than several other firms, it still audits more listed corporations than anyone else. It also retains a substantial foreign business through its contacts with affiliated firms, working in an international P.W. partnership. Haskins & Sells, which was the first major auditing firm founded by American accountants—most of the early firms were British in origin—also has a broadly based clientele, which includes the largest U.S. industrial corporation, General Motors, and hundreds of very small clients too. (In the world of the Big Eight, a small client is ordinarily thought of as one whose fees do not get above $10,000 a year.) Ernst & Ernst has built up its business substantially by moving very heavily into the "management services" field, in which it pioneered.

Because they are private partnerships, none of the Big Eight firms are required to disclose any information about their size or revenues. The last time any such data were spread on the record was in 1939, when the Securities and Exchange Commission was investigating the Mc-Kesson & Robbins scandal, and auditing practices generally. At that time the SEC report indicated that Price Waterhouse was the largest firm in the U.S. Peat, Marwick then had twenty-five partners and Arthur Andersen fifteen. The figures on partners shown below are not strictly comparable, since some firms have several classes of partnerships and others do not; however, these and other figures do at least make it clear that the relative sizes of the firms have changed a lot since 1939. The figures are FORTUNE's estimates and are based on information from a wide variety of sources. None of the firms named have confirmed these figures, but several have acknowledged that they are in the right range.*

* EDITORS' NOTE: In the July, 1966 issue of *Fortune* Magazine, Mr. Wise discusses in his article, "The Very Private World of Peat, Marwick, Mitchell," the continued growth by merger of the largest of the "Big Eight" firms and the world's largest partnership. The firm now has 600 partners operating out of 248 offices in fifty nations on six continents. In the United States alone PM has 87 offices, 345

	PARTNERS	OFFICES	EST. GROSS (In millions)
Peat, Marwick, Mitchell & Co.	190	60	$45
Arthur Andersen & Co.	171	28	40
Ernst & Ernst	132	95	36
Price Waterhouse & Co.	101	40	35
Haskins & Sells	176	36	33
Lybrand, Ross Bros., & Montgomery	126	35	28
Arthur Young & Co.	104	28	26
Touche, Ross, Bailey, & Smart	71	27	17

Exhibit 3   The P. & L. of A. & B.

In a debate before the nation's distinguished auditors last September, Leonard Spacek of Arthur Andersen & Co. and Maurice Peloubet of Pogson, Peloubet & Co. argued about accounting principles in general, and about two-profit-and-loss statements in particular. These were for two imaginary companies, A and B, which are presumed to have had the same volume and kind of business. Despite this similarity, B reported higher earnings than A. Both of them used acceptable accounting methods. Spacek deplored such flexibility in accounting and Peloubet defended it.

In general, company B has increased its reported income by deferring costs:

· B uses a first-in-first-out (FIFO) method of inventory valuation, and so has no need for the $400,000 inventory reserve set up by company A.

partners and 6,000 employees. It has boosted its United States offices from twenty-seven to the present number by absorbing over sixty accounting firms in the past twenty years. The firm, more than any other "Big Eight" member, has expanded the concept of the auditor to that of the all-purpose consultant. It is also the defendant in a series of spectacular lawsuits involving charges of faulty auditing procedures and has been subjected to much criticism for alleged conflict of interest. The firm's worldwide revenues are estimated at $150 million ($100 million in the United States) on capital of $50 million (of which the United States share is $30 million). The average partner's income is reported to be $50,000. Arthur Andersen & Co., the second-ranking firm in size, has annual revenue of approximately $75 million. However, the AA growth has been generated primarily from within, with few mergers, and with a much more precisely defined concept of professional auditing.

	COMPANY A	COMPANY B
SALES	$10,000,000	$10,000,000
Costs and expenses		
Cost of goods	$6,000,000	$6,000,000
Selling costs	1,500,000	1,500,000
LIFO inventory reserve	400,000	—
Depreciation	400,000	300,000
Research costs	100,000	20,000
Pension costs	200,000	50,000
Officers' compensation		
Base salaries	200,000	200,000
Bonuses	200,000	—
Total costs and expenses	$9,000,000	$8,070,000
Profit before income taxes	$1,000,000	$1,930,000
Income taxes	520,000	1,004,000
	$ 480,000	$ 926,000
Capital gain (after taxes)	—	150,000
Net profit reported	$ 480,000	$1,076,000
Per share (600,000 shares)	$ .80	$ 1.79

· B avoids a $100,000 charge against income by using straight-line depreciation; A uses accelerated depreciation.

· B amortizes its research costs over a five-year period, while A takes its costs immediately.

· A funds all current pension costs—i.e., it puts into a reserve an amount equal to the cost of the employee's current service and amortization of his past service. B funds only an amount equal to the discounted value of an employee's present interest in a pension plan, with this amount not to exceed the company's current legal liability.

· A paid its officers a cash bonus, while B granted them stock options, which are not charged to income—though eventually they may act as a drag on per-share income.

· Both companies had capital gains. A credited the gain to earned surplus, B to income.

QUESTIONS

1. How is the work done by an auditor different from the work done by other accountants? What kind of work does each undertake?

2. Define the following terms and specify the relationship among them:

a. accountant
b. certified public
   accountant
c. auditor
d. noncertified public
   accountant
e. internal auditor
f. junior accountant
g. senior accountant

h. accounting firm
i. partner in an accounting
   firm
j. internal accountant
k. tax accountant
l. management consultant
m. American Institute of CPA's
n. "The Big Eight"

3. Describe three stimuli to the growth of the accounting profession in the United States.

4. Why do accountants like Leonard Spacek desire strict uniformity in the preparation of financial statements for investors? Why don't men like Maurice Peloubet share this desire for uniformity? Explain your position on the matter.

5. Consider the subsection entitled "Oily Financial Statements." What are the three "generally accepted" treatments for oil drilling costs? Why do you suppose this multiplicity of practices has arisen; is there anything peculiar about drilling costs that would encourage it? Is it possible to phrase a general principle to resolve the issue without referring specifically to oil drilling costs? Try to phrase such a principle, and explain how it would secure uniformity.

6. Consider the financial statements and other information on pages 39 and 40. For each point of difference between the statements of companies A and B, decide whether or not uniformity would be desirable and justify your decision. If uniformity is desirable, then try to phrase a general principle to secure it and explain how the principle would work.

7. Why don't accounting firms like to think of themselves as *competing* for the business of clients?

8. Why do accounting firms like to think of themselves as *independent* of their clients? List several ways in which they are independent and several ways in which they are not independent.

3

The Economic Approach to Accounting

I. Kleerekoper

IT IS CLEAR that the flow of capital and the growth of international trade required for a thriving world economy can optimally be attained only if certain conditions are fulfilled. These conditions undoubtedly include "economic stability" of the countries concerned and "the opportunity for profit," in the theme of the International Congress. It is the latter condition—the opportunity for profit—that should be our primary concern here. Insofar as the possibility of making a profit is of decisive importance to the flow of capital and international trade, it will be necessary to study and, as far as possible, unify the methods of

From *The Journal of Accountancy*, vol. 115, no. 3 (March, 1963), pp. 36–40. Reprinted by permission of the publisher. Mr. Kleerekoper is a senior partner in the firm of Van der Wilde & Kleerekoper, Amsterdam, Netherlands.

measuring and recording the results of all kinds of economic activity, no matter where in the world it takes place. For effective international intercourse, people must "understand" each other; this is only possible when what the other person says can be "translated" into one's own language or—and this is to be preferred—when all those concerned are willing and able to speak "the same language."

We must realize that accounting, in a way, is a "language;" that is to say, it is a medium for making something (data or information) known to others.

Sometimes it is difficult enough for people using the same language to communicate without misunderstanding each other; how much more difficult is it, then, for people of different tongues. Consequently, our joint effort should be aimed at making accounting a universal language. The goal we have in view is a formulation of the purposes of accounting and of the postulates and/or objectives underlying the accounting principles in such a manner that they will not be misunderstood in international intercourse and, what is still more important, that they will be accepted as the basis of the practice of accounting. Not until this goal has been reached will there be reasonable certainty that the results of economic activity in the various countries of the free world are being measured and recorded by comparable and, in particular, correct methods. Then, decisions on economic matters can be taken on a sound basis; there will be no ground left for apprehension that the standards applied might differ appreciably from one country to another.

It is therefore of utmost importance that international unanimity be reached on what is a correct concept of profit and on the notions of value and cost underlying that concept. It is felt that this is one of the most significant connections between accounting and the world economy.

The goal before us will only be attained if there is a general readiness to break away, if necessary, from what has evolved in the past and from what we have become accustomed to. Practice has proved to be too much a captive of "general acceptance" and of the rules laid down in tax and other governmental laws or regulations. We fully endorse the plea made for a scientific approach to accounting by R. J. Chambers in his article "The Conditions of Research in Accounting" published in the December 1960 issue of *The Journal of Accountancy*. The writer is correct in differentiating between factual and normative problems. The first is: What *is* the present state of accounting and by what process has it reached that state? The second problem is: What form *should* accounting take? In our judgment it is not questionable that the second problem is the determining one. We fully agree with the following two quotations from Mr. Chambers' article, the first being: "To become more practical it is necessary to become more theoretical," the second: "Whenever there is an economic problem, there is an accounting problem."

In this connection, we should also like to refer to a recent Accounting Research Study entitled "The Basic Postulates of Accounting" by Maurice Moonitz, issued by the American Institute of Certified Public Accountants in September 1961. On page 6, the author writes: "We are driven to the conclusion, then, that relatively heavy reliance must be placed on deductive reasoning in the development of accounting postulates and principles. We must first recognize and define the problems to be solved, then move to their solution by careful attention to what 'ought' to be the case, not what 'is' the case."

In the Netherlands, the problems of accounting have been approached scientifically for decades in close conjunction with and on the basis of the development of a normative, i.e., directive, theory of business economics. This approach may well have partly been stimulated by the fact that there are practically no legal regulations on this subject (except tax legislation, of course, and that was no barrier; in fact this legislation adopted many of the results of the scientific study). The purpose of this paper is to provide a contribution, with a Dutch slant, to the exchange of views on the principles of accounting; a contribution that will have a strong economic flavor. According to Dutch ideas, the approach to accounting through the achievements of the science of business economics is the only true one; this approach logically meets the purposes of accounting, as will be elaborated later. This contribution will not deal exhaustively with the subject matter; such a treatment would require much more space than is available. It must therefore be confined to an indication of some of the aspects of the problem in hand.

DEFINITION OF ACCOUNTING

Any answer to the question: "What are the purposes of accounting?" should be preceded by an examination of what is implied in the concept, "accounting." The need for this may be evidenced by a quotation taken from *Accounting Terminology Bulletin No. 1,* published in 1953 by the committee on terminology of the American Institute of Certified Public Accountants. On page 8, section 7, we read: "No words are employed more commonly than these (viz., accounting and accountancy), either in the practice or in the teaching of the subject; yet many differences arising in accounting writings have their roots in different conceptions of these basic terms. A careful consideration of these words will therefore add to understanding, not only among accountants themselves, but also among those outside the profession who have to do with accounting."

There is no doubt that in the course of the years a great many different definitions of "accounting" have been formulated. Apart from the fact that it is impossible to know all these definitions in a great number of languages, there can hardly be much point in quoting and discussing many of them. As far as this study is concerned, we shall dwell upon two definitions only: the more or less official American definition, as it appears in the *Accounting Terminology Bulletin* mentioned above, and the most recent definition of Dutch origin, taken from the explanatory notes to the program of studies in administrative organization forming part of the course of study and examinations of the Netherlands Institute of Accountants. Here is the American definition:

> Accounting is the art of recording, classifying, and summarizing in a significant manner and in terms of money, transactions and events which are, in part at least, of a financial character, and interpreting the results thereof.

And this is the Dutch one:

> Accounting is the systematic recording, processing and supplying of information for the management and operation of an entity and for the reports that have to be submitted thereon.

There is considerable divergence in the wording of the two definitions. What is important, however, is not so much the extent to which the choice of words in each tallies or varies as the extent to which the fundamental points of departure coincide or differ.

Both definitions describe the *nature* of the activity of accounting ("recording, classifying and summarizing" . . . "the systematic recording, processing and supplying"); the differences evident in these descriptions undoubtedly go deeper than a mere divergence in wording, but we shall not discuss them further.

The *subject* of accounting, too, is touched upon in both definitions ("transactions and events . . . of a financial character" . . . "information"). We believe the word "information" is preferable to "transactions and events." The term "information" seems broader to us; it comprises not only "transactions and events," but can refer also to persons, objects, plans, conditions, expectations, etc. And all of these can be subjects of accounting. It is felt that the expressions "in terms of money" and "of a financial character" in the American definition are too restrictive. Accounting need not be restricted to sums of money, though it is admitted that the information recorded and supplied is very often expressed in terms of money. This, however, should not blind us to the cases where this is not so.

The Dutch definition, however, differs from the American chiefly in that it states the *purposes* of accounting explicitly. It is true that the words "in a significant manner" and "interpreting the results thereof" could be read as an implicit reference to those purposes, but a clear statement of the matter is lacking in the American definition. According to the Dutch definition, accounting—i.e., the information to be supplied—is aimed at "the management and operation of an entity" and "the reports that have to be submitted thereon."

Although we appreciate the American definition quoted, we think the Dutch one is to be preferred; it includes *all* elements of accounting— in its widest possible sense—and it indicates explicitly the purpose for which accounting activities are intended. Meanwhile, the discussion of the two definitions has elaborated the conception of the term "accounting" so far that there can be no misunderstanding as to what is meant by it.

THE PURPOSES OF ACCOUNTING

It goes without saying that the description of the purposes of accounting, given in a few words in the Dutch definition, cannot dispense of the problem. Some expansion is necessary.

One of the major characteristics of the definition is that it stresses the fact that the purposes of accounting must not be deemed to be limited to recording, processing, and supplying information on the administration of assets and liabilities, on the resulting financial position at a given date and on the results of operations for the period then ended.

This retrospective purpose of accounting, which is still given too much exclusive stress, is preceded in the latter definition—but also, in fact, in a well-run business—by an anticipatory objective. It is certainly not exclusively nor yet chiefly the task of accounting to record the history of the activities of a business. At least as important is the availability of information that can support the preparation and determination of the policy to be followed and the decisions to be made. It is therefore natural that, to a considerable degree, there is interaction between the data that serve to prepare and determine management, and those that verify it. Thus, an organic structure results, in which accounting has developed into an instrument at the disposal of management for conducting and supervising business activities.

Significance

To give a better idea of the significance of the above, the following short summary is given of the more detailed purposes of accounting:

1. Providing analyzed and summarized information on business activities and conditions, which can be used both for determining and for controlling the conduct of affairs (e.g., data on cost prices, turnover, results, financing, liquidity, efficiency, profitability, budgets, etc.)

2. Providing detailed information on persons, objects, agreements etc., as a basis for decision-making (e.g., staff documentation, purchasing documentation, data on the available capacity of plant and machinery, etc.)

3. Recording the work to be performed (orders, planning, etc.) and the communication needed to ensure a proper performance (e.g., written instructions, work preparation, co-ordination, progress reporting, payroll, invoicing, etc.)

4. Recording and summarizing information for the rendering of reports on the activities and for exercising control (e.g., internal statements for judging management, reporting by the management to owners and third parties, reporting by executives to the management at various levels of responsibility, departmental statements of results, reporting by and checking on custodians, discharge for transfer of values, etc.)

5. Complying with legal, statutory and contractual obligations with respect to the filing or publication of information.

We shall resist the temptation to pursue further the bearing and implications of the above-mentioned purposes, because that is far beyond the scope of this paper. The foregoing brief summary may suffice to stress the point that accounting in the outlined broad interpretation of the term, is a much-embracing art that is rightly qualified to be generally indicated as "a tool of management." We must recognize, however, that a mere application of a number of techniques does not attain the objectives outlined above.

The prerequisites for this are the building-up of an effective internal organization in the business and a thorough analysis of the principles to be applied in accounting. It is some of these principles that will concern us next.

ACCOUNTING POSTULATES: ECONOMIC APPROACH

The exploratory material adduced above was a necessary preliminary to the discussion of the question: "What are the postulates of accounting?" On "postulates," *Accounting Terminology Bulletin No. 1,* which has been quoted earlier, says the following on page 11:

> Initially, accounting postulates are derived from experience and reason; after postulates so derived have proved useful, they become accepted as principles of accounting.

This quotation indicates that the principles that should be applied in accounting are derived from accounting postulates, if and when they have proved useful. We shall not go into the question of how it is determined—and who shall determine—whether certain postulates are useful.

According to the quotation, postulates appear to be derivable from two sources: experience and reason. Although experience provides an important source of knowledge, it is wise to handle that knowledge with care and to guard against overestimating experience as the basis of future rules of conduct. Designations such as "usefulness," "consistency" and "conservatism" are to be regarded as typical products of such an overestimation; the derivation of accounting principles from experience-oriented postulates tends to halt or even freeze the development of thought. After what has been said on the matter above, it will not be surprising that we prefer to derive the postulates primarily from reason; as a source of knowledge we feel that more weight should be assigned to reason than to experience. Only deductive reasoning on a scientific basis—naturally after a thorough checking of its outcome against experience—opens the way for the answer to the question: "What form *should* accounting take?" It is this approach only, that can lead to normative conclusions.

In the foregoing it has been explained that accounting must provide the necessary information for the management and operation of an entity and for the reports to be submitted thereon. To arrive at the postulates on which accounting must be based, we should search for the objectives pursued by the entity. These, surely, determine the management's outline of policy and the way in which the entity should operate, while they also serve as the touchstone used by interested parties in judging the conduct of affairs.

When discussing entities in general, we should be well aware that their objectives can be most varied (medical, defense, social, economic and other objectives). We shall not deal with the question to what extent all these different objectives can be attained and judged with the aid of accounting. This does not mean that this question must be answered in the negative, but that we deem it appropriate to confine ourselves to business entities, which are links in a chain connecting basic resources and ultimate consumption. The objectives of these business entities are economic in nature; each business operates between markets, obtaining goods and services from the buying market (including the labor market) and disposing of goods and services on the selling market. It normally does this with a view to making a profit, but nonprofit entities also have an economic purpose—even if it is only that of covering costs (whereby it is irrelevant whether its costs are covered by the proceeds of the services rendered or by government or private contributions).

Within this economic framework, the management of every business entity must make a choice between alternative possibilities; its principal task is to ascertain and weigh the alternatives and then to make a decision. From case to case the guide in choosing should be the difference between the proceeds to be obtained and the sacrifices to be made. Thus, it is a matter of economic decisions, for which information with an economic content, both quantitative and qualitative, must be available. Consequently, it is economic science, and in particular the theory of business economics, that must provide the foundation on which accounting must be built in order to obtain the information that is indispensable for making rational economic decisions and controlling the activities. In other words, the postulates of accounting must, in the first place, be based on the achievements of the science of business economics. Since these achievements are the result of deductive reasoning and have been set on the proof of practice, they will not only be "useful" but above all "normative." Thus, they provide a more effective foundation for their acceptance as principles of accounting than is now mostly the case. From this basis such a unity of conception can result that no scope will be left for starting-points varying with the separate sphere of accounting that at present can still often be distinguished such as management accounting and ownership accounting. Since all parties interested in the business are primarily concerned with its economic objectives, there is no sound reason for a difference in postulates and/or principles; both management and owners require information of a similar qualitative content; their requirements only differ in detail and frequency.

QUESTIONS

1. Why do you advocate that the Dutch definition of accounting should (or should not) be adopted by the American Institute of Certified Public Accountants?

2. Kleerekoper stresses the economic aspects of accounting. Do you think that an article of equal quality might be prepared on the legal aspects of accounting? Why (or why not)?

3. State why you agree or disagree with the following quotations cited in the article:

a. "To become more practical, it is necessary to become more theoretical."

b. "Whenever there is an economic problem, there is an accounting problem."

4. Give illustrations of your position in (3).

2

The Accounting Model

4

Revenue and Expense

Carl L. Nelson

ASSETS ARE customarily shown in the accounts and on the balance sheet at cost. In most cases the assets are acquired as a result of a purchase for cash or the promise to pay cash in a short period of time; in this case cost is the amount of money which has been paid or will be paid. In other cases, assets are acquired as a result of exchanging other assets, issuing long-term obligations to pay money (bonds or long-term notes), or issuing proprietary claims. Cost here means the fair market value of the assets surrendered or the liability or proprietary equity that is created. As a generalization, the cost of any asset is the fair market-value of the cash or other consideration transferred in exchange for the asset.

Assets are sometimes (but rarely) acquired as a result of a gift. These assets are costless, but to place them on the

Special permission to publish was granted by the author. Professor Nelson is the first George O. May Professor of Financial Accounting at Columbia University.

records at this zero cost would not yield the most useful results. Accountants therefore record them at their market value. This is not a departure from the general pattern, for placing assets on the records at cost also places them on at market value at the date of acquisition; cost is the value arrived at as a result of negotiations between the buyer and the seller. The effect of this transaction is to increase proprietorship, for no other asset has been surrendered and no liability has been created. This proprietorship should be clearly segregated from other proprietorship; it has been created neither as a result of an investment by the owners nor as a result of a sale of an asset or service at a price in excess of cost.

Other assets are received as a result of a revenue transaction and hence are not shown at cost. A claim on a customer is received as a result of a sale on account. This asset (accounts receivable) is recorded at the same amount as the amount of revenue created as a result of this transaction. For this reason, the asset side of a balance sheet cannot be understood without a realization as to what revenue is and under what conditions accountants record revenue. Revenue also is the starting point for the computation of profit; how much revenue is recorded will have an important effect on the profit for a period.

The typical net income or net profit is an estimate. Revenues and expenses are both estimates until all assets are turned into cash. Normally this is done only when a business is about to discontinue activity (and sometimes not even then), so that only then can accurate results be determined. No one is interested in the profitability of the business at that time so that waiting until that time is useless. The users of accounting data want an annual (or more frequent) determination of income, even though it is an estimate.

Revenue creation is not the function of one individual or department in a business. The buyer, the personnel man, the advertising man, salesman, credit man—all play a part. For the typical merchandising or manufacturing business, the sale may be the point at which the accountant recognizes revenue, but this does not mean that the salesman produces the revenue. Rather, it is due to the existence of two conditions: (1) most of the activity necessary to produce the revenue has already been performed, and (2) a reasonably accurate measure of revenue is possible. Each of these requires elaboration.

In most merchandising or manufacturing enterprises, the sale is an important operation. Important as buying or producing may be, most firms expend considerable sums on the sale process. Thus it is a rare situation under which revenue recognition should precede the sale. When this sale has occurred (and by this the accountant means the delivery of the goods), the only remaining function is to collect the money; this is ordinarily not a time-consuming or costly process. With the sale (delivery), most of the activity to produce the revenue has been performed.

By revenue the accountant means the inflow of assets as a result of the business operations. With the sale, an account receivable is received, but the value of this receivable can only be estimated until the cash is received or the receivable sold. It is possible that a particular receivable may be worthless but in most cases the loss due to bad debts may be estimated fairly accurately and hence the revenue may be recognized. The revenue should be the amount which the firm expects to collect from the customers, that is the billed price less the estimated discounts which will be taken and the estimated amounts which will be uncollectible. The accounts receivable should then be valued at the amount of revenue less the estimated cost of collection. In practice, the sales discounts which will be taken and the collection cost which will be incurred are frequently ignored; because these amounts are ordinarily small, the error is not a serious one.

In other cases, the facts may be different. In some, the sale is an unimportant step and revenue can be estimated before the sale takes place. In others, the collection process is a difficult one and the revenue cannot be reliably estimated until the cash is received.

If the price of a product is set at a fixed amount (ordinarily by government action) and if the market (the government is usually the buyer under these conditions) will absorb any quantity at this price, the sales department has no function. When the production process is complete only delivery of the goods and collection of proceeds is lacking to complete the series of transactions. These ordinarily require little effort and their cost can ordinarily be accurately estimated. Under these circumstances, revenue can be as accurately estimated when the goods are produced as when they are sold. It should then be shown at that time. The amount will be the estimated amount that will be received from the buyer (price less discounts and uncollectible amounts). The effect is that the inventory should be priced at selling price less the cost of delivery, the cost of collection and estimated uncollectible amounts and discounts. Gold production is an illustration of this type of activity.

At times, the price may not be a fixed amount, but the market will absorb the output of a particular producer without price variation.

This situation may be described as one in which the producer faces a demand curve that is perfectly elastic (elasticity approaching infinity). The producer could sell his output when the production process is completed. To hold it (as he sometimes does) is not a costless process; this course of action is desirable only if an increase in price is forecast. The firm is then engaging in two separate activities—production of a commodity and speculation in its price. The results of each should and can be measured. The revenue from production is the selling price that could be secured less estimated delivery costs, discounts, and uncollectibles. The inventory would then be priced at this amount less collection costs. All of these adjustments to price are likely to be small. An illustration of such a producer is the typical farmer.

Some producers operate under contracts which set the price before the production process is started. Such is frequently the case for a construction company. It obtains a contract to build a structure at a price of $1,000,000. The contract ordinarily provides for monthly payments of 90% of the contract price of the work performed during the previous month. This is only an estimate, of course, but for certain types of contracts, a reliable estimate is possible. If the estimate is reliable, revenue may well be shown as work progresses; the work has been accomplished (there is no sale problem and ordinarily no collection problem), and an accurate measure of revenue can be made. Accounts receivable will reflect the estimated contract price of work performed for which cash has not yet been received.

In all the above cases, revenue recognition preceded delivery and passage of title. In others, revenue recognition should be deferred until after delivery and collection.

If uncollectible accounts are large and difficult to forecast or if the collection process is a costly one, revenue recognition at the time of sale is inappropriate. The process is not complete until cash is collected and no reliable estimate of revenue can be made until then. The account receivable should be valued at the costs incurred up to the point of delivery of the goods or services. The country doctor is often in this situation.

A special case of uncertainty exists in certain types of installment sales. If collection is uncertain or costly (both conditions may exist), the seller of goods on the installment basis should recognize revenue only as the cash is collected. At the time of sale (if no down-payment is received), no revenue should be shown; the account receivable should be valued at the costs incurred. The amount billed would be shown in the Accounts Receivable account; the difference between this amount and the costs incurred should be shown in a Deferred Profit account with the balance sheet presentation as follows:

Accounts receivable	XX
Less: Deferred profit	XX
	XX

As amounts are collected, revenue will be shown.

At times the collection of cash will precede the delivery of the product of the service. Subscriptions to magazines, the transportation of persons, the rental of real estate—in all of these cases, the receipt of cash is frequently the first step in the business process. There is then no problem of determining the amount of revenue, but the revenue has not been earned—that is very little of the activity necessary to produce the revenue has been performed. A railroad corporation's primary function is to provide transportation, not to sell tickets. Hence the receipt of cash produces no revenue; it results in a liability to provide the service. When the service is performed (or the product delivered), revenue results and the liability is eliminated.

Departures from these general principles are common in practicable application. Early recognition of revenue for income tax purposes results in early payment of taxes. If the law permits, deferral of revenue for tax purposes may therefore be desirable; the result is an interest-free loan from the government. In some cases, the income tax law requires that the accounting records be kept on the same basis as is used on the tax return; in others, this practice may be followed in order to minimize the record keeping. As the receipt of cash is usually the last step in the business process, recognition of revenue at this time is most desired by the business man. Hence many service enterprises and installment dealers use this as the basis of their accounting even though uncollectible accounts are small. Other dealers in merchandise and manufacturers are barred from the use of this method for tax purposes but may use it despite its prohibition. From this same stimulus comes the shunning of the production basis; revenue is deferred until the time of sale even though more useful results might otherwise be available.

Previous discussion has been directed to the seller of a product or service. From among the other types of activity attention will be directed to the long-term investor in bonds, and the investor in stocks.

An insurance company may purchase a $1000, 10 year, 4% bond

for $960.44. This price will result in the buyer receiving a return of 4½% on his investment. This bond entitles the owner to receive:

at maturity (in 10 years)	$1,000.00
periodically, $40.00 (4% of $1000)	
per year for 10 years	400.00
	$1,400.00

The cost of the bond being $960.44, the insurance company will earn a total of $439.56 ($1400.00 less $960.44) over the ten year period.

Although accountants are agreed that the total revenue is $439.56, there is no general agreement as to the revenue per year. Some accountants would use $43.96 (one-tenth of the total) for each year. Others would use 4½% of the investment as the revenue; the revenue the first year would then be $43.22.

During the first year revenue of $43.96 (or $43.22) would be shown but only $40.00 in cash would be received. The difference $3.96 (or $3.22) can be shown as revenue because (1) the revenue is received as a payment for the use of money and a year's use of money has been provided and (2) the amount is specifically provided for by contract. The only justifiable exception to this procedure would be if receipt of the $1,000.00 is doubtful. The revenue not currently received in cash will be received when the bond matures; hence the asset, first carried at its cost of $960.44 increases by $3.96 (or $3.22) the first year and by similar amounts in later years.

Some firms may show revenue of only $40.00, for only $40.00 is taxable during the life of the bond. This is another illustration of the effect of income taxes on accounting procedure.

Some firms own common stock which has an active market and own such a small number of shares that their action does not affect the market. On December 31, 1965 such a firm purchases 100 shares at a cost of $40.00 per share. During 1966 the issuing corporation earned $4.25 per share (total net income divided by the number of shares outstanding), and paid dividends of $3.00 to its stockholders. At the end of the year (December 31, 1966), the price of the stock was $38.75 per share.

The revenue is earned by the investor as a result of owning the stock and taking a risk for a period of time. This investor has performed this function for one year. The $38.75 (December 31, 1966 price) and the $3.00 (the dividend) are accurately measured amounts. Hence we can say that the revenue from ownership of stock is $1.75, calculated as follows:

Market value, Dec. 31, 1966	$38.75
Dividend received	3.00
	$41.75
Market value, Dec. 31, 1965	40.00
Revenue	$ 1.75

Although cash has increased by $3.00, the investment has decreased by $1.25.

Despite the measurability of this revenue, accountants ordinarily will show $3.00 revenue for this investment. This can be defended as a method of eliminating the need for judgment; at times the question of whether the investor could have realized this price is a difficult one. The number of shares owned by this firm and the activity of the market must be considered.

The determination of income requires the determination of expense as well as of revenue. In general, the accountant assigns costs to periods of time on the basis of association with revenue. If $10,000.00 revenue is recognized in 1966, the income statement should include all costs associated with that revenue, whether these costs have been incurred in past years, are incurred in the present year, or will be incurred in future years.

The cost of merchandise, for instance, is not necessarily charged as an expense in the year in which the merchandise is purchased or in the year in which payment is made. The total cost of merchandise purchased during 1966 is not treated as an expense for 1966; only that portion related to revenue is so considered; the result is an asset carried forward to 1967.

The same process is carried on with such assets as buildings and equipment. The portion of the total cost that is related to the current year is charged to current revenue (and called "depreciation"); the remainder is carried forward to be charged against the revenue of subsequent years.

Sometimes the cash is paid in the following year. Employees' services may be used to produce revenue for 1966 but may not be compensated until 1967. The expense is recorded in 1966; a liability will also be shown.

The application of this principle is one of the difficult (and still unsolved) problems of accounting. Advertising costs incurred in 1966 (to sponsor a television program, for example) will probably benefit 1966 and later years. Yet we are not sure that any revenue will be produced by the program. Even if we are, we do not know what portion of the benefit will be received in 1966 and how much in later years nor do we know how many years will benefit from the expenditure. The accountant usually is "conservative" and charges all of the 1966 advertising cost to the 1966 revenue. The same problem arises with research and experimental costs.

In the case of inventories and fixed assets, we may agree that some of the costs are expenses and some are assets. Despite this, later assignments will indicate that making this division is not an easy task; the process is largely an arbitrary one.

In some cases the problem is largely one of estimating future events. A roof applied in 1966 may be guaranteed for five years; necessary repairs during this period will be made by the roofing company. As an expense for 1966 there should be shown costs which will be incurred during 1967 to 1971 inclusive. These must be estimated and the estimation process may be a poor one. Frequently, therefore, the accountant will not show these costs as expenses until they are incurred. Revenue of 1971 may be charged with expenses that should have been shown on the income statement for 1966.

At times accounting procedure is difficult to rationalize. Sales made late in 1966, may result in collection costs being incurred in 1967, discounts being incurred in 1967, or accounts receivable being collected in 1967. It is common (almost universal among larger firms) to charge bad debts to 1966 (as an adjustment to revenue) by setting up an Allowance for Bad Debts. It is not common to follow similar procedure for collection costs and sales discounts. These are ordinarily shown as an expense (Collection Expense) and as a revenue adjustment (Sales Discounts) for 1967.

For general purposes, the following are the basic ideas which require understanding: (1) measurement of both revenue and expense requires estimates; (2) these estimates are not easy to make and will differ from accountant to accountant and from business organization to business organization, and (3) because of difficulty of estimation or the small amount involved, the revenue or expense may deliberately be placed in the wrong period.

QUESTIONS

1. What is the "cost" of an asset?
2. At what amount should gifts of assets be recorded? How should the "ownership" be reflected in the proprietorship section of the position statement?

3. Under what circumstances does the firm's net income or loss become more than an estimate?

4. How can you justify recognition of revenue at the time of sale even if there is a possibility of not collecting the receivable?

5. Under what circumstances might revenue be recognized prior to the sale? Subsequent to the sale?

6. Why may income tax considerations lead to deviation from the general principles of revenue recognition? What might be done by accountants and others if this results in departure from general accounting principles?

7. How can we justify recognizing the discount on the purchase of bonds as revenue during the life of the bond? What in essence is the discount on a bond?

8. What is the "conservative" approach employed by most accountants in treating advertising and research and development expenditures which "may" enhance future revenues?

5

Realized Revenue

E. A. Heilman

THE MOST widely enunciated principle of revenue determination is that revenue is realized as the result of the sale of commodities or services. This principle has found general acceptance in accounting literature and in business and legal practice. A number of accounting writers go so far as to state positively that this is the sole principle of revenue determination.

The concepts of "revenue" and "cost" are two of the most difficult in the whole field of economics and accounting to define in anything like precise terms. Revenue accrues to an individual or a business in something like a continuous stream and the task to which accounting has set itself, that of breaking down this stream into periodic segments, is attended with more difficulties than most of

From *The Accounting Review,* vol. IV, no. 2 (June, 1929), pp. 80–87. Reprinted by permission of the editor. The late Mr. Heilman was a Professor of Accounting at the University of Minnesota and a former President of the American Accounting Association.

us like to admit. With the large number of incomplete transactions which carry over from one such period to the next, any answer which we may give to the question of how this revenue may be equitably divided between periods is bound to be largely a tentative one, subject to revision in the light of future developments.

There can be no question that much revenue is earned as the result of the joint operations of two different fiscal periods, since only part of the services for which the final price is paid by the purchaser are performed in each period and part of the costs of furnishing these services falls into each. This leaves open three possible treatments of the costs and revenues concerned. First, the costs of each period may be considered as incurred in earning only the revenues received during that period; second, some of the costs of the first period may be deferred to the period in which the total revenue is received; third, the total revenue may be divided between the two periods on some reasonable basis.

Actually each of these methods has found acceptance in some business but the more usual accounting treatments seldom apportion the revenue, but elect to defer production costs to the period of revenue receipt and to charge commercial expenses against the net income of the period in which they arise. With the wide diversity we find in different enterprises in methods of sale, types of sales contracts, methods of production, and in collection methods it would seem reasonable to assume that no single test of revenue realization would meet all situations with the same degree of satisfaction and I hope to show in this paper that other methods of apportioning revenue between periods should be used and that there is good conservative ground for varying the test of revenue realization with the differing circumstances with which accounting has to deal. Accounting texts sometimes admit a number of situations which may need exceptional treatment but the number and importance of these situations is seldom accented and usually there is no open admission that another test of revenue realization has been applied, and only two or three authors have directly discussed and weighed other general tests which might be employed.

It is my purpose to raise this question and point out a wider range of business conditions and situations in which I think the sale test must be modified or other more adequate tests applied if we wish to arrive at the best measure of periodic net income or changes in economic position.

In the case of the sale of merchandise the chain of events leading up to the receipt of revenue begins with the purchase of the merchandise itself; in the sale of a manufactured commodity it leads back to the purchase of the raw material. In fact, we might go so far as to say that the chain of services leads back still farther to the establishment of the business itself, which was the first step in a long series of efforts and expenditures producing a continuous series of revenues during the life history of the enterprise. Through cost allocations we spread these costs over the fiscal periods and thus obtain something like an equitable relation between revenues and cost. From the time of purchase to the time of settlement of the sale a considerable number of steps are taken all of which contribute to the final result.

Generally speaking, therefore, it is illogical to assign to any one step in this whole series the whole credit for having earned the resulting revenue. In particular situations we may be convinced that the main factor in earning a certain revenue was splendid sales work, excellent purchasing, a brilliant discovery, or some increased productive efficiency, but in the usual run of accounting record we do not attempt to measure separately the revenues attributable to each step in the business process. Mr. Paton * has specifically raised the question whether it would be more logical to accrue revenue along with costs, but so far this viewpoint has found acceptance in practice only in the case of long-term construction contracts. Mr. Hatfield has also suggested situations where the credit for net income must be given to other transactions than the sale. It would seem peculiar therefore to contend that the obtaining of an order and shipment of the goods alone is responsible for the revenue earned. This would be lending too much accounting support to the feeling of salesmen and sales departments that they are the only revenue producing units of the organization and are supporting the payrolls of the other departments and would be exalting unduly the importance of mere order takers in the economic structure of the business.

The defense of the sale as a test of revenue realized lies rather in the fact that it is the last vital step in the longer business process which indicates that the task is now completed and the revenue fully earned. In the trading field and in a large percentage of that of production as well, goods are bought or produced in anticipation of sales and are finally passed on to the customer after some sales effort. Whether production or sale is the more important or costly function of the business may depend upon the nature of the business operations

* EDITORS' NOTE: Professor Paton is a notable contributor to accounting literature. Professor Hatfield also had that distinction.

but revenue is not assured until sale is assured and the sale constitutes the last important step in the process, hence conservative net income determination cannot safely precede that point. The revenue figure can at that point be considered definitely ascertainable, the certainty of final receipt is high, a legal cause of action against outsiders has arisen, and it is now possible to include the amount in the liquid funds which will shortly be available for expenditure or distribution to stockholders, all of which are highly desirable characteristics of good revenue.

It is true the business process may not yet be entirely complete and there are still a number of services which have to be furnished, involving some cost to the concern, such as carrying cost, collection expense, bookkeeping, but these are not usually large nor important and can be reduced to estimates deducted in calculating the net income. Allowances, rebates, returns, discounts, transportation may still have to be dealt with, some of which are estimated, others neglected entirely until they have to be met.

These instances will serve to remind us that "completion of the business services" in this connection can mean only "substantial completion" and the accountant may therefore be justified in asking whether the credit sale is not too early a state in the process for proper net income calculation. Accountants and business men are now quite generally agreed it is not, though in the earlier years of accounting it was not considered conservative nor safe because of the uncertainty of collection. Provisions for uncollectibles and other estimated deductions from sales revenue now considered amply safe. This may be accomplished in two different ways—by postponing the credit for that portion of the revenue which might be fairly attributable to these further services to be rendered, or by making deduction of liberal allowances for the losses or costs still to be incurred. Accounting practice in general is following the second method by setting up allowances for bad accounts, discounts, and rebates.

Those concerns which sell subject to a free service period, as do some auto dealers and vendors of oil heating plants, will make proper allowance for the further costs or losses to be borne subsequent to sale or even to collection, or possibly withhold the credit for that part of the price which is for service costs. Where the deduction for estimated service costs is made on the basis of regular selling prices of the service department, as is sometimes done by auto dealers, the service department later billing the sales department as regular prices, this amounts to calculating the net income on the service work as the service is given rather than at the time of car sale. It is a recognition of the fact that the service is a separate factor in the sale price.

From the standpoint of the exactness with which revenue can be measured and the assurance of results the sale has proved reasonably satisfactory. Where, however, realization values on accounts receivable are uncertain and collection costs apt to be high the credit sale is distinctly inferior to the cash basis. This has been the major factor in the use of the cash basis for professional men, which has had income tax approval for some time. . . . The cash basis also has its application in enterprises where accounting and business methods are unstandardized, cash in hand there constituting the most reasonable approximation of revenue.

The use of the cash or collection basis in the installment business also results partly from this higher degree of uncertainty as to collections, and collection and repossession costs. The collection basis may also be urged because it is evident that in the installment field the business process includes a longer credit step and is therefore by no means so "substantially complete" as in the usual credit sale. The handling of credits probably runs over a longer period than the whole transaction period of the business. Since installment selling in many lines has reached the point of complete segregation of trading operations from financing and collections in separate companies, we have rather conclusive evidence that the credit function in this case at least is sufficiently important to withhold revenue credits until some period of collection.

It should be pointed out, in connection with any discussion of the cash basis, that even the receipt of cash does not necessarily signify the end of business services to be furnished or costs to be incurred. A goodly number of the deductions previously mentioned would still have to be made, if accurate revenue figures are to be arrived at. . . .

Other advantages of the sale test are that it uses a regularly recurring business transaction to which to attach the revenue entry, it is simple in operation and comparatively uniform for the same establishment as well as for a fairly wide range of business. It gives us a revenue figure which is usually of importance in deciding dividend and net income investment policies. It is at least a revenue figure which represents what has already passed into the cash account or will shortly reach that destination. It, of course, cannot give any measure of the amount of that net income still on hand in liquid form, but no other revenue figure is apt to give us any such result. Some other possible tests would credit revenue, a goodly portion of which might not be available for this purpose for long periods.

Another strong factor in support of the sale is its superior legal standing. Of all possible tests it probably enjoys the highest legal recognition. The passing of title is a stage which the courts accept as evidence of the completed transaction and is the decisive element in most cases brought forward for court adjudication. . . . It is nevertheless true that accounting practice has not been very meticulous in its observation of the matter of passing of title but has more generally specialized on the fact of shipment as the indication that the sale transaction is complete, though in certain types of sales contracts title undoubtedly passes at some earlier point. The legal distinction between ascertained and unascertained goods is seldom made use of in accounting discussion of this point. Probably with the wide diversity in methods of retaining or passing title in installment sales agreements, title has become of less accounting significance.

In spite of these distinct advantages of the sale test it must be emphasized that there is still a wide portion of business in which conditions differ materially from those just assumed. It is evident that in those businesses which enter into sales contracts or take orders for goods in advance of production we have a situation somewhat different from the typical one outlined so far, and there is considerable room for doubt as to the exact stage at which revenue should be credited. The previous statement that the sale is the last vital step in the process no longer holds or it has to be modified since we are dealing with a series of steps all going to make up a completed sale. We therefore no longer have a single sale test. Let us suggest the following as some of the significant stages of the process:

1. Taking the order or signing the contract.
2. Purchase of the raw materials or placing a hedge to cover.
3. A longer or shorter production process.
4. Completion.
5. Segregation of the goods for the consignee.
6. Receipt by consignee.
7. Collection.

I am sure that the lack of uniformity between different types of business is here so complete that for each stage enumerated an industry or a number of companies might be found which use that particular stage for making the transfer to the revenue account.

It might seem absurd to calculate net income on receipt of a signed sales order before any steps toward production have been taken, though a broker, whose responsibility ceases at that point, might do so even though the company does not credit his commission until actual acceptance of the goods by the purchaser. In the milling industry where binding sales contracts are entered into in advance of production, and where sales are immediately covered in the wheat market by a purchase or a hedge, there is some considerable reason for defending a revenue procedure which takes credit for the net income on such covered sales in advance of filling the order. The amount earned on the sale can be considered reasonably certain, since we have a legally binding contract which is usually enforced. There will of course be losses on cancelled contracts but in normal times these are not so numerous as bad accounts. . . . From the standpoint of "substantial completion of the business process" such a method would be subject to criticism, since the real function of the milling company has not yet been performed. It might be justifiable to take credit for a portion of the net income at this time since substantial services have already been performed on the contract but it is scarcely timely to credit the whole revenue, no matter what costs are deducted.

On the other hand, production as a test of revenue realized has much in its favor in those cases where there is no longer any question of having to sell. Where a definite order is on hand and the goods are ready for delivery only the relatively unimportant step of delivery to the carrier remains to convert them into receivables, and it seems unnecessarily conservative to insist on the last letter of the law. A distinction between stock goods and special might be made and the justice admitted of considering one unsold until definitely segregated and set aside for the particular order, since legal title depends on these factors. Special goods, however, would not need to wait for this procedure. A more important matter from the accounting standpoint and one more frequently considered, is the practice of the business in insisting on carrying out sales contracts, and the number of cancellations which are permitted. Again reasonable provisions for such losses of net income may be made. Substantial performance is certainly present in these transactions to almost as high a degree as in the usual credit sale. A somewhat stronger case can be made for those companies whose output is contracted for in total at either a fixed price or market. Evidently the degree of certainty of result is very high and the business process of the company ceases with production and shipment. Finished goods held for shipping orders can certainly be listed at selling prices, since the only uncertainty is the exact length of time which may elapse before shipment.

In the contracting firm this procedure has been carried a step farther, at least in the case of long-term contracts, in that net income is regularly calculated at the end of the fiscal period on unfinished work on the basis of percentage of completion. The impelling reason for this method is of course that in no other way can the company arrive at anything like an equitable distribution of its revenue between periods. It appears manifestly illogical to withhold all net income on a two year contract until time of completion but the method adopted involves the acceptance of the principle that revenue accrues on every $1 of expenditure on the contract. Some good point attaches to the argument that net income depends directly on satisfactory completion of the contract and that in case of failure to complete, losses rather than earnings would result. Also final inspection may disclose deductions to be made for unsatisfactory work. But these hazards are not usually considered sufficiently important to invalidate the procedure adopted. The method is even more applicable to cost plus contracts where net income is calculated directly in connection with all work done. A rather high degree of estimate is required to obtain the result, more so possibly than in the case of manufacturing, but the need is so plain that practice has usually condoned this fault.

In the case of contracting companies which carry on a considerable number of projects each year, some of which are incomplete at the end of the year, a fair showing of revenue may be made by including only net income on contracts finished. There is therefore not the same necessity for accruing net income on unfinished work and we find in practice that the method is less often used. Such firms approach more nearly the conditions in the manufacturing plant which produces on previous order and the usual cost assumption that unfinished work represents merely costs expended is usually applied. However the arguments given above in favor of percentage of completion apply here with the same degree of validity. Since sale realization follows directly upon completion and a considerable percentage of the whole year's work may be unfinished at statement time, net income on a goodly share of the year's work may be excluded from the revenue account.

The widespread use of the time of shipment for revenue credit is based in most cases on the same conservatism which will not take revenue until results are considered assured and from the standpoint of recording convenience, this is quite desirable. Where uncertainty as to acceptance of the shipment by the customer is present, it may be better to postpone the credit until notice of acceptance has been received; especially is this true of warehouse liens or drafts with attached bills of lading where dealers sometimes fail to raise sufficient funds in time to take up the drafts.

There is another type of sales situation which needs further discussion. I have defended the sale on the ground that it most frequently is the last vital step in the business process. There are however a goodly number of industries and business situations in which the sale is not a very vital step. Wherever sale follows quite as a matter of course or presents no problem to the management it also becomes of negligible importance in revenue determination. I have already cited the case of the company which has its output contracted for in advance, which is somewhat akin to this condition. Farming represents possibly the best example, for the farmer is a producer and not a merchant, and a grain market or an elevator stands ready to take his entire output off his hands when delivered. The farm price method of inventory has long been recognized and means of course that production is the earning-point in revenue calculations.

A number of other extractive industries are in the same position since a general market stands ready to take their product at the going price and the company has merely to make its decision as to when and where it will market its commodity to convert inventory into sale. Theirs is purely a production problem and it is reasonable to calculate net income on ore inventories. There is of course the problem of fluctuations of market prices to be considered, and the exactness with which final revenue to be received can be calculated may be questioned. Any revenue figure arrived at might rather be one "realizable at the present time" rather than one realized at the actual time of delivery to the market. If the industry elects to hold its goods for higher prices, it is to that extent speculating on the market and thereby has a speculative gain or loss to deal with in addition to the net income on production.

Another situation in which the sale is quite negligible is in the case of holding marketable securities. Value-increases in the security account are convertible almost immediately into cash and this increase is much more readily realizable in cost than the net income on credit sales. A distinction has been made between owner-investors and dealers in securities. The investor is interested primarily in the annual return to be derived from his investments and in the security of his principal, so that market fluctuations do not greatly affect his investment policy.

Over longer periods, however, he will need to revalue his capital investment and is always interested in the market situation.

The dealer in securities purchases partly with the idea of making a gain on a speculative market and will convert his purchase into cash when he attains this gain. His financial position and his speculative gains cannot be determined until unsold securities are inventoried at market. A statement of net income in terms of completed sales only would give an entirely inadequate picture of his revenue. Accountants have always agreed to his inventorying at market where that is lower than cost but do not always countenance a higher valuation. The result is the same dual standard which has always obtained for merchandise inventories, losses being determined by either sale or market price, gains only by sale. In the case of the security dealer this is particularly objectionable since it results in an altogether distorted view of his net income where he holds both securities which have risen in value and some which have fallen. . . .

The same position should be taken for dealers in the other more speculative markets. Any reasonable statement of their position or profits would have to inventory all open trades and purchases at market. In some of the option markets a system of daily or weekly cash settlements converts such gains and losses into cash receipts and disbursements but the gain or loss is just as real whether this is done or not. These gains or losses are inherent in the particular trading situation and cannot be ignored without distorting both the statement of financial position and the net income. Whatever revenue is involved is highly realizable, just as available as accounts receivable, and is a regular source of loss or gain.

In this connection it is interesting to consider the peculiar position of one type of investment trust and the holder of the trust certificates. The trust is making two kinds of net incomes for its investors: if successful, (a.) income from securities and (b.) gains on rises in value of securities held. These rises in value at the end of a period may have been realized in cash by sale or may still be represented by securities on hand. A complete statement of net income for the trust would have to consider such appreciations as well as sales, at least where the investor may withdraw his investment and his share of the net income, let us say, at will. Some investors have therefore probably withdrawn both their share of net income realized in cash and those not yet validated by sale. Also no statement of the standing of the trust would be significant which did not show market values for securities.

The holder of the certificates of trust is in a still different position. Cash revenue to him is only dividends paid on the certificates, but he may realize his proportionate share of all gains of the trust by withdrawing. It would seem to me that in both these situations the best statement of net income and the best balance sheet would both have to be stated at market.

The discussion of securities has led us into the topic of appreciation; no discussion of tests of net income can pass without some reference to that topic. Appreciation of assets other than securities do not possess the element of certainty as to receipt or amount, there is usually no immediate prospect of realizing in cash or liquid funds, and it is difficult to set up a regular accounting process for recording without departing rather widely from the course of regular transactions. But there can be no doubt, it seems to me, of the importance of this factor for balance sheet purposes, and I do not see how, in the long run, appreciation of an asset like land can be kept off the balance sheet without making it a poorer statement for credit purposes and without distorting net income calculations at some point. As an example of the absurd results to which adhering to cost for land may lead us, let me cite the following instance. . . .

A farmer had purchased 200 acres of Iowa land in 1905 at $100 an acre. During the land boom of 1919 he sold his farm to this student at a price of $200 per acre, realizing a profit of $20,000 on cost; but only $4,000 was paid down. After looking about for a new place to farm he found his neighbors were all demanding $300 per acre; after a month's search he actually repurchased his own farm from this student at $225 per acre, returning the cash payment and paying a $5,000 bonus for his farm. Now current accounting methods would clearly record a profit on the sale of his farm of $20,000 and a new farm purchased for $45,000 at no loss. Evidently this is an absurd version of a transaction in which the only net result was the loss of $5,000 in cash by the farmer and an equivalent gain by the student. Surely here the sale as a sole test of revenue is inapplicable and some other basis of calculating net income or values would have to be used.

It is not possible in the brief compass of this paper to cover many of the essential details of the problem of revenue incidence, but I believe that I have been able to bring out a few of the more important considerations. I hope I have contributed some more evidence that:

1. While the sale is an adequate test of realized revenue in a large percentage of business conditions, the one-sided viewpoint that it is the sole revenue determinant must be denied;

2. That no single test can well satisfy all the varying conditions of production, sale, and credit service which are found in business practice;

3. That there is in fact no high degree of uniformity in the application of the sale test;

4. That in actual practice other tests are quite well recognized and are bound to receive more support;

5. That while the sale need not be refused because it is not the most conservative principle possible, neither can other tests be called unconservative because they are less conservative than the sale; and finally,

6. That proper accounting treatment of the revenue problem must take cognizance of the differences in business methods and operations and admit new treatments of the problems which may promise to give more accurate accounting and business results.

QUESTIONS

1. What are the three methods of treating costs and revenues relating to operations of two different accounting periods?

2. The author indicates that "good revenue" has certain desirable characteristics. Which of these characteristics are present at the time of sale?

3. Under what circumstances is there justification to use a cash-basis method of recognizing revenue from installment sales?

4. What is the legal significance of a sale?

5. The author cites a few examples of situations in which the "sale" as the last vital step in the business process may not be the appropriate basis for recognizing revenue. List and discuss.

6

Advance Ticket Sales Receipts Weren't Entitled to Deferred Tax Treatment

THE FORMER OWNERS of the Chicago White Sox received some $763,000 for baseball tickets sold in late 1961 and early 1962 in advance of some of the team's games in the 1962 season, but didn't report the prepayments as income in the fiscal year received. A successor company acquired the ball club's assets May 31, 1962, start of a new fiscal period, and was assessed a tax deficiency by the IRS for the predecessor company's claimed under-reporting. The Service's determination was in line with three recent U.S. Supreme Court decisions in different situations that tax-

From *The Wall Street Journal*, "Tax Report," vol. CLXV, no. 23 (February 3, 1965), p. 1. Reprinted by permission of the publisher.

payers had to report prepaid but unearned income in the year received.

The White Sox' new owners have appealed the case to the Tax Court. They contend the money in the case of advance baseball ticket sales shouldn't be counted as taxable income until the games are actually played.

Not until then, they argue, is the revenue earned and all of the expenses related to it incurred "to clearly reflect income."

QUESTION

1. Assuming that the calendar year is the accounting period, how should the White Sox account for $763,000 received in 1961? Why?

7

Copper-Goods Makers Consider Mill Cutbacks To Avoid Higher Taxes

NEW YORK—Several fabricators of copper products are considering curtailing mill operations to avoid the higher income taxes that would result from depleted year-end inventories.

The move further illustrates the increasing tightness of the copper supply. Normally, the fabricators would simply rebuild their stocks at the end of the year to avoid the added taxes. But this year supplies are so tight that the mills have to pay premium prices for their copper of up to twice the producer quote and therefore can't rebuild their stocks at normal costs.

From *The Wall Street Journal*, vol. CLXV, no. 93 (November 9, 1964), p. 11. Reprinted by permission of the publisher.

Copper inventories for these mills are calculated under the last-in, first-out—or LIFO—method of figuring inventory. Under LIFO, materials are evaluated at current costs rather than actual earlier costs, thus reducing taxable profit on sales in periods of rising prices.

Such higher present costs may be applied, however, only if the year-end inventory is the same or greater than that of a year earlier. As the inventory goes down, the law requires a taxable profit to be reported on that part of the inventory that has been sold or used up, with the profit on it reflecting the excess of the calculated sale price over the actual original cost.

And the recent sharp increases in copper prices mean the spread between sales receipts and original inventory costs is widening, with the result that taxable profits are disproportionately greater.

Major Producers Cut Back

The scarcity of copper, coupled with the strong demand, has already forced curtailed deliveries by three major producers. Anaconda Co. has cut deliveries by 25% to U.S. and overseas consumers because of a recent slowdown at its Chilean copper refinery. Phelps Dodge Corp. has cut its November shipments by 25% and Kennecott Copper Corp. recently reduced by 35% the shipments of its Chilean copper to non-Chilean users; none of Kennecott's Chilean production is sold in the U.S. Copper has been in short supply because of summer-long labor difficulties in the U.S. and abroad.

The price dealers quote for copper rose another cent a pound last week, to 62 cents for December delivery and 60 cents for January shipment. Copper futures contracts rose to new highs during the week but closed on Friday unchanged to off 1.4 cents a pound from a week before.

8

Swift & Co. Net in Fiscal '65 Fell 35%; Sales Up 5%

CHICAGO—Reporting on "a difficult year in the meat industry," Swift & Co. said its fiscal 1965 profit fell 35% from a year earlier, despite a 5% sales rise.

The nation's largest meat-packer reported net income in the year ended last Oct. 30 of $16,350,888, or $2.70 a common share, down from $25,294,331, or $4.17 a share, in fiscal 1964. Sales rose to $2,750,956,717 from $2,614,845,977.

"Results were reduced principally by unfavorable returns in two major product departments and the application of the last-in, first-out (LIFO) method used in valuing product inventories," Porter Jarvis, chairman, and Robert W. Reneker, president, stated in the annual report.

From *The Wall Street Journal*, vol. CLXVI, no. 120 (December 20, 1965), p. 8. Reprinted by permission of the publisher.

Soaring Hog Prices

"Both fresh-pork and processed-meat departments had poor results," they said. "This was due chiefly to soaring live-hog prices (about a 54% rise during the fiscal year) without a commensurate increase in the value of pork products (about 42%). The tight squeeze on margins persisted throughout the year."

Use of the LIFO inventory-accounting methods in which inventories last purchased are considered sold first and are thus charged against current sales, resulted in a charge of $7,444,000 against income after taxes, in contrast to a LIFO credit of $968,000 in fiscal 1964, Messrs. Jarvis and Reneker said. "When commodity prices rise sharply, the immediate effect that LIFO imposes tends to be balanced out over succeeding years," they commented. "Since its adoption in 1941, the LIFO method has proved beneficial to Swift."

Swift's earnings decline was especially steep during the fiscal second half. Indicated second half earnings plunged 45%, to $8,048,189, from the year-earlier indicated $14,662,662. Indicated earnings were obtained by subtracting first half net income from full-year profit. Swift's first half earnings were down 22% from a year earlier.

Capital expenditures in fiscal 1966 will climb sharply to about $60,000,000 from $38,219,758 in fiscal 1965, the company said.

"We are optimistic about Swift's future," Messrs. Jarvis and Reneker said. "The long-range outlook is good." On the fiscal 1966 outlook, they noted that the "ups and downs" of Swift's business "always pose problems in projecting Swift's future." But they added there are "many developments on the plus side which brighten our outlook," including rising consumer income, expanding product lines and extra effort in cost-reduction.

Numerous Plant Closings

The report mentioned numerous plant closings and consolidations being made to improve efficiency. "Tighter cost controls and expense-reduction efforts comprise an area of intense activity," the Swift officials said.

"Marginal plants with poor profit prospects are being closed," they said.

Swift plans to close its Evansville, Ind., meat plant next Jan. 29. During the fiscal year, the report said, lamb processing was ended in St. Joseph, Mo., and Omaha; the number of ice-cream processing plants fell to 23 from 29; 5 domestic-sales units were closed; and feed-mill operations in Crane, Mo., and Terrell, Texas, were ended.

Reviewing fiscal 1965 results over Swift's wide-ranging activities, the executives reported:

Beef department earnings were "slightly higher" than in fiscal 1964. Total earnings of Swift's dairy and poultry business "were the best in more than a decade." Ice-cream, feed-mill and grocery division results weren't satisfactory. Overseas operations "showed continued earnings improvement." Swift's insurance-business results were "50% greater" than in fiscal 1964. Vegetable-oil operations and agricultural-chemicals results showed substantial improvement.

Swift & Co. and subsidiaries report for the 52 weeks ended Oct. 30:

	52 wks. end Oct. 30, '65	53 wks. end Oct. 31, '64 †
Earned per share	$ 2.70	$ 4.17
Sales includes service revenue	2,750,956,717.00	2,614,845,977.00
Total income *	2,755,213,565.00	2,618,777,533.00
Net before income taxes	26,116,786.00	42,900,121.00
Income taxes	9,765,898.00	17,605,790.00
Net income	16,350,888.00	25,294,331.00
Capital shares	6,064,777.00	6,064,777.00

* Includes $1,901,408 in 1965 and $1,239,500 in 1964 as equity in earnings of affiliated insurance companies.

† Includes operations of National Wax Co., acquired during 1955, on a pooling-of-interests basis.

QUESTIONS

1. If cost prices are rising, how can LIFO result in *higher* taxable income than FIFO?

2. The article states that certain copper fabricators intended to cut production and deliveries to prevent depletion of raw material inventories.

   a. How would this action avoid higher taxes for firms using LIFO?

   b. If the copper were not in short supply, would a firm using LIFO take the same action to avoid taxes? Explain.

    c. If copper is in short supply and if copper prices have been rising, would a firm using FIFO be apt to act differently than a firm using LIFO? In other words, would the copper fabricators respond differently to a copper shortage if they used FIFO rather than LIFO? Explain.

    d. Why do you suppose copper fabricators adopted LIFO in the first place?

    3. The tax law requires that if LIFO is used for tax purposes, then it must also be used for general reporting purposes. How would this requirement thwart an attempt to resolve the inventory costing controversy by the pronouncement of a "general principle"?

    4. Why is it often asserted that LIFO is the best inventory costing method for tax purposes? Is this always the case?

9

What Is a Balance-sheet?

William H. Whitney

LIKE THOUSANDS of other accountants, the author of this article has prepared many balance-sheets. In this work, he has attempted to adhere to certain traditional procedures, which he learned from accounting texts and from men who were older and more experienced. Somehow or other, perhaps from study or experience or instinct or contemplation, a sense of right and wrong developed. Traditional doctrines, such as "provide for all losses, anticipate no profits," "value inventory at the lower of cost or market," and "do not substitute appraised values of fixed assets for cost," came to seem safe, and departures from them came to seem dangerous. There were times when departures seemed unavoidable and when forceful criticisms shook his faith in the traditional doctrines.

From *The Journal of Accountancy*, vol. LXXX, no. 4 (October, 1940), pp. 293–308. Reprinted by permission of the publisher. Mr. Whitney is a certified public accountant of Ohio. In addition, he has been an educator and an industrial accountant.
NOTE: A rejoinder to this article entitled "What Is an Asset?" by James L. Dohr follows on pages 101 to 109.

To evaluate the criticisms, to determine what acts are and are not "permissible," and to decide whether there really is a sound basis for the traditional procedures, he found it necessary to try to integrate them. Are they mere results of custom and habit, or is there a reason for adhering to them? Have they a definable purpose? Do they lead to a describable goal? Can they be integrated? Is there any reason for preferring costs over appraisals? When an accountant is engaged in preparing a balance-sheet, according to the traditional procedures, is he attempting to prepare a statement of assets, liabilities, and net worth? If not, what is he doing? Can his objective be defined in words other than "certified balance-sheet"?

This article is an attempt to answer these questions.

Some centuries ago the common-law courts in England refused to recognize the duty of one, who was entrusted with the property of another, to account to the equitable owner for the use of the property. Appeal was taken to courts of equity, and the equitable doctrines of trust and accounting developed. The accounting principles adopted by courts of equity are exemplified in the accounting statements required from executors, administrators, trustees, receivers, conservators, agents, and other fiduciaries. The accounting procedures taught in accounting texts and adhered to by the overwhelming majority of accounting firms, in spite of vigorous demands for abandonment, agree in principle with these equitable doctrines. Traditional accounting procedures seem to originate from the same sense of fairness, justice, and reasonableness, often called common sense, that has actuated the decisions of courts of equity. Perhaps the accounting procedures of court-controlled fiduciaries have exerted an important influence on modern accounting practice.

Accounting statements rendered to the courts by fiduciaries are composed of the following elements:

First: A statement of value received for the account of the equitable owner.

Second: Lists of subsequent income, and other receipts.

Third: Lists of expenditures.

Fourth: A statement of properties held for the account of the equitable owner, together with liabilities applicable thereto. On this statement, properties, which were originally entrusted to the fiduciary, are listed at the value then determined, less reasonable allowances for depreciation, when it is appropriate. Properties subsequently purchased are required to be recorded at cost, or cost less reasonable allowances for depreciation.

It is not difficult to discover the reason that courts of equity prefer accounts based on cost. Accounting on other bases is not impossible, but accounts based on cost are easier to understand and check. One does not need special training or study to prepare or comprehend such statements. Millions of fiduciaries who have never seen the inside of an accounting textbook, have prepared statements in which they have satisfactorily accounted to the courts for their use of entrusted property. Even a very young child can make such a statement. For example: Let us assume that a mother sends a child to the grocery store with a dollar, and instructs the child to buy a loaf of bread, a pound of butter, and five pounds of sugar. When the child returns with these articles he brings back a quarter, and with a little help from his mother can submit an account like the following:

Cash received		$1.00
Expenditures		
One loaf of bread	$.10	
One pound of butter	.35	
Five pounds of sugar	.30	.75
Change returned		.25

This simple statement contains the essence of all accounting to rightful or equitable owners for use of their funds. It discloses the funds received for the account of the owner, the use made of them, and the unused balance.

Like this child, and like all of those whom courts of equity formally recognize as fiduciaries, corporation managements have a duty to account to shareholders for the use of their invested funds. This duty is formally recognized in the statutes of some of the states.[1] But neither

---

[1] For example, Ohio G.C. 8623–64 reads as follows: "At the annual meeting, or any other meeting at which directors are to be elected, every corporation, except banks, shall lay before the shareholders a statement of profit and loss and a balance-sheet containing a summary of the assets and liabilities, a summary of profit earned, dividends paid, and other changes in the surplus account of the company, made up to a date not more than four months before such meeting, from the date up to which the last preceding statement, account and balance-sheet were made up, and in the case of the first statement and balance-sheet, from the incorporation of the company.

"A certificate, signed by the president or vice-president and the treasurer, or an assistant treasurer or a public accountant or firm of public accountants, shall be appended to such statement of profit and loss and balance-sheet, stating that they are

the statutes nor the courts prescribe the bases to be used in accounting to the shareholders at annual meetings.[2] Consequently, there is a great deal of honest difference of opinion about the comparative merits of accounts based on cost and accounts based on appraisals.

For example, during 1939, Kenneth MacNeal, certified public accountant, devoted the major portion of a 324-page book to a bitter condemnation of cost as a basis for balance-sheet values.[3] He advocates the use of appraised and market values on all published statements. In 1937, Judge Robert E. Healy presented the opposite view. In an address before the American Accounting Association he recounted some of his experiences on the Securities and Exchange Commission with corporations that adjusted asset values to appraisals. He criticized accountants for certifying balance-sheets containing appraised values, in these words, "I think the purpose of accounting is to account—not to present opinions of value." [4] Obviously, Mr. MacNeal believes that a balance-sheet should be a statement of assets, liabilities, and net worth, as that expression is generally understood by persons who have not studied or practiced accountancy. To such persons, the phrase means that the statement lists all of the assets at their fair or true or actual *values* on the balance-sheet date, and that the net-worth section discloses the excess of the fair or true or actual *value* of all of the assets over the liabilities.

Mr. MacNeal effectively proves that some balance-sheets which are based on cost are not reasonably accurate statements of *values* existing on the balance-sheet date, by pointing to instances when *costs and depreciated costs* are not fair measures of *value*. Differences be-

---

true and correct and that they exhibit a fair view of the state of the corporation's affairs according to its books.

"The corporation shall, upon written request of any shareholder made after notice of any such meeting, forthwith mail to such requesting shareholder a copy of such statement of profit and loss and balance-sheet."

[2] The statutes of some of the states do not permit appraised values to be used for all purposes. For example: Ohio G.C. 8623–38 (b) contains the following instructions regarding the computation of surplus for dividend purposes: "In computing the excess of the assets for the purpose of determining the fund available for a dividend payable otherwise than in shares of a corporation, deduction shall also be made for the unrealized appreciation, if any, appearing on its books unless the amount thereof shall have been transferred to or included in stated capital."

[3] Kenneth MacNeal, *Truth in Accounting* (Philadelphia: University of Pennsylvania Press, 1939).

[4] Judge Robert E. Healy, "The Next Step in Accounting," *The Accounting Review* (March, 1938), p. 6.

tween *costs* and *values* frequently are substantial if the fixed assets were purchased several years before a balance-sheet is published. The growth of cities and the character of surrounding developments profoundly affect land values. Building values are affected by the same factors, by changes in price levels, changes in style, and modern improvements in structural design and arrangement.

Even at the time when assets are acquired in arm's length transactions, cost is not always a fair measure of value. A buyer who is "hard" and "smart" will buy the same commodity in the same market for less than a buyer who is "an easy mark." [5] The value of the commodity in the hands of the former is likely to be higher than the value of the same commodity in the hands of the latter, although the cost to the former is less than the cost to the latter.

There are many other factors that cause marked differences between cost in arm's length transactions and fair value. For example, some years ago a corporation in Cleveland, Ohio, paid $371,000 for a foreclosed manufacturing plant of modern design in perfect physical condition. At the time of purchase it was appraised at $875,000. Within five years, the corporation that was created to occupy it, was earning more than $200,000 per year and in the years that have followed its net earnings have aggregated more than $2,000,000. In this instance could cost possibly be considered a fair measure of value either at the time of purchase or subsequently? Clearly the answer is no. The building and machinery sold at a low price because the corporation that had occupied it became bankrupt. The machinery was suitable only for making one line of products and most investors were afraid to take a chance in a location and in a line of endeavor where another had failed. Prejudice made this manufacturing plant sell in an arm's length transaction for a fraction of its value.

Ratio of supply and demand may determine price, or cost, but it does not determine value. Was the fair value of Chrysler stock $300 per share in 1929 and $6 per share in 1932? It sold at those prices. If costs are values, what is the present value of 100 shares of Chrysler stock purchased in 1929 and 100 shares purchased in 1932?

In the early part of 1920 a certain wholesaler of dry goods in New York City called in its salesmen and one of the officers addressed them somewhat as follows: "The goods that we are buying and selling are not worth the prices that we are giving and getting. They never were and they never will be. Go out and tell that to your customers. Don't try to sell them anything. Tell them not to buy. Tell them to

[5] K. MacNeal, *op. cit.,* chap. I., "Three Fables."

reduce their inventories to a minimum. We are going to sell our inventory and buy only to fill uncancelable orders from responsible customers." The management of that wholesale dry goods company understood the difference between the meanings of the words "cost" and "value," and used this knowledge to preserve the financial integrity of their company and of many of their customers, in the crash that followed.

Mr. MacNeal believes that balance-sheets should disclose present values. To express his concept of present values he uses market and replacement.[6] This concept of value is the layman's concept. One dictionary defines value as "worth; importance; market price; estimated worth." [7] There is considerably more to the definition. Except for "market price," it does not contain words that can be interpreted with mathematical exactness. But there is nothing in the definition that suggests the accountants' concept of the value of a fixed asset, a prepaid expense having an expiration date that is uncertain. This concept was ably expressed in 1936 in the following definition, which is the product of the joint efforts of a large number of men, well schooled in accounting principles.

> The accountant's valuation of physical assets at any given point of time involves the determination of what part of original cost should be written off to reflect consumed, expired, or lost usefulness, and what part should be carried forward as reasonably applicable to future operations.[8]

The traditional procedures by which accountants arrive at the amounts displayed opposite items of fixed assets on balance-sheets, is described in most accounting texts as a valuation process; but in reality it is something very, very different from valuation, for two important reasons. First: If accountants did what is suggested in the definition immediately above, they would not obtain an amount that any grammarian, untrained in accountancy, would admit is a value. Depreciated cost and value are different concepts. Second: In connection with physical assets, accountants do not claim that they have the ability to determine "what part of original cost should be written off to reflect consumed, expired, or lost usefulness." In order to make determinations

[6] K. MacNeal, *op. cit.*, pp. 267–270.

[7] MacMillan's *Modern Dictionary* (New York: The MacMillan Company, 1938).

[8] "A Tentative Statement of Accounting Principles Affecting Corporate Reports," formulated by the executive committee of the Amerian Accounting Association, published in *The Accounting Review* (June, 1936), p. 188.

of this kind, accountants would have to be thoroughly familiar with the details of their clients' engineering and production problems, the activities of their competitors, and the progress of science and invention. Even if the accountants' definition of value, quoted above, is accepted as valid, the traditional procedures for computing amounts to be set opposite fixed assets do not result in a value. The largest degree of responsibility that an accountant can take in connection with the display of depreciable assets is to state that the allowance for depreciation appears to be adequate. This means something, and it is important, but it is not valuation.[9]

In practice the amounts shown opposite items of fixed assets on balance-sheets are merely unamortized costs, the consequences of certain decisions by management. There is no serious attempt to determine the amounts that "should be written off" and that "should be carried forward." A serious attempt would be an appraisal. Accountants do not appraise. The usual basis of computations is historical. During the years that have passed since the depreciable assets were acquired, charges have been made to operations or to surplus to build up a credit balance in an account called "Reserve for Depreciation." The balance of that account is determined by many factors, which are neither mentioned nor suggested in the definition quoted above. Frequently the amount is based on maximum rates allowed by the federal income-tax department. In determining depreciation rates, managements ponder such questions as these: "How much depreciation do we want to charge off?" "How much can we charge off?" "How much must we charge off?" They seldom base their charges to depreciation solely on unbiased estimates of probable life and residual value. If managements did that, and if they revised their estimates yearly in the light of their experience and the fullest obtainable knowledge of future

[9] The inadequacy of accountants' examinations of depreciation rates, from a valuation viewpoint, is suggested in many publications, two of which are cited below.

W. A. Hosmer, "The Effect of Direct Charges to Surplus on the Measurement of Income," *The Accounting Review* (March, 1938), p. 36. "In many instances depreciation and obsolescence proved to be greater than the amounts charged to operations in prior years," p. 33. In the year 1936 the U.S. Steel Corporation made a surplus adjustment of $270,000,000 to correct estimates of depreciation and amortization in prior years.

Howard C. Greer, "Application of Accounting Rules and Standards to Financial Statements," *The Accounting Review* (December, 1938), p. 345. Mr. Greer made a study of extraordinary charges or credits to surplus or profit and loss, disclosed on the published statements of eighteen corporations during a nine-year period. He found nineteen identifiable instances in which charges were made covering "extraordinary depreciation and losses on sale or retirement of capital assets."

probabilities, and if the accountants' warped and stretched concept of value is accepted as valid, then the traditional method of computing the amounts to be shown opposite items of fixed assets on balance-sheets could be accurately described as a valuation process.

Accountants frankly and freely admit that balance-sheets do not portray present values of assets and net worth, when the word values is interpreted in its ordinary nontechnical sense. To corroborate this theme, Mr. MacNeal quotes the following from a letter sent to a committee of the New York Stock Exchange by a committee of the American Institute of Accountants: *

> The principal objects which the committee thinks the Exchange should keep constantly in mind and do its best gradually to achieve are:
>
> 1. To bring about a better recognition by the investing public of the fact that the balance-sheet of a large modern corporation does not and should not be expected to represent an attempt to show present values of the assets and liabilities of the corporation.
> 2. To emphasize the fact that balance-sheets are necessarily to a large extent historical and conventional in character, and to encourage the adoption of revised forms of balance-sheets which will disclose more clearly than at present on what basis assets of various kinds are stated.[10]

Accountants who develop balance-sheets by using traditional accounting procedures do not attempt to include all of the assets. By deliberate choice they omit items that have enormous values that could be immediately realized; such items as valuable franchises acquired without cost, patents developed by research departments whose operating costs are charged to expense, goodwill, or trade marks popularized by the owner (often worth more than all of the other assets combined), long-term leaseholds which have become valuable since acquisition, and enforceable contracts for the purchase of large quantities of needed materials at prices below present and anticipated market levels. Below the asset caption, accountants list items that are utterly unsalable, utterly devoid of present or future value, in the lay sense. Examples are discount on stock, premium on bonds owned, discount on bonds payable, prepaid federal capital-stock tax. In determining the amount to

---

* EDITORS' NOTE: The American Institute of Accountants has been renamed the American Institute of Certified Public Accountants.

[10] K. MacNeal, *op. cit.*, p. 319. Also, see *Audits of Corporate Accounts,* a booklet published by the American Institute of Accountants in 1934, p. 12.

be written opposite items of prepaid insurance no consideration is given to cancellation value, or replacement value, which may be substantially higher, if rates have increased since the policy was written. The amount shown is unamortized cost. It is proper to use the same amount in connection with policies which have no cancellation value or are not replaceable. Value, as that word is understood by laymen, does not affect the computation nor the propriety of showing the calculated amount preceded by a dollar sign on the balance-sheet.

The layman's concept of an asset is something of value owned. Accountants deliberately omit from their lists of assets properties that have large immediate values, because they did not cost anything or because the costs cannot easily be traced or allocated to them.[11] By admission of a committee of the American Institute "the balance-sheet of a large modern corporation does not and should not be expected to represent an attempt to show present values." [12] Items that have no present or future realizable value are listed below the asset caption.[13] A balance-sheet is not a statement of assets, liabilities, and net worth, if that phrase is given a nontechnical meaning. A statement which can be fairly described as a statement of assets, liabilities, and net worth, should include all of the assets at present values, as nearly as they can be estimated or computed by competent experts.

Investors and bankers are interested in the cost of assets in a mild sort of manner. They regard it as good information to have available. Their interest in costs does not center in the costs themselves. They are interested because costs sometimes are an index of competence of management and prospects for future profits. Investors and bankers want statements of assets, liabilities, and net worth that include all of the assets at present values as nearly as present values can be estimated or computed by competent experts. They do not want valuable assets excluded, because they did not cost anything or because the costs cannot be allocated or traced. They do not want assets listed at values which bear no relation to present realities, mere historical calculations of unamortized costs, which seldom are serious attempts to determine "what part of original cost should be written off to reflect consumed, expired, or lost usefulness, and what part should be carried forward." [14] A competent appraisal of unconsumed utility in fixed assets would interest

[11] For examples see the preceding paragraph.

[12] See quotation above, referred to in footnote 10.

[13] For examples see the preceding paragraph.

[14] See quotation above, referred to in footnote 8.

investors and creditors more than a mere statement of unamortized cost. But they really would like to have an expression of competent independent opinion on the present value of the property, an opinion which gives proper weight to consumed and unconsumed utility, and which also gives proper weight to replacement or reproduction costs, obsolescence, salability, profit prospects, and all other factors that should be taken into consideration in estimating or calculating the present value of fixed assets.

It can be said truthfully, that accountants engaged in preparing balance-sheets according to traditional procedures, are not attempting to make statements of assets, liabilities, and net worth, if that expression is interpreted in its grammatical, nontechnical sense. Traditional accounting procedures do not lead to that goal. But they do lead to the preparation of a statement which appears to be a statement of assets, liabilities, and net worth, because it contains a list of items captioned "Assets," another list captioned "Liabilities," and the excess of the former over the latter is shown in another section of the statement, often called the "Net Worth" section.

There are exceptions to the rule just stated. The assets of some financial institutions consist almost entirely of cash and items which have cash values that can be accurately determined. In such instances the traditional procedures sometimes result in balance-sheets which are accurate statements of assets, liabilities, and net worth. But the problem is different in the case of corporations that must invest large sums in fixed assets. For a few years following the organization of such corporations, balance-sheets based on cost are reasonably accurate statements of assets, liabilities, and net worth, provided costs are based on wise and prudent expenditures, and provided the corporation is moderately successful. But, even in these rare instances, the divergence between asset values and costs, or depreciated costs, grows wider as the years pass.

The time has arrived when the balance-sheets of most large modern corporations are not reasonably accurate statements of assets, liabilities, and net worth.

For some years the Securities and Exchange Commission has been struggling with the problem of obtaining statements which disclose every material fact and which are not misleading. This has been particularly difficult in connection with promotional enterprises.

The Commission has found an interesting solution. This has been described by the chief accountant of the Commission, William W. Werntz, in the following words:

In form A-O-1, for corporations organized within two years to engage in the exploitation of mineral deposits, an attempt has been made to overcome the misleading effect of financial statements of enterprises of this type by eliminating the usual requirement of a certified balance-sheet. In its place the registrant is required to submit certified schedules of (1) current assets and liabilities; (2) liabilities, other than current liabilities; (3) amounts due to and from promoters and other insiders; (4) noncurrent assets and capitalized expenses; and (5) capital stock. . . .

In the schedule of noncurrent assets and capitalized expenses the registrant is required to list and identify each material item showing, however, only the total number of units of each class of securities, the amount of cash and of anything else given therefor by the registrant. The dollar amounts are not permitted to be extended. Thus no representations as to the value of the mining property or claims are made in the registrant's financial statements and the vexing problems of stock discount and capital surplus are avoided.[15]

Amputation at the neck will end a headache. Balance-sheets cannot mislead if they are abolished. Fixed-asset values cannot be misleading if no values are stated. Abolition of balance-sheets may satisfy the Commission, but it is an unsatisfactory solution for investors who want statements of assets, liabilities, and net worth, and for practicing accountants who earn their livelihood by certifying balance-sheets. To date, the Commission has applied this extreme remedy only to mining enterprises organized within two years, but there is no promise of immunity to other enterprises. Mr. Werntz followed the comments quoted above with this sentence, "This approach has not been extended to non-mining companies, although that is under consideration at the present time." [16]

Misleading values are not confirmed to promotional enterprises. When price levels rise, fixed-asset values based on cost less depreciation, are apt to be very misleading to shareholders who are contemplating a sale of stock. Managements owe their first duty to the shareholders in the corporation which they manage. Asset or profit understatement is a violation of primary duty. Therefore, asset or profit understatements can be considered more culpable than overstatements, which violate secondary duties to prospective investors and creditors. Is it not possible that the Commission will ultimately rule that asset values based on

[15] William W. Werntz: "Financial Statements for Investors," address before the Ohio Society of Certified Public Accountants, Toledo, Ohio, September, 1939. Published by the Securities and Exchange Commission, pp. 3–4.

[16] *Ibid.*

cost, or cost less depreciation, are misleading, if they are substantially less than market or sound values on the balance-sheet date?

Values which are correct, by any standard of correctness, are misleading to many readers when they are used to describe fixed assets. Many balance-sheets display an item somewhat as follows:

Land, Buildings, Machinery and Equipment. . . . $12,480,292.46

To many readers, such a fabulous sum preceded by a dollar sign means "money, and lots of it." To the same readers, money means cash. When they look at such an item, certified to be correct, they do not see land, buildings, fences, yards, railroad sidings, bricks, concrete, smoke, grime, and so forth. They visualize huge bank deposits or mountains of currency. Perhaps they could understand better if there were no fabulous sums preceded by dollar signs to mislead their imaginations. Perhaps fixed-asset values should be eliminated from all balance-sheets, and perhaps they ultimately will be. What will be the end of this movement toward the abolition of balance-sheets and fixed asset values, which has been started by the Securities and Exchange Commission?

Years before the Securities and Exchange Commission was established, practicing accountants were attempting to prepare statements which disclosed every material fact and which were not misleading, because the principal value that attaches to a public accountant's certificate is the confidence of the public in his ability and integrity. The instances where public accountants have failed to live up to public expectations are so rare that they make the headlines when they do occur. In their efforts to make published statements better understood, year after year accountants have been lengthening the explanatory material opposite the various values; they have been abandoning meaningless, stilted phrases, and substituting descriptions that are meaningful, and that are expressed in carefully chosen English. This progress is admirable, but the principal causes of misunderstanding remain uncorrected. The quotation above, taken from a letter sent to a committee of the New York Stock Exchange by a committee of the American Institute of Accountants, proves that accountants, ranking high in the profession, know that balance-sheets are not statements of assets, liabilities, and net worth, as that phrase is understood by laymen, yet accountants continue to foster that misunderstanding by using a form of statement that contributes to it.

In the popular account form of balance-sheet, the caption found over the left-hand side is "Assets." What does it mean? More important, what does it mean to readers? Most readers believe it means that all of the items listed below are assets, that all of the assets are listed below, and that the values are correct asset values on the balance-sheet date. Accountants know that some of the items listed below the caption, "Assets," have no present or future realizable value, they know that some very valuable assets are not listed, they know that the amounts in the value columns are not correct values on the balance-sheet date, and they know how this part of the statement will be misinterpreted by most of the investors who read it. This misunderstanding will not be cleared up by the exertions of a committee of the New York Stock Exchange to attempt to "gradually" convince investors that balance-sheets are not what the form, date, and captions seem to indicate. Some more forceful method is required. Perhaps an explanatory memorandum should be added regarding the assets that are omitted. Perhaps another explanatory memorandum should be added explaining that certain varieties of deferred charges have no value, that they are merely debit balances in certain accounts in the ledger, that they have not been charged to profit and loss or surplus, and that they will be charged against profit and loss or surplus at some future date if the management decides to make the charge. Perhaps there should be another memorandum explaining that the date and the asset caption have no application to the values set opposite the items of fixed assets. Perhaps the caption, "Assets," should be changed or abolished. Perhaps accountants must tell the public what balance-sheets are, instead of merely telling them what balance-sheets are not. Perhaps another title should be substituted for the meaningless, stilted phrase, "balance-sheet."

What does this phrase mean? A sheet on which two or more columns of figures balance or equal each other. Balancing is a problem of major significance for beginning students of accounting, but probably ranks least in importance among all of the problems that face experienced accountants. Yet it is elevated to the place of chief prominence on the annual statement. Could any other title be chosen that would be more unexpressive?

Fundamentally, the account form of balance-sheet appears to be the product of fifteen minutes of not too strenuous mental exertion on the part of an unimaginative bookkeeper. Once upon a time, by chance, someone picked up a piece of ledger paper and wrote a post-closing trial balance on it. In some such way, the account form of balance-sheet was born. Its principal appeal is its simplicity. This appears to be its crowning virtue. Actually, this simplicity is its most insidious and potent vice. In this world where "necessity is the mother of invention," in this world where human beings do not think unless they must, simplicity is adored. This universal love of simplicity has led accountants to list the post-closing debit balances from accounts in general ledgers, on the debit side of balance-sheets and write "Assets" at the top. This is simpler than the caption, "An incomplete list of assets which includes current assets at present values, fixed assets at cost, or cost less depreciation, and some deferred charges valued at the cost of unused benefits, and others which have no present or future realizable value," and so forth. The caption, "Assets," is more simple, but what it gains in simplicity it loses in accuracy. It makes balance-sheets easy to misunderstand and, at the same time, it gives readers the satisfaction of believing they have comprehended correctly.

The effect of this misleading simplification, in connection with balance-sheet presentation, can be better understood if we imagine similar principles of simplification applied to profit-and-loss statements. If profit-and-loss statements are prepared in a similarly simplified account form, most of the debit balances from the profit-and-loss accounts will be listed on the debit side under the simplified caption, "Expenses." Under this caption we will find such items as beginning inventory, purchases, manufacturing costs, operating expenses, and financial expenses. On the credit side under the simplified caption, "Incomes," we will find sales, ending inventory, and financial incomes.

When the net profit is added to the sum of the "Expenses" the sum of the items on the debit side will equal the sum of the items on the credit side. If profit-and-loss statements had always been published in that form, how many readers would understand the distinction between purchases, costs, and expenses? How many would have clear concepts of cost of sales, gross profit, manufacturing costs, operating profit, and so forth? Perhaps the fine distinctions in connection with profit and loss, that are so widely comprehended, are due partly to the adopted form of statement, which is less simple, less misleading, more complicated, more informative, and as a result, more understandable, in the true sense of that word, for nothing is understood unless it is understood correctly.

SUMMARY

Many misunderstand balance-sheets and believe they are statements of assets, liabilities, and present net worth. Balance-sheets prepared according to traditional standards constitute part of the accounting that corporation managements should render to shareholders for use and care of shareholders' funds. Although the courts have not classed corporate managements as fiduciaries, their responsibilities and duties to shareholders are actually fiduciary in character. The amounts shown opposite items of fixed assets on balance-sheets should be based on cost because they are accounts of expenditures. Traditional accounting procedures are sound, because accounts based on cost are easier to understand than accounts based on appraisals, and because they comply with the equitable doctrines governing reports of fiduciaries.

In addition to the accounting now rendered to shareholders on profit-and-loss statements, surplus statements, and balance-sheets based on traditional accounting principles, shareholders and creditors are entitled to statements expressing independent expert opinion on the value of all of the corporate assets, liabilities and net worth. The need for this additional statement is growing because the differences between asset values and the account balances based on cost and reasonable allowances for depreciation grow larger and more numerous as the years pass. Statements of assets, liabilities, and net worth, which include all of the assets at present values, frequently have been prepared by accountants, in collaboration with other experts who are competent to express opinions that accountants are not competent to express. Occasions for the preparation of such statements have been incorporation of going businesses, reincorporations, reorganizations, consolidations, and mergers. Such statements are not offered as the sole opinion of the public accounting firm preparing the statement but as an expression of the combined opinions of management and of all of the independent experts. When such statements are prepared and submitted with balance-sheets in the majority of published reports, the true nature of balance-sheets will be evident by contrast. Preparation of such statements involves additional expense which managements will not incur until demanded by shareholders and investors.

Managements have authority, conferred by statute, to engross on the books of account values that violate sound accounting principles, and to give them a legal reality that accountants cannot ignore. Some shareholders and creditors who discover that balance-sheets are not statements of assets, liabilities, and net worth, bring pressure to bear on accountants to depart from sound accounting principles, and prepare balance-sheets that conform more closely to their erroneous concepts. Accountants try to adhere to sound principles. Governmental agencies lay down numerous rules and regulations that must be compiled with. The only solution to the dilemma created by such a conflict of forces is compromise. Thus published balance-sheets are, and probably will continue to be, compromises, which are partly based on adherence to sound accounting principles and partly based on legalized departures from them, and which imperfectly satisfy the conflicting desires of managements, shareholders, creditors, and the accountants who prepare them. While these conflicting forces are resolving themselves into a result that no one can forsee, accountants may discover that their best chance of preserving the traditional accounting principles is by advocating publication of an additional statement including all assets at present values as nearly as present values can be estimated by independent experts collaborating with managements.

QUESTIONS

1. Define "valuation."

2. Define "the cost of an asset" in terms of an exchange transaction.

3. Whitney asserts that the cost of an asset is not always the same as its "value." Cost is but one definition of value.

   a. How else might the value of an asset be defined?

   b. Do each of these additional definitions always result in valuations different from those that result from the cost definition? Consider examples in which the cost definition and each other definition result in different valuations.

4. Is the valuation of long-lived (fixed) assets at "cost less accumulated depreciation" different from the valuation of such assets at cost?

   a. How does Whitney think accountants determine the amount of depreciation?

   b. Why do accountants value long-lived assets as they do?

5. Do accountants value Accounts Receivable at cost? If not, define the notion of value employed (see the C. L. Nelson article on page 53). Why do accountants value Accounts Receivable as they do?

6. How would the balance sheet differ from the balance sheet usually prepared if accountants valued all assets strictly at cost? How would transactions with customers ("revenue" transactions) affect the balance sheet?

7. Which of the "needs" for accounting information does Whitney appear to regard as primary?

8. Whitney states that accountants should adhere to traditional valuation procedures but that, in order to prevent the statements from misleading investors, such procedures should be made explicit. Is this

the accountant's only course of action? Is the existence of an accounting profession justified by the single fact that it doesn't *mislead* anyone?

9. Comment on the following statement: ". . . accountants have been under pressure from shareholders and creditors to depart from sound accounting standards and publish statements that conform more closely to their misconceptions of the information that should be contained in balance-sheets."

3

Valuation in Accounting

10

What Is an Asset?

James L. Dohr

A PERIOD of economic depression brings to light many real
and fancied flaws in the economic structure, and those
who suffer are insistent in their demands for changes which
they believe will prevent a recurrence of distressing events.
As a result, a critical spirit of retrospection prevails from
which no institution or belief, however sacred, is immune.
Remedy becomes the order of the day, with prescriptions
abounding, many of which are worse than the evil they
are intended to prevent or cure.

The critical reexamination of economic concepts is, on
the whole, a salutary process. Life is not static, and the
rules by which men live require constant consideration
and frequent revision. The difficulty lies in the fact that

From *The Journal of Accountancy,* vol. LXXXIII, no. 3 (March,
1942), pp. 213–218. Reprinted by permission of the publisher. The
late Mr. Dohr was a Professor of Accounting at Columbia University
and a former director of research for the American Institute of Accountants (now the American Institute of Certified Public Accountants).

the mood of the depression carries the process too far. Not alone are the weaknesses of the structure attacked—assault is made on its very strengths. It is obvious, therefore, that in such a period careful and courageous consideration must be given to all remedial proposals.

In the current depression, accounting has had somewhat more than its share of criticism, with the result that the accountant finds himself in an intensely introspective state of mind. Fundamental accounting tenets are under critical review, and radical proposals are made for changes in accounting procedures. Among the latter is the startling suggestion that the conventional form of balance-sheet be abandoned and that financial position be indicated by other means. This "plough under" suggestion is advanced because of alleged defects in each of the three major subdivisions of the balance-sheet, i.e., the asset section, the liability section, and the so-called "net worth" section.

For one version of the indictment, reference may be made to the provocative article by William H. Whitney which appeared in the October, 1940, issue of *The Journal of Accountancy,* entitled, "What is a Balance-sheet?" * After confessing to a shaken faith in accounting procedures, Mr. Whitney advances the suggestion that conventional balance-sheets are "not reasonably accurate statements of assets, liabilities and net worth." One can readily agree as to the "net worth"; it has been repeatedly pointed out that it is not the purpose of the balance-sheet to show present worth, and it is curious that Mr. Whitney's keen analysis did not lead him to abandon the use of that term. As to liabilities, further discussion may be left for another day. As to the asset section, however, it is proposed to consider the indictment in detail.

In support of his thesis, Mr. Whitney makes two serious charges. On the one hand he suggests that in developing balance-sheets under traditional procedures, accountants "do not attempt to include all of the assets" in the balance-sheet, and that by "deliberate choice" they omit items that have enormous values. On the other hand, according to Mr. Whitney, accountants list items in the balance-sheet as assets "that have no present or future realizable value" and which are "utterly unsalable, utterly devoid of present or future value." These charges must be examined and a plea must be entered, whether it be guilty, not guilty, or *nolo contendere*.

Before pleading, the specifications of the charges may be considered. As to the first, i.e., the deliberate omission of assets, Mr. Whitney cites the failure to include (a) valuable franchises acquired without cost; (b) patents developed by research departments whose

* This article has been included as the preceding one in this volume.

operating costs are charged to expense; (c) goodwill; (d) trade marks popularized by the owner; (e) long-term leaseholds which have become valuable since acquisition; and (f) enforceable contracts to purchase materials at prices below the market. As to the second charge, the specifications involve the improper inclusion, as assets, of (a) discount on stock; (b) premium on bonds owned; (c) discount on bonds payable; (d) prepaid federal capital stock tax; and (e) insurance at unamortized cost, particularly where there is no cancellation privilege.

In examining these specifications, a preliminary question is presented as to whether there is *accounting sanction* for the acts in question. If not, the matter is one of practice rather than principle and, for present purposes, may be dismissed as such. If, on the other hand, the acts are sanctioned, the propriety of the sanction involves a basic question as to the nature of an asset.

WHAT IS AN ASSET?

In preparing statements of financial position, the accountant endeavors to present a summary of the facts with respect to financial or pecuniary matters. Those facts are divided basically as between two groups; the first includes the *favorable* facts of financial position, while the second includes those which are *unfavorable*. The favorable group includes in general the facts with respect to the ownership of valuable property, the ability to pay debts or to obtain credit, earning power, freedom from governmental restrictions, exclusive privileges, etc. In a broad sense there is, therefore, a great variety of favorable or "asset" factors in financial position. In addition to such obvious items as cash, accounts receivable, inventories, land, buildings, machinery and equipment, etc., there are such things as a pleasing appearance, a college education, a wealthy aunt, innate managerial skill, special talents, etc.

As a matter of balance-sheet presentation the accountant endeavors, so far as possible, to reduce the various asset factors to the common denominator of money. In this process three general types of situations are encountered. Some factors can be satisfactorily valued; others are of uncertain, doubtful, or widely and rapidly fluctuating value; some factors cannot under any circumstances be stated in terms of money. The three situations may be illustrated by real estate used in the conduct of business, patents, and managerial ability, respectively.

Real estate can be valued at its cost. Consideration may also be given to its present market value, and if that value is slightly above or slightly below cost, the difference is not significant and it may be ignored in a going concern. If the present market value is substantially above cost, it may still be ignored on the ground that the property is not available for sale and is required for the continuance of business. The same is true if present market value is substantially below cost, so long at least as the land serves its purpose in the conduct of business. In the two latter situations, however, it may be advisable to call attention to the present value by footnote or comment, particularly if the difference is great.

Patents may be shown at their cost. They may of course have a substantial present value whose amount, however, is extremely uncertain. That value is dependent mainly on earnings which may fluctuate widely, which may not be established, or which may not be accurately determinable. Wide variations in value may result, dependent upon the valuation method. In this situation it is better to value the patents at cost, leaving it to the reader to formulate his own conclusions as to present value, which he must do largely on the basis of the income statement.

Managerial ability may be the most important factor in the financial condition. It is not, however, susceptible of valuation and its financial significance can only be reflected in the results of business operations.

Items of the first class are obviously listed in the schedule of assets as such. Items of the second class may be shown in that schedule at cost, with appropriate footnotes or comments to indicate their full significance. Items of the third class need not be mentioned, since they are implicit in the results shown by the earnings statement.

For balance-sheet purposes, then, an asset may be defined as (a) a favorable factor in financial position which is susceptible of satisfactory *valuation*, i.e., expression in terms of money, or (b) a favorable factor in financial position which is not susceptible of such a valuation and to which attention may be directed only in general terms, i.e., by footnote or comment.

Speaking generally, it may be said that the term "asset," thus defined, corresponds closely to the legal concept of property. As used by the lawyer that concept includes:

(a) Ownership of physical objects. In this sense assets include inventories, land, buildings, machinery, equipment, etc., which are commonly designated as tangible property.

(b) Legal rights to the payment of money or its equivalent. In this sense assets include bank accounts, trade receivables, notes receivable, bonds, mortgages, prepaid insurance, etc.

(c) Legal privileges of various kinds. In this sense assets include prepaid rent, prepaid interest, franchises and licenses, patents and copyrights, goodwill, trade marks and trade names, etc.

In addition to the foregoing, which constitute the great bulk of assets currently shown in balance-sheets, the committee on terminology of the American Institute of Accountants has pointed out (Accounting Research Bulletin No. 9) that there are a few situations, perhaps, in which the asset is not, strictly speaking, a matter of property, but rather a deferred cost properly chargeable against the future. It is to be doubted, however, whether there are many such instances in which no property or legal rights are involved.

AS TO "ASSETS" OMITTED

Applying the foregoing to Mr. Whitney's specification of "omissions," the situation with respect to such items as franchises, patents, goodwill, trade marks, leaseholds, contracts, etc., is clear. These items may be listed *as assets* provided a reasonably satisfactory base of valuation, such as cost, can be found. In the absence of such a valuation they may properly be omitted from the schedule of assets; where there is doubt as to value or its amount, it is frequently better to refrain from any valuation. It is obvious, of course, that under these circumstances, the statement of financial condition is not complete except as reference is made, by footnote or otherwise, to items of this kind.[1] Their importance is indicated, in the final analysis, in the earnings statement; the accountant shows the earnings and leaves it to the reader to judge as to their significance.

The answer to the first of Mr. Whitney's charges may now be made. The balance-sheet may not be presented without a notation as to the items to which he refers, but owing to the difficulties of valuation, it is not advisable, necessary, or even possible in some cases, that such items be valued and included among the assets as such. This being the case, it is hardly fair to accuse the accountant of not "attempting" to show assets or "deliberately" failing to show them. The accountant's conduct is entirely intelligent in the circumstances, and there seems to be nothing in the situation, therefore, which would in any way

---

[1] It is now generally recognized, for instance, that significant purchase commitments (one of the items in Mr. Whitney's specifications) must be so set forth.

warrant or require the discontinuance of the conventional form of balance-sheet. Despite these difficulties, it is desirable to show the amount of *capital invested* in the enterprise; all that can be reasonably required in addition is that the accountant exercise great care in order that all significant facts in financial position be brought to the attention of the reader.

AS TO IMPROPER INCLUSIONS

It must be admitted, of course, that the various items referred to in Mr. Whitney's specifications relative to improper inclusion are, as a matter of practice, shown as assets. If they are properly so shown, a plea of guilty must be entered. Each item cited by him must therefore be considered in turn.

As for discount on stock, it is difficult to see how anyone can argue that such an item is an asset. Its presence in a balance-sheet indicates generally that the corporation in question has received something less than what it should have received upon the issuance of its shares of stock. To treat a failure to receive assets as an asset is, of course, indefensible. It may be that the corporation, in such cases, has a claim against the stockholder, in which event the item of "discount on stock" may be justified as representing that claim. As such, however, a description of "discount on stock" is unenlightening. As to this item, therefore, it is suggested that Mr. Whitney's criticism is sound but only *as a matter of accounting practice.* The practice is without accounting sanction,[2] and the obvious answer is that stock discount should *not* be presented as an asset.

As for premium paid on bonds owned, it is difficult to understand Mr. Whitney's position. A bond is in substance a right to receive a *principal sum* at a specified date plus a series of rights to receive *interest* in stipulated amounts at stipulated dates. Where bonds have been purchased at a price above par the purchaser evidently believes that the rights are, in the aggregate, worth more than the principal sum; the unamortized portion of the premium is therefore simply a part *of the cost of the bond;* where the bond is to be held to maturity it may be shown at amortized cost; no attention need be paid to present value *unless such value reflects a doubt as to ultimate collection.*

---

[2] A casual review of the authorities support this statement. See Sanders, Hatfield, Moore, *A Statement of Accounting Principles,* p. 86; Paton, *Essentials of Accounting,* pp. 188, 663; Kester, *Principles of Accounting,* p. 426; S.E.C. Reg. S-X Rule 3–17; *Accountant's Handbook,* p. 300; Montgomery, *Auditing Theory & Practice,* p. 142.

The bond is clearly an asset and there is, therefore, no merit whatsoever to the charge of improper inclusion.

As for the item of discount on bonds issued, it is here that Mr. Whitney's criticism is most effective. This item is not an asset, although it is usually so justified on the ground that it is, in substance, prepaid interest. In theory the item is a part of the bond *liability,* and the suggestion has been advanced that it be deducted from the face amount of that liability to reflect its present significance.[3] Accountants are loath to follow this suggestion because of the fact that it may mislead the reader of the balance-sheet as to the *amount* of the outstanding obligations. The problem is a difficult one, and it is probable that the best solution lies in accepting the fiction that the asset in question is prepaid interest.

As for the item of prepaid capital-stock tax, it is difficult to see how such an asset could ever be present in a balance-sheet. The tax paid in July, 1941, for instance, covers the privilege of doing business from July 1, 1940, to June 30, 1941; it is held, however, that the doing of business on a single day in that period gives rise to the liability to pay the tax. It appears, therefore, that the tax *accrues as a liability* in the ordinary case, on July 1, 1940, and that unless payment is made before that date (a most unlikely occurrence) there would be no prepaid-tax item in the balance-sheet. The answer is that, properly considered, the capital-stock tax becomes a liability on July 1, 1940, and remains in the balance-sheet as such until payment in July, 1941.

As for prepaid insurance, whether subject to cancellation or otherwise, there is clearly an asset in the conditional legal right to be reimbursed if specified losses occur. So long as the enterprise in question is a going concern, the legal right is a financial advantage; the payment of the premium represents in substance an investment or advance of capital which can be "recovered" in the conduct of business. The unrecovered or unamortized portion at any point of time is therefore properly shown as an asset. If Mr. Whitney's criticism goes to the statement at "unamortized" cost, it is fully answered by the fact that there is no sanction for such practice.

While the foregoing paragraphs cover the items specified by Mr. Whitney in support of his second charge, it is only fair to point out that there are a variety of additional items, to which he has not referred, which are commonly shown an assets, such as experimental and development expenditures, "suspense" items, promotional costs, unad-

[3] See "Accounting Principles Underlying Corporate Financial Statements," *Accounting Review* (June, 1941).

justed debits, etc. None of these items is properly shown as an asset, however, unless it meets the tests set forth above. It must be conceded that a broader authority for the inclusion of these items is advanced by those authors who suggest, for instance, that a balance-sheet "is a summation of debit and credit balances" and that the term "asset" includes items "which the company has not been able to write off," "amounts held in suspense," "abnormal losses which it is not yet convenient to write off," and "a capital loss which for some reason is being carried forward." This is unfortunate, but clearly the remedy lies in correcting these views and not in abandoning the balance-sheet.[4]

It is apparent that there is nothing in Mr. Whitney's second charge, except as to the item of bond discount, which need give rise to alarm. In all items of a similar nature, the test is simply whether the enterprise in question has economic capital invested which can be "recovered" in the conduct of business. If it is so recoverable, it is an asset and is properly shown as such; if it is not, the item should be excluded. If these rules are applied, there is no basis for the sweeping charge that accountants show as assets items which are "utterly unsalable, utterly devoid of present or future value."

CONCLUSION

The questions raised by Mr. Whitney go to the heart of the accounting problem. As ordinarily conceived, the accounting processes are developed with a view to showing the "financial position" of an enterprise through the medium of a balance-sheet. The purpose of the statement is frequently misunderstood as that of showing the "present worth" of the enterprise. The profit-and-loss account is then treated as a subsidiary statement showing some of the changes which have occurred in a period between two balance-sheets.

It is submitted that this concept must be abandoned. The primary purpose of the accounting processes is to record gains and losses—

---

[4] It is interesting to note in passing that Mr. Whitney, curiously enough, does not specify patent-development costs in his list of improper inclusions. If they are not shown as an asset, the accountant may be charged, as he is by Mr. Whitney, with omitting items of "great value." If they are included, may he not be charged with showing as assets items which are "utterly unsalable, utterly devoid of present or future value"? What then shall the accountant do with this item?

It is suggested that much of Mr. Whitney's difficulty arises out of his desire, at least implied, to combine in one statement cost, market value, and liquidation factors; ordinarily the accountant elects to proceed on the basis of a going concern and his objective should be to indicate proprietary investment.

to show how proprietary capital is increased or decreased as a result of the conduct of business. The accounting begins with the capital invested by the proprietors—that is the initial balance-sheet. From that point on the accountant considers each transaction to determine whether the proprietary capital has been increased or decreased. Appreciation is not generally considered as an increase; decline in value, if substantial, may be recognized. Additional contribution of capital or withdrawal of capital must obviously be taken into account. The periodical profit-and-loss statements summarize the various transactions in which a gain or loss is involved, and in the balance-sheet at the close of each period the increased or decreased proprietary investment is shown. The balance-sheets are, therefore, simply the connecting links of a series of income statements. It is only by a proper consideration of this historical development that the financial statements are to be understood.

QUESTIONS

1. What does Dohr mean by the statement, "Some factors can be *satisfactorily* valued" (p. 103). In the light of his remarks early in the article, why do you suppose he insists that valuations be "satisfactory"?

2. How does Dohr justify the exclusion of certain assets from valuation on the balance sheet? Give several examples of such items and justify their exclusion in specific terms. Does "exclusion from valuation" imply "exclusion from the statements"?

11

The Crucial Importance of Valuation in Accounting

Howard I. Ross

IN THE YEARS in which I have been involved in the work of our Institutes, and particularly in my year as president of the CICA, I have had a chance to appreciate the fascinating problems that arise in organizing and developing a modern profession. The hardest problems—the ones we should be worrying about most—are, I believe, those that arise from the tremendous changes that are taking place in the world in which we operate. It would be relatively simple, for example, to develop satisfactory financial statements for use in a static economy. One would at least be able to hope that by gradual improvements, effective statements could eventually be developed. But gradual improvements are quite inadequate in the world which we attempt

From *The Journal of Accountancy*, vol. 48, no. 4 (October, 1964), pp. 68–70. Reprinted by permission of the publisher. Mr. Ross is a prominent Canadian Chartered Accountant who has served as President of his country's professional accounting organization.

to serve—because the rapid and fundamental changes that are occurring in business are developing new problems faster than we are solving old ones. Thus while we are doing many admirable things, our backlog of unsolved problems is growing rather than diminishing.

Rather than generalizing on this theme, I would like to select a specific problem—which is of great importance in itself and which will also serve as an example of the sort of problems that should concern all of us. For this purpose I select, as an important and typical problem, the lamentable state of financial reporting.

No one can hold us entirely responsible for the fact that even the best of financial statements published today are inadequate. The corporations issuing these statements have obviously a primary responsibility for them. However, our profession must surely consider itself to be the custodian of the art of financial reporting if it is to justify its existence. The public corporations who must issue financial statements are entitled to rely, in technical matters, on the chartered accountants who are on their staff or who act as their auditors.

The basic problem on which I would like to concentrate is posed by the paradoxical fact that accountants appear to divide their time, perhaps about equally, between preaching, on the one hand, the great importance of publishing regular financial statements and insisting, on the other hand, that one who relies on financial statements, in almost any of the circumstances in which one would normally turn to them, is likely to be misled. In other words, it would be iniquitous to issue securities without providing a prospectus containing a ten-year earnings statement and balance sheet—yet the balance sheet is not even intended to be a valuation document. Despite appearances to the contrary, the balance sheet is simply a summary of the ledger balances that may be properly carried forward under a set of unwritten, unwritable (but nevertheless generally accepted) principles which accountants have devised as their contribution to the art of financial communication.

I think it is important to establish at the outset that I am not exaggerating this paradox. Presumably we can take for granted that accountants emphasize the importance of financial statements—but do they really insist that a balance sheet could mislead an investor or creditor attempting to estimate the value of his security? Well, our own Institute's excellent and authoritative *Terminology for Accountants* defines a balance sheet in these terms: "A balance sheet is a statement of current resources, unexpired costs, liabilities to be met and sources of ownership funds, *rather than a statement of worth*." This view could of course be confirmed by innumerable references to serious accounting texts and pronouncements, not only here but also from England and the United States, from whence we have learned so much. In fact the committee on terminology of the American Institute of CPAs has been so concerned lest the unwary public should assume that a balance sheet is a valuation document, that it has been at pains to discourage the use of even the qualified term "book value." In one of its bulletins, this committee has suggested that "the term ledger balance or a term such as the amount shown in published financial statements would more clearly and accurately convey an exact meaning." This is of course true, and indeed unarguable. But the important point is, if we are ever to evolve better (that is to say more useful) financial statements it has got to cease to be true. It is high time we came out from behind our barricade of technical jargon and rushed to the attack on the very grave problems that face anyone who attempts to produce a valuation document for such a complex economic entity as a modern corporation. No one knows better than we do how tough some of the problems will prove—but I do not see how any progress can be expected until we abandon the idea that there is any merit in a balance sheet which does not even purport to show current values. The values will naturally always be estimated values—but we must not reject them for that reason—we must simply devote our energies and ingenuity to devising the best and most reliable procedures available for making fair estimates.

Accountants have, of course, always been aware of the unsatisfactory aspects of the balance sheets they have produced but, I suggest, instead of facing up to the problem, they have tended to take evasive action. It has been common, for instance, to soft pedal the balance sheet and place primary emphasis on the income statement—on the grounds that investors and creditors are really interested more in earnings and earning power than in current resources. This is probably true, but it does not get us off the hook. The income statement includes (often as a crucial item) the amortization of the balance sheet "values" for fixed assets—and if the balance sheet figures are irrelevant past costs, it follows that the resulting figure of net income must be equally irrelevant. Moreover, it is not only the question of fixed asset valuation that causes the trouble—an even broader problem is raised when we ask ourselves what use a figure of net income can be if it does not eventually reflect itself in an increase in value. The income account can be considered as a statement to explain the change in successive balance sheets, and the figures in income account and balance sheet are so inextricably connected that it is perhaps better to consider these statements as divisions of one single statement, rather than as separate. I can see no justification for shrugging off balance sheet items as merely technical accruals and still claiming that the resulting all-important net income figure has some genuine significance.

I do not underestimate the difficulties of evolving satisfactory valuation techniques, but I insist that, however hard the problems, they are problems we must tackle. Moreover I would like to emphasize one other point. No matter how successfully we cope with valuation difficulties, there is no possibility that we will ever be able to produce a statement from which an investor can simply read off a figure which will tell him what his investment is worth. This is not even theoretically conceivable. The modern corporation is far too complicated an organism for its value to be thus mechanically pinpointed.

The basic problem here is that while some of the factors that go to make up the value of a corporation are measurable in terms of money, others are not. The assets with which we have been accustomed to deal have measurable values—and so perhaps have some of the other assets which we have tended to ignore or exclude in preparing statements. However, the value of the shares of a corporation is influenced by many factors—the state of the president's ulcers or of the general manager's love life—factors which even the most dedicated and desiccated statistician might hesitate to convert to cents-per-share.

However, I do not believe that the fact that certain relevant factors cannot be measured should absolve us from estimating the measurable items as well as they can be measured. Those using financial statements would then, and only then, be assured that they were using the best statements that could, in the nature of things, be prepared. I do not see how the investing public could expect anything less from a first-class profession.

It is, of course, an oversimplification to suggest that assets are either measurable or not measurable. There is rather a shading between those that are clearly measurable and those that are by nature clearly not measurable. This can be appreciated by running down the typical balance sheet. Cash in bank presents few problems—when we move to receivables the question of collectability enters to raise an element of doubt and estimation—with inventories there are further complexities with which we are all familiar—and so on. It is more debatable still whether reliable current values for fixed assets can be established—and goodwill presents problems we have hardly started to consider seriously. Thus, one serious problem we face is what assets should be included—but I have dwelt on valuation because I do not see how we can tackle any of the multitude of complex problems before us unless we decide clearly and firmly what we are trying to do. In my opinion our aim should be to provide the most useful statements that can be produced—that is statements in which the measurable factors that affect the value of the corporation are estimated as accurately as they can be. George O. May warned of the dangers ahead many years ago when he told the profession that we tended to be so worried about the possibility that someone might be misled that we were apt to forget the importance of providing information.

In my various appearances as president of our Institute during the past year, I have hammered away on the subject of the inadequacy of our financial statements. I must say very few of our members have argued with me. This worries me as it suggests that these criticisms may be dismissed as the rambling theorizing of an elderly member, with little practical interest for the busy accountant in mid-career and in possession of most of his faculties. I wish I could believe this were so, but I cannot escape the feeling that this is an urgent practical question for our profession.

The production of financial statements is largely a matter of data processing—and this is increasingly true as corporations grow in size and complexity. At the moment we are in the midst of a revolution in data processing techniques. Computers provide the dramatic example of this revolution—but there are many other radically new processes coming in, some of which are the result of new "hardware" and others of the adaptation to accounting of advanced mathematical techniques. Financial data are not the only data subject to these revolutionary forces. There is also a great deal of statistical, scientific and research data being handled by computers. The result of all this is a reappraisal by corporations of the whole problem of accumulating and analyzing information. This is too large a subject to get into here, but I call your attention to this revolution to remind you that the field of data processing is inevitably being invaded by skillful and highly trained technicians with nonaccounting backgrounds. This adds a new urgency to these problems for us because if, as I think, better financial statements are needed, someone else is eventually going to produce them if we do not.

QUESTIONS

1. How would Ross define the professional responsibility of the accountant?

2. Why aren't the measurement of earnings and the valuation of assets separate problems? What happens when accountants regard the measurement of earnings as more important than the valuation of assets?

3. What is meant by "general acceptance"? Whose "acceptance" is required? Is the notion of "general acceptance," as a basis for establishing the propriety of a particular valuation method, consistent with the notion of "usefulness"?

4. What is the Canadian Institute of Chartered Accountants' definition of "balance sheet"? How does this differ from the traditional accounting definition?

5. Since the balance sheet is often considered to be a poor valuation document, greater emphasis is placed on the income statement. Indicate why this may be illogical.

6. "It is, of course, an oversimplification to suggest that assets are either measurable or not measurable." Which assets are clearly measurable? Which assets are less clearly measurable?

7. Why does the increasing use of data processing equipment, particularly computers, make the accountant's problem of improving financial statements even more urgent?

8. The author sees only two possible ways of achieving a change in general acceptance of financial statements. These are (a) "by discussion among experts in an attempt to get agreement in theory," and (b) "by individuals producing actual new forms of presentation and submitting such new forms to general criticism." (1) Which methods would probably be the more effective? Why? (2) What are some other possible ways of achieving "general acceptance"?

9. How do you reconcile the paradoxical fact, as stated by the author, that accountants on the one hand stress the importance of uniform reporting and yet they are among the first to belittle the validity of financial statements?

12

The Unsolved Problem of
Fixed Asset Valuation

Howard I. Ross

IT IS SOMEWHAT discouraging to find how much good work
can be done on the theory of financial reporting, while
such relatively small progress is made in the practical task
of producing better annual statements. There have certainly been plenty of good technical articles, some excellent
panel discussions, some devastating criticisms of the in-
adequacies of conventional statements—but it is hard to
detect all that much radical improvement in published
accounts. Auditors are essentially critics, and it may be
that they are more effective in complaining about what is
wrong with statements than in producing better ones.

From *The Canadian Chartered Accountant*, vol. 84, no. 4 (April,
1964), pp. 276–279. Reprinted by permission of the publisher.

Good Talk—Poor Action

This whole problem is excellently illustrated in the discussions about changing money values, which have been going on now spasmodically since the end of World War II. Many interesting solutions have been suggested but only in rare cases have companies attempted to reflect changes in money values in their published accounts. The question gets discussed under a number of headings: "constant dollar accounting" or "accounting for inflation." These and many similar descriptions indicate the confusion that surrounds the subject and perhaps give a clue to one of the big difficulties encountered when we attempt to find a solution: we are not too sure what the problem is.

The Exaltation of Procedures

The accounting profession tends to be dazzled by the ingenious and brilliant device of double entry bookkeeping. Thus, instead of regarding itself as the custodian of the art of financial communication, the accounting profession at times appears to behave as though it considered itself the custodian of the art of double entry bookkeeping. Some pronouncements by accounting experts would almost suggest that the most important objective for accountants is the disposal, in a systematic manner applied consistently from year to year, of the balances thrown up by the double entry bookkeeping system, rather than to provide the most informative financial statements that can be produced.

This tendency to focus on the problems of producing statements instead of concentrating on the use to which the statements can be put is a sort of occupational distortion with accountants. Here again our struggles with constant dollar accounting are illuminating. Part of our trouble is that accountants have tended to plunge into the question of the techniques by which changing money values can be worked into financial statements, instead of trying to find out what those who use financial statements want from them.

Tax Considerations Hold Sway

Another complicating factor is that no proposal to change accounting principles can ignore tax implications. The hard fact is that a large part of our taxes are collected on the basis of net income as determined for accounting purposes. Much of the criticism of conventional historical costs was no doubt prompted by the notion that historical costs did not produce a sufficiently large depreciation charge in determining taxable income. Thus, much of the ginger went out of the movement for statement reform when other, as it seemed, simpler methods were devised for getting larger write-offs for tax purposes. The combination of diminishing-balance depreciation and the provision that depreciation could be claimed for tax purposes without being booked, knocked the prospective tax advantage out of replacement value accounting, and discussion of this interesting question palpably cooled off. But accelerated depreciation allowances (however calculated) tend to be short-term solutions to tax problems, and there is some indication that they have lost their attractiveness now that the heavy write-offs of earlier years are tending to reduce current allowances.

Historical Costs Are Virtually Meaningless

There seems little doubt that better statements would be produced on some other basis than historical costs. Despite the difficulties and objections raised to some of the solutions that have been put forward, the fact remains that historical costs are virtually meaningless in present-day contexts. If it is important to produce better statements (and who would deny this?) the first thing to do is to get clearly before us the purpose of the statements we wish to produce. We have had quite enough in the way of bright ideas, stimulating suggestions and interesting possibilities. What we really need is a little clear-headed analysis of just precisely what we are trying to do.

To begin with we might as well be clear that what we are talking about is simply the sort of general-purpose statements that companies produce for presentation to those shareholders interested in various aspects of credit, and for use (with such amendment as required by the Tax Act) by the Tax Department in determining taxable income.

Exclude Statements for Management

It should perhaps be mentioned that there are many types of financial statements that need not be considered in tackling the problem of changing money values. Particularly there are statements required by management. These are very important, and, indeed, perhaps the most important financial statements of all, but they do not present any problem in respect to generally accepted accounting principles.

Management can produce any form of statement management finds useful. They need not worry about what other companies are doing. They may value assets any way they find useful. It is only when we come to statements produced for circulation to shareholders and other "outsiders" that any problem of accounting principles is encountered.

It is important to have standardization in general-purpose statements and such standardization can only be based on a general agreement as to how the statements should be prepared. Here enter the problems of generally accepted accounting principles.

Basic Purpose of Financial Statements

We must have a clear picture of the purposes to which general-purpose statements are put. For example, it is safe to assume that in the summarized sort of statements we are thinking of (such as the balance sheet and income statement) there is only a limited amount of information that one can expect to provide. While bankers, suppliers, tax authorities, bondholders and others may have recourse to general-purpose statements, as well as shareholders, and while each of them has a somewhat different point of view, basically what they all want is some general notion of the liquid position of the company and its profit earnings capacity. It would seem then that the purpose of the sort of general financial statements we are here considering is to give a fair and useful view of two aspects of a company's operation: can it pay its debts and is its position improving or worsening?

It should be fairly clear even at this preliminary point in our discussion that, whatever anyone wants in looking at a set of financial statements, it is most unlikely to be the historical cost of its fixed assets. Historical costs are in fact almost completely irrelevant. If they have any sort of relation to the values in which the reader of a financial statement is likely to be interested, it can only be by coincidence.

What Is the Appeal of Historical Costs?

If historical costs are meaningless, it is perhaps worth asking ourselves how they have come to be so firmly entrenched. The enthusiasm of accountants for historical costs—or rather their distaste for venturing on any other basis of valuation—presumably arises out of the search for objectivity. Value is such a tricky and ephemeral matter that accountants have tended to cling to costs that have an illusion of objectivity. They at least represent what someone actually paid for the assets at some point in time. Thus amongst all the varied opinions there can be about the value of an asset, here at least is an appraisal that was once backed up by ready cash. It is easy to understand the attractions of historical cost from this point of view. But has no one ever got a bargain? or been persuaded to pay too much for an asset? When your wife comes home with a new hat are you necessarily satisfied that it is worth $69.95 just because she paid that much for it? Moreover, even if an asset changes hands at fair value, if the transaction took place twenty years ago, of what interest is the price to anyone today? In adhering to historical costs in the face of all the unanswerable criticisms of them, accountants are really maintaining that they prefer a value based on an actual transaction, however irrelevant this valuation may be, to a value based on someone's unsupported opinion. And yet if the opinion is given honestly and seriously, there is every possibility that it is a more useful value than a jumble of historical costs, some of which are current and some of which date far back.

Joint Ventures—Background to Historical Costs

Another reason for the survival of historical costs as the basis of fixed asset valuation may be the historical accident that the first serious attempt at financial statements arose from the development of joint ventures. In joint ventures, historical cost is a satisfactory valuation, particularly in joint ventures that are completed within a reasonably short period of time. When modern corporations began to appear it was perhaps natural to adopt the form of accounting that had been developed for joint ventures. The influence of the joint venture approach has probably survived because, for teaching purposes, it makes some sense to start with the simple statements of joint ventures and then to introduce the increasing complications presented by a corporation with a long life, and the consequent necessity of producing periodic financial statements.

However, the operations of a large modern corporation have almost no resemblance to those of a joint venture. It is dangerous to even draw an analogy between them. The shares of modern corporations are bought and sold continuously and it is only by coincidence that any shareholders, assembled at any given annual meeting, have any connection whatever with the historical cost of the assets.

The persons participating in a joint venture normally buy certain merchandise, resell it and wind up the venture. In such circumstances the actual cost of everything acquired has an obvious sort of relevance to the venture. But to the shareholders of a large public corporation the historical cost of its assets is largely meaningless. When a shareholder makes his investment he may pay a price for his shares that reflects (amongst other things) an increase in the value of the corporation's assets since acquisition, and indeed, under today's conditions, this is more likely than not to be the case. The original cost of the assets ceases to have any significance to the average investor.

Questions That Statements Should Answer

The sort of questions that a general purpose statement should help to answer are: Is the company a good buy at the quoted market price? Will the company's position be likely to improve or deteriorate from operations? What sort of return on investment can be expected from it? Is it a good credit risk?

The passage of time is likely to have a decisive effect on asset values. Financial statements that purport to tell what has happened during a period of time and what the position is at a certain date must be of limited usefulness if they ignore the changes in value that the passage of time always brings about. Clearly such changes should be reflected in the statements. But before jumping to the conclusion that we should work out some machinery to incorporate the changes, we need to consider the nature of these changes and to decide what the reader of financial statements really wants to know.

Accounting for Inflation?

Let us consider the effects of inflation. The extent of inflation can be measured by various index numbers. Some of these measure the change in the value of a specific type of commodity and others are composite indices that attempt to measure the general trend of inflation. As to which type of index is most useful, the answer depends on what we want to know. If our aim is to measure the general effect of changing money values on a company, all its assets and liabilities must be adjusted and a composite index is appropriate. There is quite a good deal of literature on this question and a number of adequate indices have been recommended. Under this view a rise in the value of money increases asset values and liabilities generally and, if there is an excess of assets, leads to an increase in owner's equity. The net assets of a company and net worth both go up.

If adjustments of this sort are attempted in actual practice, many difficulties arise, but all such difficulties can be satisfactorily solved. A number of plans have been put forward for this purpose and statements can be produced to reflect the general trend in rising or falling prices. But is this what we want? Composite indices are all very well, but what merit is there in adjusting assets upwards to reflect a rise in the general level of prices if, as may well be the case, the sort of asset the company owns is actually declining in value, remaining stationary, or increasing in value at a different rate from the general price level. This is anything but an uncommon case. It might therefore be argued that the adjustment appropriate in a balance sheet is not to increase the assets and liabilities on the basis of a general composite index but to bring the values of the company's actual assets up to date to reflect more accurately what such assets are now worth. The advantage of the latter approach is that technical changes, which alter the value of assets, are taken into consideration as well as changes in the general value of money. Surely this must be sensible—that is to say, must be generally useful. There seems little merit in sorting out one element of change in value and going to a great deal of pains to reflect this element, while ignoring other changes.

We may thus move from the idea of accounting for inflation in general to the concept of replacement value. While this has some similarity to accounting for inflation (in that it involves the abandonment of historical costs), it is really quite a different concept. The general notion in replacement value accounting is to maintain the value of the enterprise, as an indication of how much may safely be paid in dividends without impairing "real" capital, and so on.

Replacement Value Accounting Pro and Con

There are many arguments against replacement value accounting, the most devastating of which is the simple consideration that, in modern enterprises, assets normally are not replaced; they get superseded by newer types of equipment. However, no matter how unanswerable some arguments against replacement value are, when choosing between replacement values and historical costs one faces the simple question of which of these bases is likely to give the most useful picture of the company. Even if it is unlikely that the company's assets will literally be replaced, it may still be argued that replacement value nevertheless does give some notion of the value of a concern, while historical costs do not. In an attempt to make the intention clearer it has been suggested that the word "replacement" could well be dropped altogether in order to emphasize that there is no assumption that the assets will actually be replaced. The "replacement" value is simply an attempt to bring valuation up to date. It is not a question of whether such values are logical; it is merely a matter of whether such values are more useful, in providing a fair picture, than actual cost.

One way to answer this question is to consider the position you would be in if you attempted to size up a corporation, of which you had no previous knowledge, by studying its financial statements. Would you be more likely to reach reliable conclusions about the company if its assets (and depreciation) were stated on historical cost or on replacement cost?

Need to Produce Useful Statements

It is quite wrong to expect an ideal solution in the field of financial statements. The problem is simply to choose the best method available. The whole art of accounting is utilitarian. Our job is to produce the most useful statements we can. An ideally best statement, not subject to any reasonable criticism, is never available. The task of accountants is to grope for something better than we now have.

To make progress in this area we will have to stop worrying about procedures and the technical methods of reflecting changed money values. These problems either have been solved or can be solved. What we must do now is to get down to a serious and clear-headed analysis of what we want. There have been enough good studies published to prove that various techniques can be adapted to the business of producing better statements. But we must first make up our minds as to just what it is we want.

QUESTIONS

1. Ross considers five definitions of fixed asset value: (a) Cost; (b) Cost less accumulated depreciation; (c) Cost adjusted for changes in the general price level; (d) Cost adjusted for changes in specific prices; and (e) Replacement cost. How is each of the five values measured? What problems of measurement arise with each value? How do accountants assess the usefulness of a measure of value?

2. Ross notes that accountants tend "to focus on the problem of

producing statements instead of concentrating on the use to which the statements can be put . . ." (p. 117). How does this tendency lead many accountants to prefer historical cost (see page 119)?

3. Is there any inconsistency between requiring a *single* statement for external users of data and asserting that the statement must be useful? Explain.

13

The Meaning of Depreciation

Sidney Davidson

THE TOPIC of depreciation is one of the most disputed in all the relationships between accounting and business. And, of course, optimum practices and policies with regard to depreciation are still far from settled.

More than a quarter-century ago, Henry Rand Hatfield wrote a very entertaining essay on the subject, "What They Say About Depreciation," * in which he pointed out some thirty-six different approaches or procedures to be used in connection with the depreciation question. The quarter-century which has passed since that time has resulted not in consolidation of ideas but rather in a multiplication of approaches, so that this whole question of

* EDITORS' NOTE: The late Professor Hatfield's article appeared in *The Accounting Review* (March, 1936), pp. 18–26.

From The University of Chicago Graduate School of Business, Selected Papers, No. 2, 1962. Reprinted by permission of the author. Mr. Davidson is Arthur Young Professor of Accounting and Director of the Institute of Professional Accounting at the University of Chicago.

what depreciation is, what it means, what should be done with regard to it is one that is subject to a good bit of controversy.

One of the things that has certainly helped to heighten the controversy in this area is the important place that depreciation plays in income-tax calculations, especially when income taxes reach a 52 per cent rate.

As far as the general nature of depreciation is concerned, there can really be no question. Depreciation is—and must be recognized as being—a cost of doing business, one that nobody can deny. The cost of a boiler is as much a cost of doing business as the cost of the coal. It is true that plant expenditures may be more sporadic; nevertheless, these expenditures have to be made. We all know that these facilities are used up in the carrying-on of the firm's activities. Therefore, as you can readily see, depreciation is a cost of doing business that nobody can deny.

However, depreciation is a joint cost par excellence. It is joint with respect to the several time periods during which a plant asset is used. It is joint with respect to the products that are turned out utilizing any piece of equipment. It is joint with respect to the individual units of production that are turned out during any given time period. Economic theory suggests to us that joint costs cannot be allocated satisfactorily. Yet in a variety of circumstances we are faced with the problem of allocating these joint costs—costs which are joint to an extent unmatched by almost any other kind of cost.

The problem is complicated by the fact that the period of usefulness of most plant assets—the period over which this association is made—is usually relatively long. Changes in the economic significance of the units that we use to measure the expenditures that we have made can come about fairly readily and, in fact frequently do.

The depreciation problem, in essence, boils down to three questions.

The first is: What kind of base should we use in measuring depreciation? Should it be related to the historic dollars that have been expended, or should it approximate some measure of the current cost of assets that have been utilized?

Second, over how long a time period should we attempt to allocate these costs? What is the service life of the assets?

Third, what pattern of charge-off over this service life should we use?

With this background for the problem and the uncertainty about depreciation, what does depreciation mean to the business firm and to the economy as a whole?

We can say that to the individual firm depreciation means a tax deduction, a factor in the preparation of external reports, and an ingredient in internal analysis.

To the economy as a whole, depreciation is a factor in determining the base for income tax. The procedure with regard to depreciation in the legally defined notions of taxable income has had considerable effect upon the equity of the income-tax law and upon the rate and structure of economic growth within the economy.

Let us start with what depreciation means to the business firm. Here let us turn to one area where, I think, we can speak with a relative degree of confidence, with relative assurance. This, of course, is the area of depreciation as a tax deduction for the business firm.

Within this area it seems clear to me that the goal of the firm should be to maximize the present value of the reductions in tax payments from claiming depreciation. In a flat-rate tax situation this is the same as saying we want to maximize the present value of depreciation deductions. Of course, we can always deduct the cost of the asset over its life, but the earlier deductions are worth more in this cash-hungry world than the later ones. Therefore, our goal should be to maximize the present value of this stream of depreciation deductions and with this to minimize the present value of the stream of tax outpayments.

Congress has presented business firms with several permissible alternatives to follow in determining the amount of depreciation to be charged off each year. The pattern of depreciation charges is, to at least some degree, within the control of the business firm. It seems clear that the firm should choose that alternative which meets the general goal that we have set forth—to pay the least amount of tax as late as possible.

We can put this more strongly by saying that management has an affirmative obligation in our economy to carry on operations and activities so as to minimize all costs—to minimize the present value of these costs over the long run. This is an obligation of management to the stockholders and, indeed, to the competitive system, because to fail to minimize costs is to put a roadblock in the wonderfully effective system of allocating resources by market processes. This applies to tax costs as well as all other costs, and, except in a highly unusual circumstance, tax costs are minimized by taking depreciation as rapidly as legally permissible.

Any management that fails to take depreciation as rapidly as legally permissible to minimize the present value of tax payments is remiss in its responsibility to stockholders. This is something that must be done, and, in fact, I would say that any management that does not seek to maximize the present value of this stream of depreciation deductions is suspect in a sense and that we must look for the exceptional circumstances that justify this sort of procedure. In this connection, one of our Ph.D. candidates is writing a dissertation which is an effort to analyze firms that do not take rapid depreciation for tax purposes to see what the unusual circumstances are which explain their failure to do so. There is the question of what procedure does minimize the present value of tax payments. The tax law spells out three general types of procedures—the straight-line method, the sum of the year's digits, and something described as double-declining balance. It is clear that either of the two latter, the sum of the year's digits or double-declining balance, will, almost without exception, give a more rapid rate of charge-off than the straight-line method. However, the choice between these two, the SYD or double-declining balance, is dependent upon several rather specific circumstances, such as the estimated service life of the assets, the discount rates that are appropriate for the firm and the salvage value of the assets. Several of us worked up a paper last year on the selection of the optimal depreciation method in a capital-budgeting situation.*

Is there a danger that these goals of the least and latest tax payments may conflict? For instance, in taking depreciation deductions early, may we be faced by the problem of increasing our tax payments in a later period by a greater amount? You see, if we take more depreciation now, then in a simple situation we will have less to take later. If tax rates should turn out to be higher later, when our taxable income would be higher, we would have a larger total tax bill.

This might be the case if we were considering a single-asset firm, although even here the interest saved from postponing tax payments might very well offset the higher payments later. However, if we move from a firm that has only a single asset to the more realistic situation of a balanced firm, the higher depreciation on new assets that are acquired regularly will serve to complement the lower depreciation on the older assets, with the result there can be every expectation that the tax savings in the earlier years will not be offset by higher taxes in the latter years. Indeed, if the firm is a growing one, there will be more newer assets than older ones, with the result that, rather than having

* EDITORS' NOTE: This article, "Capital Budgeting and the 'Best' Tax Depreciation Method" by Sidney Davidson and David F. Drake appeared in *The Journal of Business,* vol. XXXIV, no. 4 (October, 1961), pp. 442–452.

repayments of the earlier tax savings, we will have increasing tax savings year after year.

If we turn from the notion of depreciation as a tax deduction to depreciation as a factor in external reporting, we are up against a different sort of problem. In the tax situation the regulations are prescribed by the Internal Revenue Code. However, the place of depreciation in the external reports is prescribed by generally accepted accounting principles.

The goal in the tax case is to minimize the outflow of funds. The goal in the external reporting case is to seek a statement of income which is realistic in measuring the consumption of plant assets—one which is rational or accurate in the measurement of the expiration of the plant assets. The only trouble is that no one knows how plant assets depreciate realistically, rationally, or accurately. In this calculation we are faced with a multiplicity of subjective estimates. How long will the asset last? What is the pattern of its expiration of useful life? What will be its salvage value?

Arthur Hadley, former president of Yale University and a noted transportation economist, once said, "God Almighty does not know the cost of hauling a ton of freight from New York to Boston." The same thing might be said with respect to what the realistic, the accurate, depreciation charges are in any given year. However, it does seem to me that there are some that are more realistic, more accurate than others.

Recognizing that there has to be a considerable amount of skepticism about any measurement of annual depreciation, yet we see some reason for feeling that depreciation should be tied in with the capital-budgeting estimates made when we decided to buy the asset. We have another Ph.D. dissertation in process which seeks to analyze and describe the procedure of basing depreciation charges on capital-budgeting estimates of cash inflows. Whatever specific procedures are used in measuring depreciation, our goal in external reporting should be to state, as realistically as possible, the amount of the expiration of cost of the assets used in operation.

What if this realistic estimate of expiration of costs differs from this maximum charge-off that we seek under the tax laws? What if the charge-offs for tax purposes do not coincide with what we think is appropriate for external reporting purposes? There is some tendency here, I believe, to let tax rules be controlling and allow the possibility for more meaningful income reporting and more meaningful asset valuation to go by the board—to accept the tax-depreciation charges. There is some element of clerical convenience in doing this, but this impresses me as a minor advantage.

Far better, it seems to me, is to report in the financial statements the depreciation charges in line with the best estimates of expiration that we can make, based on generally accepted accounting principles, and simply allow this figure to differ from the one shown in the tax return. Since generally accepted accounting principles do limit depreciation to cost and since we try to charge that cost off as rapidly as we can for tax purposes, it is likely that the external reporting of depreciation charges is going to be lower than those shown for tax-reporting purposes. Therefore, we are likely to show a greater income on our financial reports than we show on our tax returns.

This, it seems, is an altogether appropriate, permissible, legal, moral thing to do. Many of my colleagues in the accounting profession say that taking higher deductions for tax purposes today than we take on our financial reports means that in the future tax charges will be based on a higher income figure than that shown on the financial statement. In some future years, taxes will run more than 52 per cent of reported financial income because in those years there will be smaller depreciation deductions to be taken, and so taxable income will run higher than reported financial income. This means, they say, that we have borrowed tax deductions from the future and that we should recognize something described as a deferred tax liability.

I disagree emphatically with this view, but my protests have had no effect. The American Institute of Certified Public Accountants and the Securities and Exchange Commission now virtually require all firms, except some public utilities, to recognize a deferred tax liability if they claim depreciation deductions more rapidly on tax returns than in financial statements.

What is the nature of this deferred tax liability? Will it require the expenditure of corporate funds at some future date, or is it, for all practical purposes, part of the stockholders' equity?

If a firm continues replacing assets, there will always be as large a deduction on the tax return as in the financial records, with the result that the deferred tax liability will never have to be paid. I have searched hundreds of balance sheets for evidence of payment of this deferred tax liability, and I have found none for the firms that have remained on an accelerated depreciation basis for tax purposes. I am not saying that there are no cases. It is just that after hunting through a few hundred published balance sheets, covering a seven-year period, I have not found any case where this deferred tax liability is drawn down, where the depreciation deductions on the tax return are less than they are on the published statements. The reason, of course, is simply that this will come about only in the case of a declining firm and one which is declining in that happy state where its profits are remaining undisturbed through the liquidation period; this is somewhat hard to visualize.

Finally, what about depreciation in internal analysis? There are a multitude of problems here we could discuss, but we will skip over all but a few.

As far as investment decisions—certainly one of the central problems in internal analysis—are concerned, what part does depreciation play in the decision to purchase new equipment? It seems to me that, here again, this decision is affected only in terms of reducing cash outflow for taxes.

There is the myth that depreciation provides funds for the replacement or expansion of capital assets. If depreciation is viewed as providing funds, it ought to be sued for nonsupport as Charles Gaa * says—there are no evidences that it is a good provider. The only way that funds are provided is by making sales to customers. Depreciation simply gives us a tax shield so that less of the funds received from the customers need be turned over to the government. Unfortunately, no amount of accounting legerdemain can produce funds. It would be wonderful for accountants if it were the other way, if somehow by making a few marks on our books we could bring a substantial flow of funds into the firm. However, the only way funds can be provided is by finding customers willing to purchase our products.

The central question regarding investment acquisition decisions is whether the after-tax cash flow is sufficiently high to enable us to recover the cost of the investment plus a reasonable profit. The effect of depreciation is simply one of cutting down the tax out-payments. This increases the rate of return; it increases the excess present value; it shortens the pay-back period. Whatever test is used for investment analysis purposes, the reduction of tax flow benefits it. That is, the effect of depreciation in this capital investment area is measurable solely in terms of the improvement in the amount of cash inflow that remains from sales to customers.

This is a point that has great relevance when one considers how changes in tax laws affect the volume of capital formation in the economy.

* EDITORS' NOTE: Professor Gaa is Professor of Accounting and Financial Administration at Michigan State University.

One other place in internal analysis where depreciation has an important and growing significance is in measuring divisional performance. In this question of decentralized operations, which seems to appeal to people these days (and with good reason, I believe), the question of depreciation and asset measurements plays a central role. One general approach to decentralized operations is to say that each division should show a satisfactory rate of return: that we are willing to set the division managers up in almost a separate business if they will show a satisfactory rate of return. This of course has to be a rate of return based on some figure. The amount of assets turned over to the division is the denominator of the rate of return calculation; the income that the division earns is, of course, the numerator. Depreciation figures in the calculation of both the income and the asset base.

Most firms that I have been able to survey follow an arrangement that is similar to the duPont procedure, in which, as I understand it, the denominator is the original, undepreciated cost of the assets and depreciation charges are taken as some percentage of this original undepreciated cost. A composite depreciation rate is applied to this original undepreciated cost. When we retire an asset, no gain or loss is recognized. We simply reduce the asset total that is being charged off.

It seems to me that this approach, despite its success, has several shortcomings. It gives a powerful incentive to retire assets prematurely because retiring an asset reduces the denominator. There is no point in keeping standby equipment even though it may have potential usefulness. As a matter of fact, this kind of notion would say that, if we bought a piece of equipment last year for $100,000 which we thought would have a twenty-year life and now this year a new piece of equipment comes along that will save us $1,000 a year, we ought to junk the old $100,000 piece of equipment and buy the new one because by decreasing operating costs by $1,000 it will increase the income numerator and will have no effect on the denominator, since both old and new equipment is carried at the original cost terms. Obviously, no division manager is going to do anything quite as flagrant as this. However, the plain fact is that this type of depreciation and asset valuation approach may very well serve to make the division manager's interests incompatible with those of the firm as a whole.

An alternative treatment would be to recognize losses on retirement of assets within the division. Of course, this tends to have the exactly opposite effect of making us unwilling to bring about retirements, even though they would pay off in the long run. In the long run, of course, the division manager hopes he is going to be holding another job, and what he is going to be judged on are the profits of this year and the next.

What we need is a different approach, one which admittedly is followed by a great many firms, where what we do is to set up assets for the divisions in terms of net book values—where we attempt an appraisal of the assets in terms of their economic significance and then keep the record at cost from then on, with a revaluation every time we get a new division manager. We would use composite depreciation with no gain or loss recognized on disposition of assets. This method also has shortcomings; however, the fact is that there is no ideal method of charging depreciation in a decentralized operation so that the division manager's goals and the goals of the firm can be made to dovetail—all of such plans do have certain drawbacks. However, it does seem to me that using depreciated economic values as a base, with a composite rate of depreciation, is probably the best way out of this difficult situation.

What is the meaning of depreciation for the economy as a whole? Here, it seems to me, its entire meaning is tied in with the tax laws. Depreciation has had a checkered history here. In the first English temporary income-tax law of 1842, which has had its one hundred and twentieth renewal this year, depreciation was not permitted as a deduction. In one of the renewals of the temporary law, that of 1878, provision was made for permitting depreciation of equipment and machinery.

Our own 1894 law, which was ruled unconstitutional for other reasons, specifically disallowed depreciation as an income-tax deduction. Almost all the twentieth-century laws, including our own, have contained a provision which does permit depreciation as a tax deduction. The idea has been that this is necessary in order to get an equitable measurement of income and also that it does have an effect upon economic growth.

Since World War II, almost every country has tinkered with the depreciation provisions of its income-tax laws in an effort either to make the laws more equitable or to stimulate economic growth. Of course, it is difficult to separate the two because any changes made in the name of improving equity usually speed up the rate of depreciation deductions for tax purposes. This simply frees funds and makes investments that much more profitable, even though it is done in the name of equity rather than in the name of economic growth. . . .

QUESTIONS

EDITORS' NOTE: The effect of the investment credit may be ignored in answering these questions.

1. What is meant by saying that depreciation is "joint with respect to the several time periods during which a plant asset is used" (p. 126)? Which one of the "three questions" at the bottom of page 126 is raised, at least in part, by the fact that depreciation is joint with respect to time periods?

2. The author implies that we need three pieces of information in order to determine the periodic depreciation for an asset: (1) the cost of the asset in "historic dollars," (2) the "service life of the asset," and (3) the "pattern of charge-off over this service life," including the amount of the salvage value.

   a. Given the first two pieces of information, the cost and the service life, how does the firm decide whether one "pattern of charge-off" is better than another for purposes of reporting to investors?

   b. How would you answer question (a) if the purpose were to determine the depreciation for taxable income?

   c. Given your answers to question (a) and (b), will a firm always be led to the same pattern of charge-off for both tax and investor purposes?

   d. Why might a firm allow tax considerations to determine the pattern of charge-off for investor reporting?

3. Does your knowledge of statements of net working capital flows and statements of cash flows bear out Professor Davidson's assertion (p. 131) that "there is a myth that depreciation provides for the replacement or expansion of capital assets"? Is it really a myth? Explain. How is the myth perpetuated by accountants?

4. "The only way that funds are provided is by making sales to customers." Do you agree? If you do agree, then might we argue that the statement of flows should always be a single number? Discuss.

5. It is observed that "Sweden had 100 per cent write-off for more than a decade and a half." What does this mean? Under such a write-off procedure, how would the long-lived assets section of a Swedish balance sheet appear? What assumption must you make in order to answer the latter question?

6. "Accounting for depreciating assets would be greatly simplified if accounting periods were only long enough or the life of the assets short enough." What is the point of this quotation?

7. How can depreciation enter into the calculation of managerial efficiency in a decentralized firm?

8. To what extent is depreciation relevant for internal analysis purposes?

14

Tale of the Ledgers

FOLLOWING PRECEDENT set for Presidential candidates by
Dwight D. Eisenhower and Adlai E. Stevenson, President
Johnson and Senator Barry Goldwater have released resumes
of their financial holdings. The Goldwater holdings are
listed at approximately the current market value; most of
the Johnson holdings are listed at the value they had when
they were acquired:

Goldwater Family Wealth

(Source: Trust Department, Valley National Bank,
Phoenix, Ariz.)

OWNED BY MRS. GOLDWATER:	VALUE
5,278 shares, Associated Dry Goods	$ 311,400
2,491 shares, Borg-Warner	119,568

From *The National Observer*, vol. 3, no. 34 (August 24, 1964), p. 2.
Reprinted by permission of the publisher.

Goldwater Family Wealth (continued)

OWNED BY MRS. GOLDWATER:		VALUE
1,576 shares, Valley National Bank		113,478
1,690 shares, American Electric Power		77,740
798 shares, General Motors		75,000
Municipal bonds		71,000
700 shares, Standard Oil (N.J.)		61,600
350 shares, Honeywell		44,450
87 shares, IBM		40,225
500 shares, Maryland Casualty		33,550
348 shares, General Electric		29,232
400 shares, Texas Utilities		25,600
417 shares, Hooker Chemical		18,765
200 shares, Continental Casualty		15,600
349 shares, Arizona Bancorporation		7,330
186 shares, Universal Match		2,418
	Subtotal	$1,046,956

OWNED BY SENATOR GOLDWATER:		
7,555 shares, Associated Dry Goods		$ 445,700
Cash		37,000
937 shares, Arizona Bancorporation		20,400
Cash value life insurance		20,000
90 shares Borg-Warner		4,320
	Subtotal	$ 527,420
HOME (title in Mrs. Goldwater's name)		$ 166,600
	TOTAL	$1,740,976

Johnson Family Wealth

(Source: Haskins & Sells accountants' report)

OWNED BY MRS. JOHNSON:	VALUE
313 shares of Texas Broadcasting Corp., plus dividends left in company, plus accrued salary, plus interest in company profit-sharing trust, less minimum Federal income tax applicable if dividends withdrawn	$1,629,154
State and local bonds	239,270
One-half interest in Texas real estate, including ranch home listed at the $79,936 paid for it in 1951	227,114
Cash	64,150

Johnson Family Wealth (continued)

OWNED BY MRS. JOHNSON:		VALUE
Miscellaneous assets, including cash surrender value of life insurance, notes receivable		42,633
Alabama real estate		17,804
Missouri real estate		5,509
LESS $75,000 note payable to Texas Christian University and other liabilities		(—)99,336
	Subtotal	$2,126,298

OWNED BY LUCI BAINES AND LYNDA BIRD JOHNSON:		
184 shares in Texas Broadcasting Corp. stock		914,684
Texas real estate		48,250
Miscellaneous assets		12,538
Cash		4,247
	Subtotal	$ 979,719

OWNED BY THE PRESIDENT:		
One-half interest in Texas real estate		227,114
State and local bonds		159,270
Cash		64,150
Miscellaneous assets		26,883
LESS $75,000 note payable to Texas Christian University and other liabilities		(—)99,336
	Subtotal	$ 378,081
	TOTAL	$3,484,098

QUESTIONS

1. Which of the two statements conforms most closely to conventional accounting? Why?

2. Which of the statements do you consider to be most useful? Why?

15

Lakers' "Sale" Again Comes into Attention

Bill Hengen

WHILE THE Los Angeles Lakers basketball team, in an apparent atmosphere of serenity, looks ahead to the National Basketball Association playdowns, the inner turbulence among Laker stockholders has not subsided.

The question now revolves around a possible sale of the team. Mentioned as interested are Alfred Bloomingdale of the Diner's Club and Dan Reeves, now associated with the Los Angeles Rams pro football team and the Coast pro hockey club.

President Bob Short, who holds 51 per cent of the Laker stock, says he has not been approached with a firm offer. "There have been a few 'fishing' expeditions," he said Sunday.

From *The Minneapolis Star,* vol. LXXXIV, no. 86 (March 5, 1962), p. 1F. Reprinted by permission of the publisher. Mr. Hengen is a newspaper sports writer.

Short says that as far as he is concerned, talk about selling is premature. "We have a good chance to win the World championship. Wouldn't that make the Lakers a more valuable property?"

If that happens, Short revealed, "For the first time I would seriously discuss retiring my interest in the team. Of course, this would need the consent of the minority stockholders."

What's Lakers Worth?

How do you value the Lakers?

"It's a nebulous thing. How much money it makes? Then there is not much value," mused Short.

"Owning a World championship team is another thing. Location —the Los Angeles area has a drawing power of seven million, which is very important with a majority of fans seeing only one, two games a year.

"The team? This is a young, building club. This is important.

"Players? Together Jerry West and Elgin Baylor could be worth $500,000.

"Comparison with others? Both Boston and Philadelphia figure their worth in excess of $1 million." (There is a report that Philadelphia will sell to San Francisco at approximately $850,000.)

"The building? Los Angeles has a tremendous arena which the fans enjoy, too."

It has been reported before that once the Lakers were offered $750,000 to sell. Short doesn't deny the offer but says it was "mostly words, not money."

Apparently the majority stockholder feels that the Lakers are valued at around a million dollars, especially if they win the title.

Other Side

On the other hand, the minority stockholders have a few ideas of their own.

"When the Lakers were moved to Los Angeles it was with the thought after one year of building up its value the club would be sold," says Johnny Dorek, an original $2\frac{1}{2}$ per cent owner.

"There are roughly 10,000 shares of original value of $25. Then it slipped to where some was sold for as low as 10 cents on the dollar."

But now, says Dorek, there is a possibility of an offer which would level out at around $80 a share. He and some of the other active minority shareholders feel the original plan of selling the Lakers should be followed through.

Small Profit

The minority group, which obtained the right to examine the books, says that the Lakers could finish with a profit of $19,000—if they win the playdowns.

"This doesn't seem to make the team a money-maker," remarked Dorek. "Yet it undoubtedly could make more money if it were owned by Californians and not through absentee stockholders."

The minority also has legal action pending which would ask more clarification of Short's 51 per cent control. This is scheduled for around May 7.

Meanwhile, there is a chance that some of the minority stockholders will be in contact with any prospective bidders. There has been a renewed interest on the coast with a reported effort to purchase some Laker stock.

QUESTIONS

1. If Short is correct and the Lakers won the playdowns, how much would Dorek's stock be worth?

2. Supposing Dorek is right, how much are his shares worth? If this differs from your answer in (1) above, how do you explain the difference?

3. Why might the value per share of Bob Short's shares be different from that for Johnny Dorek's?

4

Management Planning and Control

16

Classification of
Cost Distinctions

Joel Dean

	DICHOTOMY		BASIS OF DISTINCTION
1	Opportunity costs	Outlay costs	Nature of the sacrifice
2	Past costs	Future costs	Degree of anticipation
3	Short-run costs	Long-run costs	Degree of adaptation to present output
4	Variable costs	Constant costs	Degree of variation with output rate
5	Traceable costs	Common costs	Traceability to unit of operations
6	Out-of-pocket costs	Book costs	Immediacy of expenditure

From Joel Dean, *Managerial Economics,* ©, 1951. Prentice-Hall, Inc.,

	DICHOTOMY		BASIS OF DISTINCTION
7	Incremental costs	Sunk costs	Relation to added activity
8	Escapable costs	Unavoidable costs	Relation to retrenchment
9	Controllable costs	Non-controllable costs	Controllability
10	Replacement costs	Historical costs	Timing of valuation

QUESTIONS

1. Show how all of Professor Dean's dichotomies might be utilized in a single managerial decision.

2. What are some other cost dichotomies that are extensively utilized in accounting? that might be utilized?

p. 271. EDITORS' NOTE: In his book, Professor Dean explains that the distinctions in this table are basically of two different kinds. In one, he views costs from an accounting as contrasted with an economic viewpoint—included here are numbers 1, 2, 3, and 10. In the other kind of distinction, he divides total aggregate accounting costs in various ways—included here are numbers 4, 5, 6, 7, 8, and 9. Thus *costs*, including *accounting costs*, do not mean the same thing in all circumstances. Quite the contrary, the appropriate cost concept will depend upon what is relevant to the kind of decision to be made. Professor Dean is a member of the Graduate School of Business faculty at Columbia University.

17

Direct Costing

Alphonse Riverin

BUSINESS GROWTH has created complex administrative problems. To face them administrators need more information in a form they are able to understand. Management's essential task is to make decisions in every phase of business transactions.

Cost accountants have developed systems that provide management with some information, usually timely and useful but frequently little understood by administrators. Absorption costing has long been the only way accountants thought information should be conveyed. However, for many years now, another system, called direct costing, has been adopted to an increasing extent.

This system for providing cost information has created antagonism among those who support the more traditional method.

From *The Canadian Chartered Accountant,* LXXI, 4 (1957), 345–350. Reprinted by permission of the publisher. Mr. Riverin is an Assistant Professor of Accounting and Finance at Laval University, Quebec.

WHAT DIRECT COSTING IS

First, it has to be stated that the procedures used in conjunction with direct costing do not convey the meaning usually attached to direct costs. In cost accounting direct costs are the costs directly identified with the product, such as direct labour and direct material. All other costs are called overhead or manufacturing expenses. The cost of the product, under absorption costing, includes direct material, direct labour and overhead.

Under direct costing all the variable manufacturing costs (direct and indirect) are included in the cost of the product, all other costs being considered as period costs and charged off currently to profit and loss instead of to cost of sales. However, selling and administrative expenses are not included in the cost of sales, and consequently in inventories are taken into account before arriving at what is called the marginal income. Therefore, the method would be better described as variable costing.

The essential difference between absorption costing and direct costing is that the first emphasizes the distinction between production costs and all other costs whereas the second emphasizes the distinction between fixed costs and variable costs. Absorption tends to stress inventory valuation whereas direct costing is primarily interested in cost analysis.

In EXHIBIT I, an example has been set up showing the differences in profits arising out of the two methods. From the study of this exhibit, the following inferences can be made:

1. When sales and production are the same, there is no difference in profits.

2. When production is lower than sales, profits are higher under direct costing because there is no fixed overhead coming from inventory charged to cost of sales.

3. When production is higher than sales, profits are higher under absorption costing because of fixed overhead having been carried to inventory.

4. When sales are constant and production varies, the direct costing method shows a gross profit ratio more constant.

5. Variances in profits due to any one method tend to zero in the long run. Production and sales can vary over short periods, but a business can never sell more than it produces.

Exhibit I

	1953	1954	1955	1956
Production	5,000	3,000	4,000	5,000
Units sold	5,000	5,000	3,000	6,000
Variable manufacturing cost (unit)	$ 1.50	$ 1.50	$ 1.50	$ 1.50
Variable selling and administrative costs	.50	.50	.50	.50
Fixed manufacturing costs	1.00	1.00	1.00	1.00
Selling price	5.00	5.00	5.00	5.00
Total fixed costs	5,000.00	5,000.00	5,000.00	5,000.00
Fixed selling administrative expense	2,000.00	2,000.00	2,000.00	2,000.00

PROFIT AND LOSS STATEMENT

	1953	1954	1955	1956
Absorption Costing				
Sales	$25,000	$25,000	$15,000	$30,000
Cost of sales	12,500	12,500	7,500	15,000
	$12,500	$12,500	$7,500	$15,000
Unabsorbed overhead		2,000	1,000	
Gross profit	$12,500	$10,500	$ 6,500	$15,000
Fixed and variable general expenses	4,500	4,500	3,500	5,000
Net income before taxes	$ 8,000	$ 6,000	$ 3,000	$10,000
Direct Costing				
Sales	$25,000	$25,000	$15,000	$30,000
Variable manufacturing costs	7,000	7,500	4,500	9,000
	$17,500	$17,500	$10,500	$21,000
Variable general expenses	2,500	2,500	1,500	3,000
Marginal income	$15,000	$15,000	$ 9,000	$18,000
Fixed manufacturing costs	5,000	5,000	5,000	5,000
	$10,000	$10,000	$ 4,000	$13,000
Fixed general expenses	2,000	2,000	2,000	2,000
	$ 8,000	$ 8,000	$ 2,000	$11,000

POSITIONS OF PROFESSIONAL BODIES

Direct costing is not yet used in a sufficient number of companies to be called a generally accepted principle of accounting.

Moreover, accounting associations have not yet given official recognition to this new convention. In bulletin No. 43, which super-seded all its previous bulletins, the American Institute of Certified Public Accountants did not speak of direct costing as such, and the bul-letin is not very clear as to the position adopted. In the chapter on inventory pricing, Statement No. 3 reads: ". . . cost means in principle the sum of the applicable expenditures and charges directly or indi-rectly incurred in bringing an article to its existing condition and location." But in the following paragraph, it is stated: ". . . general and administrative expenses should be included as period charges, ex-cept for the portion of such expenses that may be clearly related to production and thus constitute a part of inventory costs. Selling ex-penses constitute no part of inventory costs." Yet it is further stated: "It should also be recognized that the exclusion of all overheads from inventory costs does not constitute an accepted accounting procedure." This last sentence leaves an open door to direct costing. If it is not proper to exclude all overheads from inventory costs, it might be proper to exclude only fixed costs.

On the other hand, The American Accounting Association ad-heres strictly to the cost principle in its statement on Accounting Concepts and Standards Underlying Corporate Financial Statements: "Adherence to the cost basis of accounting requires that there should be no suppression or unwarranted assignment to expense of the costs of existing assets."

In its Research Bulletin No. 5, The Canadian Institute of Char-tered Accountants seems to recognize the two methods. In effect, it says, the cost of finished goods in inventory includes the price of raw mate-rial, direct labour and usually the share of overhead that can be trace-able to production. On the other hand, the Institute recognizes im-plicitly direct costing when it states that in some cases it is proper not to include fixed overhead if its inclusion would impair the significance of the profit figure due to fluctuations in the volume of production.

From the positions taken by professional associations, it can be seen that no agreement has been reached. It should be noted, however, that practising accountants seem almost ready to accept the direct cost-ing method in view of its practicability and simplicity.

ADVANTAGES OF DIRECT COSTING

Direct costing has been devised to produce useful statements more easily understood by management. It shows clearly, without re-quiring any additional work, the cost-volume-profit relationship. Hence by looking over the report, management sees the effect of production and sales variances on profits. As the profit figured is not influenced by the fixed costs which must be incurred whether the facilities are producing at full capacity or not, direct costing makes administrators more conscious of the importance of costs. It also reveals the influence of fixed costs on net profit before taxation.

Once all variable costs (variable manufacturing, selling and administrative costs) have been deducted from net sales, the remainder is the contribution of operations to fixed costs and profits. This figure, usually called marginal income, is very useful to management. When it is expressed as a percentage of sales, it gives the marginal income ratio which allows the computation of the break-even point by dividing fixed costs by this ratio. This essential computation brings to light the sales figure above which the firm is building profit and under which it paves the way to failure.

Moreover, direct costing supplies the data needed by management in profit planning, make-or-buy decisions, pricing decisions, and decisions relating to capital expenditures, whether for replacement, cost reduction or expansion.

Any item which covers part of overhead increases the net profit of the firm. All products do not contribute equally to profits. Thus when information is given in detail by departments and by products, eliminating the fixed costs from the computation, it allows management to make decisions as to what item is more profitable, what lines should be promoted and to what extent a non-profitable item can contribute to fixed costs. Hence pricing is facilitated and selective selling can be made. Undoubtedly, absorption costing could give the same information, but with much more clerical work, since its procedures are not directed to that end.

Due to proper classification of expenses, it is possible to place responsibility for variable and fixed costs control. Fixed costs are no longer classified by departments or function but by item of expenses.

Cost information should not be more expensive than the value of its service to management. By developing cost information only when it is useful, direct costing has the advantage of simplicity and economy.

Inventory valuation derived from direct costing does not always comply with generally accepted accounting principles. However, because of its usefulness for internal reporting, it should not be an insurmountable problem for external reporting. To bring inventory into conformity with accepted practice, the procedure is to add or subtract from the inventory figure obtained by direct costing the amount of fixed costs that would otherwise have been taken into account under absorption costing.

To take this step is to resort in large measure to what absorption costing does, except that in direct costing it is done probably once a year, while in absorption costing it occurs constantly.

DISADVANTAGES OF DIRECT COSTING

The most difficult problem in direct costing seems to be the classification of costs as variable or fixed. Even in practice some costs that pertain to the cost of production are classified as periodic costs due to the complication resulting from their allocation to products. A good example would be discounts on purchases which are often classified as period costs because of the difficulty of assigning them to the proper batch of raw materials.

Variable and fixed costs are classified by the following principle: fixed costs are those providing the capacity to produce and expiring with the passage of time, regardless of extent to which the facilities are actually utilized. All other costs traceable to products are considered to be variable costs because if there was no production, such expenses would not have been incurred.

Consequently, fixed expenses are treated as profit-reduction items, not as value-creating items. This position is quite objectionable since if there were not any facilities to produce, there would not be any production at all. Facilities are used to create values, not reduce profits.

Moreover, some expenses usually considered fixed are sometimes variable, whereas other expenses ordinarily classified as variable are fixed. For example, the depreciation charge takes into account wear and tear of the facilities and their obsolescence. Only the latter can be said to expire with the passage of time. The first is due to the use of facilities. Consequently it is as variable as direct material or direct labour.

In some companies a large part of direct labour is fixed and will not vary with production volume. This is usually true of the highly-skilled groups of workers. Whether or not to separate these expenses into variable and fixed depends upon the proportion that the costs bear to the total cost of production.

In its essence, direct costing is an application, at the accounting level, of the traditional marginal analysis which may be stated this way: marginal cost is attained at the level of output where the incremental unit cost (traditionally presumed to increase as output increases) is equal to the price per unit which may be obtained for that output.

The conclusions reached by marginal analysis as to price policy and output are applicable only to short run analysis and are valid only in the short run. Obviously, a firm that would take into consideration only variable cost in pricing its products would gradually consume its investment in long life assets and cease to exist as a going concern. Consequently, even if variable and differential costs are important for short run decisions, management cannot ignore the aggregate costs in planning the future strategy of the business.

It is often advanced that management must strive to maximize profits in the short run. However, nowadays another motivating force of management is the desire to assure the continued existence of the business with reasonable profits.

As previously mentioned, direct costing understates the value of inventory for reporting purposes. In the balance sheet, the working capital ratio is thus understated. This situation might create some problems for credit purposes.

Finally, direct costing when first adopted prohibits comparison with any prior year, unless a good deal of extra work is done to change the past periods to a direct costing basis. There is also a lack of comparison with other firms in the same industry which have not adopted the direct costing method.

QUESTIONS

1. What is the distinction between "direct costs" and "direct costing"?

2. Is there any difference between "direct costing" and marginal costs?

3. Is the case for "direct costing" diminished if an objective of the firm is to survive? How?

4. Illustrate Riverin's statement that "the most difficult problem in direct costing seems to be the classification of costs as variable or fixed."

5. Defend the following proposition: Resolved that the usual classification of expenses on income statements included in annual reports be changed from a functional (i.e., cost of goods sold, selling and administrative) or objective (i.e., wages, electricity, depreciation) basis to a "direct costing" basis.

18

Approaches to Pricing: Economist vs. Accountant

William T. Baxter and Alfred R. Oxenfeldt

THIS ARTICLE examines the part played by the cost accountant in fixing a firm's prices, and especially his assumption that cost plus or full cost is a useful and logical basis for price. It also undertakes the difficult task of reconciling the almost flatly contradictory views of the cost accountant and the economic theorist on pricing.

Generalizations about the two professions must, of course, be unsatisfactory. Since the terms "cost accountant" and "economist" cover many persons with a wide range of views, a short article must omit many desirable qualifications and do injustice to many individuals. However, few who are familiar with both costing and economics would fail to recognize the gulf that often separates the respective

From the *Business Horizons*, vol. 4, no. 4 (Winter, 1961), pp. 77–90. Reprinted by permission of the publisher. Mr. Baxter is Professor of Accounting, University of London, and Mr. Oxenfeldt is Professor of Marketing, Columbia University.

approaches to price. It is generally true that the cost accountant fails to state his assumptions about the firm's aims and pays scant attention to demand; he collects cost data and arrives at price by manipulating these. The economist, on the other hand, starts by assuming that the firm is trying to maximize something, for example, profit; he then shows how the firm should study demand as well as cost in an attempt to find this maximum output level.

COST PLUS

The cost-plus procedure is too familiar to need extended description.[1] In the multi-product firm, the formula for finding the price of a job runs somewhat as follows: (1) find the job's direct costs—mainly material and labor; (2) add a charge for indirect costs (by allocating these overheads as a rate on a unit such as the wages or hours of direct labor, or machine-hours); and (3) add a further sum for profit —often calculated as a percentage of the total under (1) and (2).

Objections to Cost Plus

It is not hard to ridicule the logic of the cost-plus doctrine. Its "cost" is objectionable on at least three grounds—time, jointness, and opportunity.

TIME The avoidable cost of any job depends on the firm's degree of commitment at the time in question. Since this may change with each decision and act, a job has not one cost but a range of costs varying with its stage of completion and at best a cost figure can be right at only one stage. The cost accountant's sums, however, are based on historical records that do not change with changing commitments.

JOINTNESS A job is normally a joint product in the sense that other jobs use the same resources. The cost of such resources is thus common to many jobs and there is seldom an unimpeachable basis for dividing it among the jobs (since the resulting figures rarely show what will actually be saved if a given job is not done). Yet full cost includes an allocated slice of common cost.

[1] Costing practices are described in countless textbooks. For a description of U. S. pricing practices, see Theodore Karger and C. Clark Thompson, "Pricing Policies and Practices," *Conference Board Business Record*, XIV (September, 1957), 434–42; Joel Dean, *Managerial Economics* (New York: Prentice-Hall, 1951), pp. 444–57; Alfred R. Oxenfeldt, *Industrial Pricing and Market Practices* (New York: Prentice-Hall, 1951), pp. 156–65; and A. D. H. Kaplan, Joel B. Dirlam, and Robert F. Lanzillotti, *Pricing in Big Business* (Washington: The Brookings Institution, 1958).

OPPORTUNITY Costing tends to concentrate on expenditures of a given work program. It seems to ignore the alternatives open to the enterprise, or to assume that the alternative is idleness. Yet displaced opportunities are vital in making a business decision, which might indeed be defined as the process of selecting among alternatives.

The objections to the "cost" in the cost-plus formula are only part of the problem; economists criticize the "plus," too. The use of a somewhat rigid margin suggests that the firm does not want to find the price levels at which its total profits will be highest—or at least that it is oddly indifferent to the power of demand and of competition. Yet competition in some cases may be strong enough to take price decisions right out of the firm's hands. In other cases, surely the starting point in pricing should be the study of demand (whether, for example, it is elastic or inelastic) and the realization that each possible price may entail a different output and profit.

Superficially, it appears that if a firm adds a margin to cost to cover overheads and profit, it thereby ensures itself some profit. But, of course, this is true only in favorable markets. If cost plus produces a price so high relative to customer valuations that few sales are made, losses will be sustained. No mechanical pricing formula can guarantee a profit, although, unfortunately, cost plus gives the impression of doing so.

Cost and Displaced Alternatives

Costing thus seems to violate a central cost principle of the economist, that cost can be measured realistically only by taking into account the alternative opportunities open to the firm. To find the sacrifices that will result from the decision to do a job (the economist argues), we must logically look only to the period that still lies in the future at decision date, and must estimate the changes in future expenses and revenues that result from the decision, a procedure that obliges us also to estimate what these expenses and revenues would look like if the job is not done.

It will therefore be helpful to classify costs under two heads. The first agrees with what is commonly understood by "cost" (except that it insists on a cause-and-effect relation between decision and sacrifice), while the second differs from the everyday definition of the word in that it is concerned with potential gains displaced by the given job.

First, compare expenses if the firm does Job A, with its expenses if it does nothing. In this way, we find the expenses that should appear in an ordinary budget—the sacrifices that the firm can avoid by not doing A or anything in its place. We shall call these potential savings *avoidable costs.*

Second, compare the firm's balance sheet after doing Job A with its balance sheet if it instead puts its assets to their next best uses (for example, employs plant on other work, or lends cash at interest). The net revenue that the firm would gain by applying its resources to their next best use is part of the sacrifice of doing A. We shall henceforth use *opportunity cost* in this narrow meaning of net revenue foregone. The total sacrifice involved in doing Job A may thus include both avoidable cost and opportunity cost.[2]

Business Acceptance of Cost Plus

The objections to cost plus sound formidable in the classroom, but cut remarkably little ice outside. The cost accountant often concedes that they have some validity in private discussion; yet he ignores them in his published writings, and his accounts continue in the main to be filled with historical costs and allocations. These seem to impress executives and to serve as satisfying guides to policy. Cost plus is probably the primary method of fixing price in American industry (and is perhaps even more usual abroad).

The main attraction of cost plus is, of course, that it offers a means by which plausible prices can be found with ease and speed, no matter how many products the firm handles. Moreover, its imposing computations look factual and precise, and its prices may well seem more defensible on moral grounds than prices established by other means. Thus a monopolist, threatened by public inquiry, might reasonably feel that he is safeguarding his case by using cost plus; also when the "just price" of part of a firm's output is at issue (as in contracts for military supplies), cost plus may be the best short-run method of fixing price. For these and other reasons, the appeal of cost plus to harassed executives is plain, even though some of them may look on it privately as no more than an expedient ritual. We must indeed ask whether those of us who are its spoken critics would in fact wholly reject it if we were ourselves responsible for pricing.

[2] This approach to cost assumes that the cost figures are to be used only for decision on pricing or the like. Some accountants now say that the merits of costing lie more in *control* (of waste, and so on) than in pricing. For control, the right cost may well be historical cost, possibly compared with standard or budget figures.

The gulf between practice and doctrine is thus extremely wide.[3] In an effort to appraise the issues, we shall now look more closely at the cost accountant's figures under various circumstances. We shall, for instance, compare different market structures and contrast single-product with multiproduct firms.

SINGLE-PRODUCT FIRMS

Where a firm makes only one product, the cost accountant generally summarizes his results as averages. Average cost seems at first sight to serve many useful ends. In particular, it can readily be compared with price and for this reason it is a handy test of whether the firm is earning profits—provided the implied guesses at total cost and volume prove correct. However, average cost becomes less attractive when we distinguish various markets in which the one-product firm may find itself, and consider the pricing problems that these markets sometimes pose.

Where Markets Are Purely Competitive

Although examples of pure competition are probably not to be found anywhere, rough approximations to the economic theorist's model do exist. Agriculture, organized commodity markets, and some branches of the textile industry come fairly close. In such purely competitive markets, the businessman needs no cost data for pricing purposes. He has no power over price, being compelled to accept the prevailing one, or wait to sell his wares at another time, since price

---

[3] Considering the size of the gulf, it has excited surprisingly little comment. Costing authors are usually too swamped in massive computations to say what their end-figures mean. Economists tended to ignore costing until the late thirties, when articles by R. H. Coase and R. S. Edwards—republished in David Solomons, ed., *Studies in Costing* (London: Sweet & Maxwell, 1952)—criticized costing theory; and when, for example, R. L. Hall and C. J. Hitch, "Price Theory and Business Behaviour," *Oxford Economic Papers*, No. 2 (May, 1939), pp. 12–45, pointed out that businessmen's descriptions of their own behavior fail to tally with those in economic writings. P. W. S. Andrews in *Manufacturing Business* (London, 1949) went on to suggest that the economist's description is therefore wrong. Such backsliding evoked many retorts, including: Austin Robinson, "Pricing of Manufactured Products," *Economic Journal*, LX (December, 1950), 771–80; and Fritz Machlup, "Marginal Analysis and Empirical Research," *American Economic Review*, XXXVI (September, 1946), 519–54. The virtues and limitations of the economist's approach are ably set out by R. A. Gordon, "Short-Period Price Determination in Theory and Practice," *Studies in Costing*, pp. 183–208.

is determined by the interaction of all buyers and sellers, and is not subject to perceptible influence by any one of them. Therefore, cost cannot be the basis for price.

Accounts, however, may still be guides to business policy. Every firm should consider whether it can better itself by altering its scale of operation; the cost accountant would be doing useful work if he drafted budgets of total cost and revenue at various levels of activity. These would show which level is the most profitable, or even that none of the levels is profitable, in which case the firm would do better to switch to other products, or go right out of business. With change in scale comes change in cost; thus, under pure competition, it is price that fixes cost rather than vice versa.

Where the Product Differs from Competing Products

A firm making a single product that differs from the offerings of rivals generally has some discretion over price.[4] Its price decisions will influence, perhaps strongly, its physical volume of sales. It should presumably try to find the price and volume that bring the highest profit; it may decide to charge a price far below what its rivals ask for competing wares, or to sell at a premium. Only rarely will its best price be the same as its rivals' prices. More important, only rarely and by accident will its most profitable price (in the short run or the long run) be average cost plus a constant conventional margin. Sometimes the firm with the lowest unit costs can command the highest price because of attractive features in its product. To reap the rewards of its skills, such a firm must depart from routine cost plus. As a minimum, it should raise its "plus" when it produces an outstanding product; conversely, when its model is a failure, it may be forced, in order to get rid of the batch, to shift from cost plus to cost minus.

Where Different Prices Are Charged

Under the two kinds of markets outlined above, we have assumed that the firm sells all units of its one product at the same price. In practice, however, a firm often sells at different prices. The price may be changed rhythmically over time (with seasonal shifts in demand, for instance), or different prices may be charged at the same time in different markets—customers being ostensibly distinguished by location, size

[4] Certain market imperfections have the same result. Firms may, for example, be too widely scattered to experience severe competition.

of order, or promptness of payment, but in fact by intensity of demand. Many firms believe that they raise their profit by varying price in this way; indeed, there seems to be a trend in retailing away from the one-price system and back to old-fashioned higgling.

On occasion, the prices of some units may with advantage be put *below* average cost; as long as sales in the low-priced market exceed the avoidable costs of the extra goods, the firm's net profit is raised. For instance, hotels and airlines sometimes gain by cutting off-peak rates to less than average cost. Comparison of the cut rates with average cost serves little purpose, except perhaps as a clumsy reminder of the deficit to be made good at the peaks.

When one-product firms vary price in such ways, they have presumably rejected cost plus. Here then are cases where our opening statement about the widespread use of cost plus does not apply, and where firms apparently agree with the view that cost plus can impair profit.

For the reasons just given, one might almost say that any reference to average cost will be downright harmful at the pricing stage. Average cost becomes useful after the firm has chosen the best price for the given output program, because comparisons of price and average cost then form a handy miniature budget for predicting period results, and may well suggest a need to change the program. But a miniature budget of this kind cannot give a more accurate financial picture of total revenue and cost than a full budget; in fact, it is likely to be less accurate.

MULTIPRODUCT FIRMS

The firm with many products is, in its extreme form, the individual job shop that makes unique goods to order—for instance, the engineering shop that bids for special projects. Most common is the firm producing substantial numbers of several standardized products. In such firms, both cost accountant and price fixer are confronted by far harder tasks and, consequently, are all the more apt to take refuge in cost plus.

Demand Difficulties

As we have said, the economist insists that demand should be consciously weighed when price is being fixed. But labor and skilled guesswork needed for making detailed demand studies for a wide range of items would generally be prohibitive. Systematic comparison of the firm's prices with those of rivals is perhaps the simplest part of the task, and yet this is often burdensome and confusing. Even the firm that is a price leader might well throw up its hands at the costs of fully estimating demand for each product. Clearly, no firm selling hundreds of products could afford to make careful demand estimates for each; in any case, many of the estimates would be out of date by the time they could be used.

Thus, the accountant has a strong argument in that his system is simple, quick, and cheap. Moreover, and this is a most important point, it lets a manager delegate pricing. Such advantages, coupled with the inevitable vagueness of demand estimates, no doubt go far to explain its wide acceptance.

On the other hand, inability to estimate demand accurately and in time scarcely excuses the substitution of cost information for demand information. Crude estimates of demand might substitute for careful estimates of demand, but a cost gives remarkably little insight into demand.

Allocation of Indirect Cost

If asked to explain his charges for indirect costs, the accountant will perhaps explain that a job makes a drain on the firm's manufacturing resources—its plant and space, supervisors, design talent, and the like—and this drain is a cost of the job. Since a big job makes a big drain, cost varies with size.

Here the views of accountant and economist are poles apart. The accountant in effect believes that the total historical cost of providing the plant can be divided up into separate sacrifices for each job. The economist contests the worth of such figures and offers instead his opportunity cost argument: If the firm has excess capacity (plant supervisors, cash, and so on), *no* sacrifice is involved in using these idle resources on the particular job; [5] if the firm has other uses for the resources, then the cost of assigning them to this job is the sum they would earn (less avoidable costs) in their best alternative uses. Opportunity cost in a range from zero to a large sum is very different from the accountant's layers of overhead. [6]

---

[5] Any extra expenditure due to the extra wear and tear on equipment and so on *is* a sacrifice caused by the job, and should be included in avoidable cost. This is a good example of the way in which the accountant's direct cost (based on the arbitrary classification of the ledger) can differ from true avoidable cost.

[6] A job's full cost may include, besides the load for factory overhead, a second load for more remote overheads such as administration (usually found as a percentage of the job's direct cost plus the first load). The second is even harder to justify

Overhead allocation is arbitrary in that the choice of any particular basis (for example, direct wages or machine-hours) is hard to justify; in addition, each of the possible bases gives figures that may differ greatly from those found on another basis. Moreover, allocation invests the "fixed costs of the job" with an air of reality that at times deceives some managers, who may, for instance, let plant stand idle rather than use it on jobs that yield less than its full slice of overhead. However onerous—even disastrous—fixed commitments like rent and interest are to the firm, they are not sacrifices for which the individual job is responsible, and are irrelevant in pricing it.

Costs bind the firm, not its customers. In the case of a product, if the avoidable costs exceed its price, the firm can at least stop making it, but where allocations of fixed costs are concerned, this remedy may not help. A firm that cannot turn to more remunerative jobs should carry on with those that fail to cover their share of overhead; such a firm can only hope that the gross margin (revenue minus avoidable cost) on all jobs will meet fixed cost and leave a profit.

RELEVANCE OF THE MASTER BUDGET

In a firm of any sophistication, job costing (whether in forward-looking budgets or backward-looking accounts) is intimately linked with the firm's plans as stated in its master budget, the budget of total revenue and total cost for the next period. Sometimes such budgets merely give combined figures for the firm's total operations, but generally—if subdivision is feasible—they allow individually for each of the main products. The master budget's projection of revenue implies a specific level of price (hopefully resting on the most competent analysis of market conditions that management can make). Both revenue and cost figures similarly imply forecasts of volume and mix.

From the master budget, with its implicit price and cost per unit, one can derive an average margin per unit. In other words, it is the master budget that gives the rates of allocated overhead and profit for each job. This holds whether the budget is full and formal, or merely a tentative forecast.

If costing and pricing are integrated with a master budget, then several extremely important corollaries seem to follow.

PRICING OBJECTIVES   The master budget presumably states the firm's realistic plans and expectations, and reflects what it is trying to

than the first, since a given job is not likely to add much to administrative expense or make much drain on administrative services.

maximize. The economist summarizes the relevant forces in his diagrams of total or marginal cost and revenue, and suggests that the firm will trim its output until it arrives at the point of maximum profit. The master budget seems to be the firm's forecast of its costs and revenue at that point. The *maximand* may in fact be profit—probably for the long rather than the budget period alone; more likely, it is some compromise among such advantageous factors as profit, a safe cash position, growth, and prestige.

Considering the importance of the master budget, costing writers are curiously silent about its construction, and add little to our scant understanding of the mental steps behind the big decisions. Their reticence compels the critic to put his own interpretation on this fundamental part of costing theory, but it is doubtful that these writers seriously challenge the economist's view of the firm's aims and methods *at the budget stage.*[7] They must surely regard maximum long-run profit as an important part of the goal—at least in the sense that the less costly method is better than the more costly, and a very low profit is a danger sign.

MEASURES OF ACTIVITY AND SIZE OF JOB WITH DIVERSIFIED OUTPUT   Some multi-product firms have no obvious unit with which to measure the size of jobs. Such firms cannot readily link budget figures with units produced, or speak of unit cost and unit price, nor can they in any direct way compare the profits and costs of different jobs.

We suggest that the one object of job costing is to overcome this difficulty, and to find units where these are not provided by the nature of the job. In a few cases, an artificial unit of output can be devised, such as the "bus mile" or "passenger mile" of a motor bus. Where no common unit of output can be found, the accountant for want of something better may take a unit of input, like wages or hours of direct labor, or machine-hours. The master budget can thus be regarded as a plan for a certain volume of activity measured in man-hours, or some other selected unit. The cost estimate for each job likewise makes use

---

[7] For instance, the concept of profit target as a round percentage on past investment may strike many accountants as no more than a convenient simplification, which can be amended without inconsistency when circumstances demand something less crude. Again, the accountant (like other practical men) sometimes illustrates the master budget with a break-even chart whose lines are straight, in contrast to the economist's curves—thus seeming to imply that output and profit can expand indefinitely. If pressed on the point during discussion, the accountant will freely agree that the implication is absurd; he may explain away the absurdity by saying, for example, that nonmonetary factors, such as strain on management, will in fact check expansion.

of the same unit for allocating indirect costs and finding price; in this way, cost and price are linked with the job's size.

AVERAGE COST PER UNIT WITH DIVERSIFIED OUTPUT If this interpretation is right, then the accountant's measure of indirect costs for a job is often akin to an average that is weighted to allow for the job's size, measured in the chosen input units. It has therefore much the same demerits and merits as average cost in the one-product firm. It fails to show the real sacrifice involved in doing the job, but it serves under some circumstances as a miniature forecast of the firm's annual results, and so gives advance warning of a need for revising, say, the scale of operations.

THE COSTING MARGIN AS A PROCESSING CHARGE Again, just as the one-product budget shows both the number of units to be produced and total revenue, so a multi-product budget shows planned production in input units and total revenue. But the one-product budget may sensibly deal with unit price whereas to speak of average price per unit in the multi-product firm usually does not mean much.

If the margin added to direct cost to arrive at price is explained as so much indirect cost and profit per input unit, it has little to recommend it. But if it is regarded as a price per unit—for example, the firm's estimate of the best average price to charge per man-hour for the service of converting direct materials into finished goods—it may be both useful and intellectually defensible. The price quoted for a job could then be regarded as avoidable cost plus a processing charge—with no mention of overhead cost. This idea comes close to the method called "contribution costing," which is used by certain cost accountants when they express the margin on a job as a rate per machine-hour, that is, as the earnings per hour of some key machine that the job utilizes.

A firm in its master budget should presumably try to forecast the number of input units and the average price for each that will give best results. Then, in its day-to-day decisions, it should implement the budget strategy. Suppose, for instance, that the planned costing margin is $\$m$ per man-hour. A job needing x man-hours is priced at $\$mx$ (plus direct costs), not because $\$mx$ measures meaningful slices of overhead, but because this is the price that the firm must charge if it is to carry out its budget decisions. Cost plus, then, represents an administrative trick for putting a price policy into action.

THE COSTING MARGIN AND OPPORTUNITY COST Our interpretation thus implies that a costing margin should be regarded as a tacit allowance for opportunity cost, among other things. The firm first decides that it can maximize profit by selling so many input units of service at a certain price; given this assumption, to do Job X at a lesser rate is to lose greater potential revenue. The loss may arise because X's buyer would in fact be willing to pay more, or because X displaces a better job, or because the firm would need to cut prices all round when X's price became known.

This view, if correct, would go far to explain why costing seems to serve business needs despite its shaky logic. It does not do what it professes to do, but it may do something better; the traditional costing margin—overhead plus profit—may serve as a rough guide to opportunity cost. On the other hand, if costing derives its virtue in this way, then recognition of its true nature would prevent errors based on misinterpretation and would enable accountants to improve their figures.

There are obvious objections to our interpretation of the costing margin, to which we shall return shortly. It does, however, stress one important point; in real life, the alternative to Job X is usually not a known Job Y that neatly duplicates X in everything save profit. The alternative, which may still be unknown when a price is put on X, may consist of several small jobs or part of a large one; it may demand more or less time, space, and money than X. Job-by-job comparisons of profit may, in fact, be impossible or meaningless. Conceivably, operational research will someday help to simplify this issue; in the meantime, probably the best the firm can do is to allow roughly for X's displacement power by means of a load that depends—like the costing margin—on how much of the firm's resources are engaged in the production of X.

JOB COSTS AND MARGINAL ANALYSIS

A further conclusion may perhaps follow if the foregoing argument is correct. The conflict between accounting and economics seems, in this area, somewhat unreal; both may simply be dealing with different stages of the production program.

When the economist considers the problem of profit maximization, he is generally thinking of the stage at which the firm is still trying to find its best scale of operation for the next period. He considers, for instance, the results on expected cost and revenue of expanding the next period's output from n units to $n + x$ units. (x is here the marginal quantity, and its avoidable cost is the relevant marginal cost.)

Costing is more often concerned with what happens after these plans have been made. As we have seen, estimates for single jobs or small batches assume that the master budget for the period has already been drafted and that the figures of the budget (including planned physical activity of n units, however these are measured) have been used to find rates for burden and profit at the start of the period. Later, at some point during the period, a given job is considered. Costing tries to estimate inputs of this job, its size (x units), and, thus, its weighted average cost. But the master budget is not changed by the job; output is still expected to total only n (not $n+x$) by the close of the year, for x is merely a part in the planned flow of output. Consequently, the job, its cost, and its revenue do not appear to be marginal in the economist's usual sense; a textbook diagram whose horizontal axis shows total output is helpful for explaining the composite program, but is irrelevant to any job within that program. We suspect that, when economists question businessmen on how the fundamental decisions are made, there may be sad muddling of budget strategy with costing tactics.

OBJECTIONS TO THE COSTING MARGIN

In our attempt to interpret the costing margin as a measure for pricing, we have deliberately passed over the flaws in the argument.

1. One weakness is that the interpretation has never to our knowledge been put forward by a cost accountant.

2. Another lies in the notion of omniscient budgets and clear-cut budget periods; plainly, a costing margin found by a master budget cannot measure opportunity costs at all closely, for the budget assumes such costs to be the same for every date during its period and for all the products. The day-by-day state of the market ought to change a manager's views on the period's possibilities; if he gets a big order, he must, at least mentally, revise his budget totals somewhat. Consequently, a cost margin found at the budget stage may soon be out of date.

3. Again, the argument makes sense only where the firm can in fact switch from one product to another. This is often difficult or impossible, because, for instance, the products emerge in fixed proportions, or plant is built to do only one job. If there is no alternative, there is no opportunity cost.

4. Further, the argument assumes that the chosen input unit correlates with costs and demand in much the same way as the output units of the single-product firm. This is a tall assumption. In some firms, any given input unit seems likely to vary too much with each job's peculiarities to be a good general index of size for all jobs, and there

may be no common denominator for size if each job is a distinctive bundle of materials, skills, and services.

5. A customer, to take the demand point of view, will not base his valuations on any internal unit used by his supplier. His test of a job's size is how much he wants it, and his price ceiling is the lower of this subjective value and the price he must pay for a similar article elsewhere, or for substitutes. This composite force on the demand side, and not the supplier's cost and effort, is what enables the supplier to charge more for the big job—and indeed to earn any revenue at all. Accordingly, a prime criterion in choosing a unit should be that it serves as a guide to the bids of rivals; the more their productive methods differ from those of the given firm, the less sound will the latter's input units be as guides.

6. Finally, just as one-product firms may find that it pays to charge different prices in different markets, so the multi-product firm may benefit by varying its margin per unit on its different products. A firm of jobbing engineers, for example, may make each of its tenders in somewhat different demand conditions; here the case for flexible pricing is very strong.

Although these objections to the use of the costing margin as an indicator of opportunity cost and price are formidable, the pricer in the multi-product firm must have some measure of the size of each job in order to determine how much of the firm's productive resources (man power, machinery, space, and executive direction) the job will consume. Even when these resources involve no added expense or outlay, they do represent the firm's opportunity to create net income, and some price must be placed on their use if the firm has alternatives. The costing margin may be a crude and imperfect tool, and yet be the least objectionable one that is available.

Perhaps the correct attitude toward the costing margin is to regard it in practice as the best starting point for pricing. When the appropriate price for the size of the job has been found by this omnibus formula, management can consider whether the master budget's assumption about the general state of trade still applies or whether demand for the particular article warrants a change in the margin. Considering such factors, they may, perhaps without realizing the extent of their intervention, modify the costing price substantially.[8]

8 I. F. Pearce showed in "A Study in Price Policy," *Economica*, XXIII (May, 1956), 114–27 that in one firm, whose managers firmly believed they worked on cost plus, job prices found by cost plus became actual prices in only a minority of cases.

The Firm with a "Line of Products"

A good example of the need to modify prices found by means of a costing margin occurs when a firm sells many different products to the same customer. Such firms may be said to sell a "line of products." A new customer means sales of many products; a lost customer means lost sales of many products.

Cost plus, strictly applied, would often rob the firm of the benefits that come from pricing its wares as a "team" in which some items clear the ground for others. The price line, with the low-price, low-margin items whose function is to "build traffic" and arouse customer interest, and the high-price, high-margin, and high-quality item that brings prestige to the entire line and aids the medium-priced items, is commonplace in many industries. Other firms use the variation of periodically cutting prices of some items for a short time.

Could costing at least show which items to promote and which to drop? There are several difficulties in using accounts to this end. First, the cost side would include some arbitrary allocations; many of the overheads charged to the item under scrutiny would not be reduced to nil by dropping it. Second, the revenues are likely to understate the item's contributions; inclusion of an item in the line may well explain how important customers have been won and held. Finally, the decision maker must look to the item's future rather than its past.

Accordingly, this kind of firm is likely to be led astray—both in fixing prices and in deciding whether to promote, drop, or maintain items—if it relies on traditional accounts. It is far better for an expert price fixer to guess clumsily at the right factors than to measure precisely those that are irrelevant. He should estimate the demand for those products that are unique in some degree and arrange prices on the team principle; when he is considering whether to drop an item, he should guess at what it adds to revenue by boosting the sale of other products. The mechanical application of a generalized budget formula is here most unlikely to measure opportunity costs. A cost estimate of the savings from dropping the item may be useful, but it should be an *ad hoc* estimate, confined to costs that will in fact be changed by the omission.

SUGGESTED PROCEDURE

Early in this article we posed two problems. Why is cost plus so popular, despite its crude logic? And, would we, if we were in positions of business responsibility, reject this approach? We shall now try to answer both questions by outlining the way in which we think the cost accountant should help with pricing.

Formula vs Individual Analysis

The central problem is whether any general formula, such as cost plus, suitably reinterpreted, can with advantage be put in the place of individual decisions about each price.

The two main factors to be weighed by a pricer are demand and cost. Demand should ideally be studied with the utmost care by persons of outstanding discernment. We believe that no formula can accurately assess all the pulls and shifts of the living market, and that management must in the end bear full responsibility for estimating demand. A formula can be defended only on the grounds that careful judgments on each separate price are either not feasible (because of the need for quick decisions on many articles) or not worthwhile (because of the high risk of error). The retail shop provides an apt analogy: its owner might well maximize profit by bargaining afresh with each customer on each visit over each unit of stock, but in practice he is usually forced by the difficulties of doing otherwise to put the same price ticket on all like units.

Cost may at first sight seem easier to reduce to a formula. If, however, it is looked on as a choice between alternatives, it too becomes subjective and hard to weigh. Ideally, a job's cost should be estimated by senior managers after full consideration of the likely alternatives and all their impacts on future possibilities. We accept that no formula will do justice to a host of dimly foreseen and hypothetical events, and that management must shoulder the task of choosing between alternatives. But a formula may still be defensible, if only on the grounds that it winnows out the obviously unattractive plans, and leaves managers free to work on plans that offer a good prospect of success.

In short, the formula can be defended only as a last resort. Our task is to consider the circumstances in which it is most likely to be a useful supplement to special studies, and the means by which its defects can be minimized.

Building the Master Budget

As we have seen, the formula implies the existence of some sort of forecast—at its best, a full budget of the firm's revenue and costs. Such a budget seems desirable in any case. Before it is drafted, certain basic questions might well be explicitly posed. Is it the firm's aim to win maximum profit, at least in the long run and with various provisos? Is there a point on the firm's scale of activity at which profit is maximized, and on either side of which profit declines through the combined action of cost and demand forces? Practical men will know that such questions cannot be answered without qualifications, and that no one can pinpoint the quantities at stake. The important thing is to be clear on the objective and plan of attack.

Demand and price should play a big part in the plan. Our discussion has stressed the major influence of demand, and how this varies in different markets. In some markets, the firm has no discretionary power over price; the only major decision concerns scale of output. In others, the firm must simultaneously envisage price, demand, volume, and cost as interrelated parts of the budget problem.

In firms facing several types of demand, or making several products with very different cost patterns, the budget should be split up between home and foreign markets, or time of year, or type of product, and so forth. The firm must study demand in each market, and try to map out the best price policy in each; it must also draft separate budgets for each department that has a fairly uniform cost pattern.

The Task of the Formula

The budget establishes the general plan—scale, level of prices, and so on. The formula tries to put this plan into effect when the minor decisions are later made on each job.

One must in each case ask whether the firm can foresee the future clearly enough to establish such an all-embracing plan. If conditions change so fast that even supplementary budgets soon lag behind events, then a predetermined formula seems likely to do mischief. The same holds if the various jobs differ greatly, whether on the side of demand or costs. The formula presumably assumes stability and sameness in day-to-day operations; it relies on "what things usually cost" or "what we can usually charge," and thus breaks down if there is no "usual."

For reasons set out earlier, we cannot accept the normal wording of the formula in terms of allocated overhead, and so on. We prefer to interpret it as a measure of contribution, that is, what the firm believes to be its best price, per unit of activity, for converting direct inputs into finished goods.

If the formula is to work well, it must allow for three quantities that would otherwise need to be found by special estimate:

1. Concealed and remote avoidable costs.
2. Opportunity costs, that is, the contribution to overhead and the profit that could be obtained by doing other jobs instead.
3. Any further contribution from this particular job.

The formula's claims may be tested by following the build-up of a price, step by step; we shall, if we do not state the contrary, deal with single jobs rather than large flows.

BUILDING A PRICE The first step is to find the avoidable costs. Though the direct costs of the accountant may often be very similar to the obvious avoidable costs, the accountant's figures are based on clerical convenience rather than a cause-and-effect relationship between decision and sacrifice.[9] They will thus on occasion need amending in two ways: The money values attached to some ingredients must be changed, for example, by substituting current for historical cost; and the list of direct costs must be extended to include those avoidable costs that accounting classes as indirect. By their very nature, items on this extended list may be hard to detect and evaluate; even a special study for the job might end with a very vague guess at the sums in question. Therefore, it does not seem unreasonable to allow for them roughly with a rate per unit of size, unless the job has individual peculiarities that call for a special estimate. Size in this context seems more likely to be a function of time (man-hours or machine-hours) than of direct expenses.

If we ignore odd cases like the loss-leader, avoidable cost will be the lowest price at which the firm will ever take on work. This minimum will, however, need to be raised if the given job displaces other profitable opportunities. Accordingly, the next step is to estimate opportunity cost.

OPPORTUNITY COST The alternatives to the given job may be known and clearly measurable. If they are, straightforward comparison between the job and the best alternative should be easy, and will show which work yields the biggest margin. If they are not, then a margin based on normal yields per unit of activity seems likely to be helpful,

[9] For instance, a clerk can trace the historical cost of raw materials through his records from their purchase until they enter the final product, but the resulting "direct cost" may not show the sacrifice due to the decision to use materials in stock. This decision probably causes the purchase of new materials; if so, the sacrifice is not a figure already in the books, but the outlay on replacement.

at least as a starting point. However, since such a margin cannot be more correct than the master budget from which it springs, the pricer should consider whether the budget still holds good. There may be a temporary change in activity, or new trends may be emerging, in the light of which the load for the given job should be trimmed. Unless the margin rate keeps pace with the order book, it is a poor guide to opportunity cost.

Which unit of activity from contenders such as direct labor cost or machine-hours should the formula employ to measure opportunity cost? Presumably the firm must find out by experience which unit best satisfies a double test: (1) prices based on this unit must attract the desired volume of activity; and yet (2) the items bought at these prices must not displace more remunerative items. The right unit is thus part of the price mechanism that equates demand with supply; customer reactions to the unit are important as well as the firm's internal workings. When one starts to find out whether a given job will displace other work, one's first inclination is perhaps to look for any scarce factor that acts as a bottleneck in production. Such a factor may exist; if, for example, labor is short, man-hours may be a good index of displaced jobs. Under imperfect competition, however, a firm may have plenty of "slack" in a physical sense, and yet continue to charge a margin. Here the bottleneck is not physical; it is the firm's own policy of restricting sales volume by keeping up prices. In this case, therefore, one should not search for bottlenecks in the plant, but should use the unit that rations sales most profitably (particularly in markets that are subject to destructive price cutting). Once again, a unit based on time seems most likely to work well; but, conceivably, the best unit for measuring opportunity cost is not the best for measuring concealed avoidable cost.

PROFIT MARGIN   When the pricer has estimated the job's avoidable and opportunity costs, his next and final step is to ask how much more can be added as pure profit.

In many cases, the ceiling is obvious—the price charged by rivals (adjusted to allow for any special features in the firm's own product). If this is less than total cost, the firm will withdraw from the race. If it is more, the pricer must judge how near it to pitch his figure, a calculation for which direct comparison would seem a better guide than the formula.

But, where the product is new or a tender has to be made for a special job, the firm may not yet know the competing prices. Here one of the chief aims of the cost department might be to guess the prices charged by rivals. If the latter rely on a formula, then a formula may be a useful tool for predicting their prices; indeed, the normal full-cost estimate may be defensible on the grounds that it suggests not the firm's own costs, but the prices of competitors (actual or potential). Presumably the formula should not be used blindly, but should be adapted in the light of what is known of the rival's ways. For instance, a special estimate might be needed if the rival has a different method of production.

There may be a wide space between the cost floor and the demand ceiling. In that case, bargaining skill rather than economic factors may fix the position of price, or the firm may gain by charging a low price, perhaps because this will mean many future sales. An omnibus formula can scarcely respond to situations of this type. Nor can it weigh the eagerness of particular customers or the merits of a particular product. Such factors strengthen the case for using individual decisions to modify the formula's figure for profit.

COST AND PRICE FOR LARGE BATCHES Our approach must obviously be modified when we pass from the individual job to many sales of like units. Here the pricer faces nearly all the complexities of the complete budget in a single-product firm: cost may vary with volume, which may vary with the price that he is trying to find. No mechanical approach that relies on the use of a formula can do justice to such a problem.

The accountant can help by providing cost estimates at several points of the scale of output; the pricer must try to guess demand at corresponding points, and so find the optimum scale of operations. As the drafting of many precise estimates would involve much work, there may be good reason for using a formula in the preliminary stages. When the choice has been narrowed, special studies of avoidable and opportunity cost may become worthwhile, particularly if the given batch of new articles is big enough to suggest that it amounts to a change in the master budget.

IMPORTANCE OF DEMAND Our review of the forces at stake has emphasized the supreme importance of demand. Though this force is hard to gauge, the pricer's success must in the long run depend on his flair for assessing it.

Part of his problem stems from the effect that frequent price changes may have in the long run on customer relations. He should be equipped with a clear statement of the firm's policy on this point. Does the firm feel that isolated price concessions will involve a serious handicap in the future? The top executive might even be called upon to set a figure that measures the size of the handicap; for instance, he might estimate that price stability would in the long run justify a drop in current profits of up to $25,000.

The pricer may sometimes get helpful impressions from other members of the firm. If, for example, he is trying to set prices for a line and to employ the team-pricing concept, men in the sales department are likely to be the best source of information about which items to treat as promotional numbers, how much to charge for a prestige model, and the probable gain in general sales from having a particular item in the line.

The pricer should gather data and impressions from others within the firm, including data from specific studies specially undertaken for him by the market research department. In the end, however, he must size up all the relevant forces for himself. He cannot move directly from cost to price; he cannot even assign clear values to many of the forces. He can probably do his job best by drawing up a schedule covering the main factors at stake, and by making his own estimate, however crude, of their values. Such schedules would call for different information according to the type of product and market. Once prepared, however, they would be helpful starting points the next time a price decision for the same product was needed.

In the procedures described above, costs are still important, and it is to be hoped that the cost accountant will help to make the estimates. Since he is the man most at home with the firm's cost structure, he can give much useful information.

However, if the cost accountant is to play his full part, he must adopt an approach that is still alien to his tradition; any attempt to kill two birds with one stone (that is, to use his ledger balances for pricing as well as for their more fitting task of control) will fail. He must abandon a classification that depends on clerical traceability; he must look forward rather than back, and must cease to imagine he can perform the miracle of splitting common cost. Further, he must recognize the need for a wider range of information, much of it subjective; opportunity cost depends on factors about which the accountant in many firms is at present not kept informed, such as the nature of the market and the state of the order book. Thus, he must keep in close touch with other departments, notably the sales department.

Such a task would be an exacting challenge to the cost accountant. But it would make for much closer ties between him and the managers, since he would have to be privy to their intentions and alternative plans, and, in consequence, it would greatly enhance his status.

Our approach can in part be summarized as a plea for cost statements with more precise words and less precise figures. The words ought to serve as clear explanations of the different kinds of sacrifice—obvious avoidable costs, hidden avoidable costs, and opportunity costs. Many cost figures must inevitably be guesswork, and this should be made plain; on occasion, they will be none the worse for being expressed as a range of probabilities, or for being sprinkled with question marks. Such vagueness accords with the facts of business life better than a façade of precision.

Clear words would also show the nature of each computation, whether it is the passive product of a formula, or a special estimate. A pricer must choose between the two. The special estimate is plainly superior in the sense of being more logical and flexible; but, as none of us has boundless wisdom, time, and energy, there may often be a sound case for the critical use of a formula.

QUESTIONS

1. In general, how does a cost accountant arrive at a price to charge for a given item? What are the criticisms of this approach?

2. Does adding a percentage profit margin to the "total cost" of producing and distributing an item ensure that the firm will make a profit?

3. How do the authors differentiate among total, avoidable, and fixed costs?

4. Referring to question 3, which class of costs is probably most subject to control procedures?

5. In market situations approximating pure competition, how is price determined? What major contributions might a cost accountant perform is such a situation?

6. Under what circumstances might it be advisable for a firm to set the price of a product at less than its average cost?

7. Why is the "cost-plus" method of pricing likely to prevail in a multi-product company?

8. Do you think that a given product should be charged with a proportionate share of plant depreciation in arriving at a decision to either add or drop the product? Why? Would your answer change if the plant were operating at "less than capacity"? If operating "above capacity"? (Note: Assume fixed costs remain the same at capacity or less and increase in fairly constant increments if capacity is exceeded.)

9. The goal of profit maximization may be modified because of

other factors. In addition the time horizon is often long-run rather than short-run. Discuss the other factors that a company may consider in pricing decisions.

10. What method of adding a profit margin to direct costs would bring the accountant and the economist closer to agreement on pricing policies? Explain.

11. Would you ever recommend that a company sell a product at a price less than avoidable cost? Explain.

12. Would you recommend the use of the same records and procedures for pricing and control purposes? Explain.

19

Contributions of Accounting to Measurement in Management

William J. Vatter

THE QUANTITATIVE aspects of business management were left almost entirely in the hands of accountants prior to the advent of "scientific management" some seventy-five years ago. Although this term has fallen into disuse, the emphasis upon quantitative bases for decision-making and control has increased as the management problem has become more complex. Needs for additional data and for more comprehensive analysis have brought changes in accounting to provide more frequent and more detailed information. New systems for processing data have been developed; in some cases these appear to have replaced or to have amended the traditional notions about accounting. Actually, none of the new methods really alters the basic situation: no one approach to managerial measurements is completely

From *Management Science*, vol. 5, no. 1 (October, 1958), pp. 27–37. Reprinted by permission of the publisher. Mr. Vatter is Professor of Business Administration at the University of California (at Berkeley).

effective in all circumstances. What is really needed is a combination of techniques; traditional and novel methods, census and sampling techniques, general- and special-purpose analyses all contribute to the measurement objective. We should strive to combine all available quantitative techniques in such ways as will provide optimum service to meet the needs of management.

Accounting is the most venerable measurement method in economics. It was born with the earliest notions of production and exchange— probably even before money as we now know it existed. Accounting records of crude types originated from memoranda used to supplement personal recollections; as business transactions became more numerous, the need for systematic records increased, and accounting procedures grew in response to the need for information. The invention of credit (which probably preceded if it did not precipitate the invention of gunpowder) served further to develop the use of accounting as a management device. The "venture" profit and loss statement was well developed before the Roman Empire existed, and the principles of double-entry bookkeeping were clearly enunciated when the New World was discovered. However, fairly elaborate accounting systems were operated in commercial and governmental institutions much earlier; there is at least one example of manufacturing accounts and cost allocations dating from the beginning of the 16th century.[1] The growth of accounting is a continuing story of matching needs for information with improved accounting methods.

The beginnings of the industrial revolution also started renewed development of accounting methods. The device of corporate organization put a new and different emphasis upon financial reports; colonial expansion and industrial developments made it more and more necessary to measure and report results of operations to those who could not observe them at close range. Scientific management engendered new advances in the analysis and recording of costs; the pressures of growth, recession and recovery, stringent competition and heavy risks have in recent years placed heavy emphasis upon management planning and control in the form of budgets, standards, and other systematic devices designed and implemented by a new kind of staff-executive, the controller. Still more striking developments have started with the recent improvements in data processing. These new methods make it possible to satisfy demands for management information more effectively than ever before; even now, there are strong pressures for the redesign of

[1] Florence Adler, "Cost Accounting in the Sixteenth Century," *Accounting Review*, XII (September, 1937), pp. 226–37.

systems and reports to make them into more effective management tools.

This abbreviated historical résumé shows two things clearly: first, how long it takes for human beings to learn relatively simple things; but second, it shows that accounting has been the creature of the needs and uses it has served. From its very inception, and through all of its development, accounting methods and measurements have been closely intertwined with managerial processes.[2] Long before there were such things as trade associations, the Securities and Exchange Commission or the Federal Income Tax, the need for analytical measurements in the management areas has been met by accounting. These needs persist and grow with the complexity of managerial problems; indeed, they are greater as better means of serving them are developed. However, in this ever-growing demand and development of the supply of quantitive data for managerial purposes, accounting shows several notable and distinctive features which contribute to the measurement process in management.

1. UNIFIED EXPRESSION OF DIVERSE DATA

The central problem in any measurement process is the selection of the measuring unit. This is often quite difficult, since there are many variables or attributes which do not readily lend themselves to quantitative expression. The attempt to measure qualitative things, such as attitudes, feelings, and preferences is always fraught with error when the units of measurement are (as they often must be) selected arbitrarily. This has caused more than one person to question the results of such operations. Kelvin's dictum—"unless you can measure, your knowledge is meager and unsatisfactory" is not without its critics.

However, measurement units selected *ad hoc,* with limited rational basis, may be useful and desirable, within their limitations. The arbitrary nature of the unit employed to measure the hardness of metals, for instance, does not detect from the usefulness of such quantifications.[3] Most measurement units are arbitrary in some respects; the

[2] A. C. Littleton, *Accounting Evolution to 1900* (New York: American Institute, 1933) and Edward Peragallo, *Origin and Evolution of Double-Entry Bookkeeping* (New York: American Institute, 1935).

[3] Hardness seems to be itself a somewhat vague concept. It may mean solidity and firmness of outline, resistance to permanent indentation under static or dynamic loads, energy transmission under impact, resistance to abrasion or machinability. Yet we can specify hardness in a metal part, and deliver to specification in terms of a Rockwell or Brinnell number.

basic test of any measurement is whether or not it can be fitted into a broader logical framework, there to be used to further understanding or to establish other relationships.

For example, the measurement of temperature cannot proceed from mere sense-impressions, even though in some cases this may be the real issue to be met; when I "feel cold" no measurement can supplant my feelings. The range of feelings does not cover the span of temperature variation, so we try to quantify by other means, such as measuring thermal expansion in a thermometer. But the difficulties engendered by this are worth noting.

The coefficient of expansion is not exactly a constant for any substance; what is measured is an average relationship over a limited range; although most substances expand equally in all directions when heated, others expand faster in one direction than another, even contracting in one dimension while they expand in another.[4] The measuring medium must be selected with care. The range for the temperature scale is established by the boiling and freezing points of water; because several factors are known to affect boiling and freezing points, we use a substance relatively easy to purify. But to extend the range of measurements, we use mercury which has a wide "space" between its boiling and freezing points, and which has a fairly high rate of expansion, equal in all directions. This liquid must be inclosed in a tube which is transparent, and of constant dimensions to avoid distortions of the measurement. Since the tube itself expands and contracts, it is made of material with a low expansion rate. Then, since there are differences in the time rate of response to heat changes in the mercury and the glass, a time lag must be specified if the reading is to be accurate. The measurement device is thus seen to be quite complex; with all these complicating factors at work, the task of measuring temperature is not easy; we can hardly look upon the process *a priori* as a highly satisfactory job.

Still, the pragmatic knowledge of temperatures has facilitated technological progress in many ways; the usefulness and adaptability of temperature-measurements has been demonstrated experientially. To cite an example still in the physical science realm; if it can be established that all substances which do not ionize in solution depress the freezing point by .186° for each gram-molecular weight of solute [5] the measurement of temperature must be accepted as valid, for such an

---

[4] A. L. Kimball, *College Physics* (New York: Holt, 1923), p. 160.

[5] H. N. Holmes, *General Chemistry* (New York: Macmillan, 1922), p. 95, pp. 138–9.

extension of quantitative relationships cannot be the result of mere chance. Where such homogeneity of substance has been empirically established, something has been measured and measured well. The validity of the measurement has been established by the way in which it fits in the wide framework of reference to which it can be related.

Accounting provides this framework into which the variables of managerial measurements are oriented. Business operates in terms of financial results, and the structure of accounting serves to tie together the combined effects of the forces and factors with which management is concerned. Relating such units as man-hours, ton-miles, kilowatts, to a common pattern of systematic observation and comparison in financial terms is the way in which accounting provides that necessary frame of reference.

Management is a continuous process of making choices among various courses of action. Although these choices may be set, individually, in special terms applicable to each situation, something more is needed to make the overall pattern effective. The whole range of individual choices must make sense in the general scheme. In our industrial and commercial society this general scheme is a pecuniary one; even though the basic criterion of effective results may be something different from profit-maxima, the financial result of business decisions is the way in which we judge the overall effectiveness of management. When we do employ profit as a test of effectiveness, it can only be used over a fairly wide area of operations, such as a division or a product line.[6] Solutions to problems such as the routing of transportation, the selection of machines for given tasks, the establishment of standard procedures for given operations, are typically achieved by "suboptimization" in terms of minimizing costs, utilizing available capacity, or achieving balance. However, the correctness of these individual choices can be evaluated for the firm as a whole only by reference to some central value-scale. Some basis of interpretation or expression is needed, to carry over from isolated decisions to combined effect—the train of decisions must be put together into a consistent whole, in a continuing medium, to permit an overall evaluation.

Another way to say this is to note that what may appear best for one department, section, problem or situation can usually be determined by the use of "local" data and methods. But production, mar-

[6] Even for a division or a product, the jointness of costs and revenues gives trouble. See Joel Dean, "An Approach to Internal Profit Measurement," *N.A.A. Bulletin*, March 1958, pp. 5–12. Also W. J. Vatter, "Limitations of Overload Allocation," *Accounting Review*, XX, April 1945, pp. 163–176.

keting, or personnel programs need to be put together for *overall* evaluation. This task is done by accounting techniques so that general policy and broad strategy may be evaluated in the interests of the enterprise as a whole.

This function of accounting is important, even when the judgments to be made are qualitative rather than quantitative in nature. The effect of a given managerial decision on employee morale may be difficult to quantify—not only because of uncertainty, but because there is no easy way to express feelings or attitudes in an additive number-pattern. Even though employee morale cannot readily be expressed quantitatively (much less by dollar amounts), it may be easier to judge such effects if they cannot be related to financial measure: it may not be "worth" such an amount to disappoint a customer or an employee, even though we may not be able to measure the disappointment itself.

Marshalling financial data against a problem adds depth to the analysis; the use of an overall financial measuring scale makes certain kinds of summaries and comparisons possible, which otherwise would require tedious, circuitous, and inaccurate methods. The "homogeneity of substance" arising from the fact that accounting is related to *both* the detailed choices of method and the overall test of effectiveness, makes accounting an effective backdrop for judging managerial decisions in the aggregate.

2. OBJECTIVITY

Segregation of the accounting function in the typical organization chart is no accident; just as there are good reasons for the separation of planning from performance, there are considerations which demand the separation of operating activities (both planning and performance) from the measurement and reporting function. Nearly all measurement devices and methods are subject to some kind and degree of bias. Sometimes, the measurement methods are themselves prone to errors; but errors of observation and interpretation are common. Some of this is mere ineptness or lack of understanding; but it should always be recognized that nobody is able to be completely impersonal about a project or problem on which he is at work. The very fact of our interest leads us to anticipate, and we sometimes fail to observe and interpret as we should. Data must of necessity be selected in some way, and it is easy for "fringe" patterns or side-effects to pass unnoticed. There is a real advantage to have data collected from a position and a viewpoint that are detached and independent. One of the basic merits of accounting is that it can be kept independent, and that its measurements may be made, its reports prepared, apart and separate from the activities and decisions of the management.

This does not imply an unsympathetic attitude or a lack of interest of the accountant with respect to managerial problems. The measurement and reporting device simply functions best when it is separated from decision-making, to maintain its objectivity. Further, the measurement system must stay "out of the way" of operations; otherwise, the responsibility for decision-making cannot be kept separate from that of data-collection and processing. This is essential if the measurement system is to interpret and report the effects and results of decisions without bias. The separation of data-collection in the accounting system leaves management free to manage, using the reported data as independent benchmarks which may or may not be important for given purposes. In other words, data may be used, or they may be left unused in the process of decision making, depending upon whether they are judged relevant or essential to the decision. The independence of the accounting function should insure that the data are not set in too narrowly conceived dimensions; it should help maintain the objectivity desired, both in the making of decisions, and in appraising their effects.

However, it is worth noting that information is not collected in a vacuum of abstraction; it has meaning only in terms of the problems and issues against which it may be used. The objectivity that is maintained in the separation of accounting from managerial areas is of full usefulness only if steps are taken to bridge the gaps in communication between the collectors (or reporters) of accounting information, and those who are expected to use that information. Accounting figures (for that matter, *any* numerical data) are not "brute facts" of absolute significance; they must be fitted to the uses that are to be made of them. Costs relevant to the measurement of efficiency may be irrelevant for problems of price and output decisions; various classifications of controllable, incremental, out-of-pocket, alternative, and avoidable costs must be related to the independent and dependent variables in the problem at hand.[7] The effectiveness of accounting data often depends vitally upon the proper communication between the accountant and the operating management.

One contribution that accounting can make to managerial measurements is thus to increase the objectivity of the quantitative

[7] J. M. Clark, *Economics of Overhead Costs* (Chicago: University of Chicago Press, 1924).

data that are collected and reported. An intelligent objectivity that combines absence of personal bias and impersonal treatment of data, with an understanding of the content and uses of data relevant to managerial problems, is one of the major contributions of accounting to the managerial process.

3. LOCALIZATION OF DATA IN TERMS OF MANAGERIAL RESPONSIBILITY

As has been pointed out, data may be marshalled in different patterns to fit specific problems, and such classification and reporting is an essential to proper discharge of the accounting function. However, there is one set of classifications that has basic, overall, and continuing importance in an organization or an enterprise. The delegation of authority (or even its seizure) necessarily implies a responsibility for a part of the enterprise activities, and a pattern of supervision and evaluation. One of the important tasks of the accountant is to associate costs with the jurisdictional areas of organization, not merely to tie costs to projects or programs, but to assign them to managers responsible for implementation and execution.[8] Many plans are failures, not because of any lack of brilliance in conception or of "correctness" in analysis, but because of misunderstandings or ineffectiveness in the implementation and execution of those plans. Often the task of implementation is such as to require cooperation and "follow-through" on the part of several administrative units. Management looks to the accountant to furnish a "ready-made" and continuous procedure for following up the implementation of programs and policies. This is the channel through which most management people have contact with accounting, since the use of accounting for this purpose is nearly universal.

There is more here than a mere reporting *ex post,* and this function is not identical with the overall accumulation of data referred to previously in this paper. The processes of management are facilitated by the use of accounting data to judge between alternative comprehensive plans of action, to work out in advance the ways in which problems of the future will be met, in the form of budgets or standards. The preparation of budgets and standards is not an accounting function; although they may be based upon data furnished by the accounting system, the decisions made must be those of the managers, not the

[8] See "Responsibility Costing" in Eric Kohler, *A Dictionary for Accountants* (New York: Prentice-Hall, 1952), p. 365.

accountant.[9] But the accountant will usually suggest (at times he may have to argue) that the plans should be set to state detailed tasks for subordinate divisions or lesser jurisdictional areas, so that results may be matched with planned responsibilities at all levels. It is not so important to know merely that the total plan has succeeded or failed, as it is to know where and how errors have occurred or advantages have been foregone. By pinpointing plans and results in terms of specific jurisdictions, the accounting system helps management evaluate its own effectiveness. Responsibility accounting shows *where* trouble exists; if we know where to look, it is not usually difficult to establish the conditions that need attention.

4. COMPLETENESS OF DATA

Accounting is by nature a recording process, and its basic task is to preserve information about day-to-day transactions in such forms as may be useful. The really important reason for collecting information is not that the past is important *per se*. Historical data are important because the future may be expected to be somewhat like the past; if we allow for differences, we may extrapolate from our understanding what has happened to plan the future with confidence. However, data used for such purposes must not only be additive, objective, and related to problems under review; it must be at least reasonably complete. In many situations, incomplete data may be useful; in some cases, incomplete data are all that should be required. But any measurement system must recognize that partial analysis runs the risk of overlooking important factors. The whole story ought to be available; and the aim of the accountant is to make available the relevant information for the specific situation, without detracting from the overall frame of reference.

Although it is true that partial data may be adequate for dealing with certain managerial problems, especially if the samples may be selected rationally or in accordance with randomization or other plans, it is also of some importance to know what the total picture is.[10] Not only does the availability of totals and aggregates serve to check the partial data, but the aggregates frequently suggest the need for other analyses. There is a real use for aggregative data to supplement and to implement managerial measurements.

[9] T. F. Bradshaw and C. C. Hull, *Controllership in Modern Management* (Chicago: Irwin, 1949), p. 62, *passim*.

[10] D. R. Anderson, *Practical Controllership* (Chicago: Irwin, 1949), Chapter XIII.

To accomplish the aim of providing complete data concerning enterprise activities, the typical accounting procedures insist upon certain standards. For instance, every sale should be recorded on appropriate forms, arranged to insure the collection of all wanted information on the form itself. Even though much of this information is of minor significance for the purposes of routine reporting, it may be collected for its availability to meet other needs. To illustrate, we may not care to have sales classified by size of order, or by weights of shipments, as a routine matter; however, if the sales order form is designed to collect such information, it may be used whenever it is needed. So long as the cost of collecting such information is not too great, the sales order forms may be made a mine of statistical information whenever such data may be of service. The use of punched cards in accounting (and more recently magnetic tapes) have served to demonstrate the advantage of such procedures. But more important is the fact that every systemic aspect of accounting contains some procedure to make sure that all the data of a given class are indeed present in the totals. Serially numbering the sales invoices or other records makes sure that no part of the data as collected is lost in the process of handling the forms. The importance of this for pure accounting objectives is obvious; no report that pretends to show what has happened in financial terms over a period can be satisfactory if it is based upon information that may be incomplete, or that may exclude certain kinds of data that may be of importance. Since the accountant takes no firm position as to what parts of the data may be significant for the questions that may be raised, he has no alternative but to be sure that all wanted information is in fact included in his reports. Often, the accounting method aggregates data that could be better interpreted if analyzed in detail; it thus may cover up unobserved trends or relationships. However, this need not happen because of the *absence* of such information; the basic vouchers and memoranda may be referred to for such supplementary and detailed study as may be indicated. Then, the sampling process may be expected to be established on more meaningful grounds by stratification or other use of knowledge of the universe. Accounting provides a systematic pattern of data collection which insures that all wanted data are available for study, and that impressions and analyses are not distorted by ignorance of relevant facts.

It should be stressed that initial recording controls the ultimate availability of information. Data not recorded in the routines of accounting may be had by other means, but special purpose methods are expensive, and they are subject to errors of various kinds. Data processing may of course classify available figures and other data in almost any desired pattern, but it cannot *originate* information; the initial record must be adequate and complete, or the job of collecting information must be done over again. This raises a serious question which accountants and others must try to answer: just what information is to be contained in the original record?

It is uneconomic to record everything, even when this is possible. There would be little value in collecting data on age and other physical characteristics of department store customers unless they are to be used. Yet, it is obvious that no realistically meaningful data should be overlooked. The compromises implied are not easily settled, especially because the aggregative aims of accounting reports are not the same as those involved in special-purpose studies. Within the limits of cost and errors in the recording process, we should probably be generous in getting as much useful information as can be justified; but we should probably be cautious in the processing and reporting of information on a routine basis, unless it meets needs of management. The fact remains, however, that data collection must be systematic and continuous, if we are to rely upon it for representative and dependable orientation of the measurement problems in management.

5. "VARIANCE" MEASUREMENTS

One of the more recent innovations in the application of accounting measurements to the problems of management is that of measuring deviations from established norms in so-called variance accounts. This has a similarity to budget comparisons, in that the actual data are compared with some preconception of what they should be, and the differences observed are used to make judgments as to performance as well as to decide upon corrective action.[11] It is also closely allied to the idea of "responsibility" accounting suggested earlier; but standards and variances go farther than this. The measurement of variances begins with a refinement of the cost concept (or revenue concept) which attempts to state what the cost or revenue should be under the given conditions; in this conception, certain factors are held constant in the cost or revenue notion so that their fluctuations may be observed. For instance, if the cost is stated in terms of a given price for materials, and the deviations from that price are recorded in a separate account, the net algebraic effects of the purchase transactions

[11] C. W. Bennett, *Standard Costs* (New York: Prentice-Hall, 1957).

at prices varying from the "standard" are shown in the variance account. Similarly, if the quantity of materials required for a given volume of product are known, the additional amount used may be recorded as an excess material usage. Other factors thus isolated by variance accounts are wage rate differentials, labor efficiency, spending, volume, and capacity variances for indirect costs. Similar procedures may be used for the analysis of sales costs, engineering projects, repairs, and maintenance; any operation that can be specified in terms of identifiable factors may be treated in this fashion. The data collected may be analyzed in detail, so that even isolated products and processes may be thus analyzed. These deviations are useful not only as general sources of information, but also to separate known from unidentified factors, or irrelevant from relevant data. For example, one factor in cost data that can be the source of much difficulty in management problems is price-fluctuation. For some purposes, there is a real need to know just what prices have changed and how much; the change in the price of materials may be a good reason to use more labor time in reduction of materials costs. But under other circumstances or for other purposes, price changes may be entirely irrelevant. Unless the production process can be varied to exploit price-shifts, price changes may be merely uncontrollable forces about which the manager can do nothing. Indeed, it is possible for price changes to conceal important data. To blame higher prices for rising costs may be correct, but it may be wrong to measure efficiency by costs, unless the price factor is removed from the comparison. Thus cost intended to measure efficiency in routine operations should be shorn of price-change factors, because they do not relate to the problem. Variance accounting makes it possible to separate diverse influences in the day-to-day record of operations, so as to achieve more useful comparisons and more meaningful reports.

Management literature is full of references to the principle of exceptions; this is, that management must operate by making plans and establishing methods for carrying them out; assuming the plans to be correct, attention is given only to those conditions and results which are different from expectations.[12] To review all the data, observe every event, and deal with each item of data is unnecessary, undesirable, and in some cases impossible. What is needed is a system of reporting and analysis that reports things which require attention as promptly and as clearly as possible. The standard cost approach is a basic contribution

[12] E. Peterson and L. G. Plowman, *Business Organization and Management* (Chicago: Irwin, 1949), pp. 286-7.

to managerial measurements, because it stresses those things which should be stressed under the principle of exceptions. Here accountants may use the other quantitative tools to supplement accounting method. Standards may be established through regression analysis, time and motion study, or mathematical programming. Further use of such techniques may be useful supplements to the accounting measurements of variance. But there is still a real need served by systematic, day-to-day follow up and reporting of those factors to which management should pay attention on the principle of exceptions.

6. THE RAISING OF SIGNIFICANT QUESTIONS

All of the foregoing discussion finds summarization in that function of accounting measurements which really ought to be better understood. That is, that the overall and most challenging task of the accountant is to raise issues, not to settle them. The really useful accounting system is one which serves to prod management by bringing issues to attention which require action. The principal task of a modern controller is to keep management informed as to these issues, and to make sure that their nature and importance are understood.

Management is a complex process; the task of making detailed plans to establish policies, strategic campaigns, and procedural routines throughout the enterprise is one that takes all the talent, acuity, and industry that can be put on it. This task is spread over wide areas of authority, in various patterns of geographical, commodity, and functional organization; it involves many specific decisions on the part of various officers, each of whom is able to visualize his own problem in terms of his own background and experience. This process is intended to be completely integrated and articulated, so that each manager acts for the best interests of the entire organization; whether it really *does* operate that way is but imperfectly known. However, there is reason in all this to regard the managerial process as analogous to scientific experimentation. That is, the only test of validity is prediction. If expected results do not appear, there can be only two reasons: either we do not understand the forces with which we are dealing, or else we have erred in our attempt to apply what we think we know.

The annals of science are full of examples to show that the unsuccessful experiment is often the basis for new knowledge; so it is also with management. We learn not only by setting up hypotheses which work, but also by trying ideas which fail; but neither of these is an absolute. The question of how well a program has succeeded or why another one has failed is never answered completely. The task of accounting in management is not to give the definitive answer, but to raise leading questions: the controller who has learned this has gone a long way towards furthering managerial efficiency. A budget report or a cost comparison is not merely a set of numerical comparisons showing "overs" and "unders," the real problem is to determine what factors lie behind these differences. A budget comparison which agrees precisely with the actual data may really suggest that perhaps the budget needs re-thinking, because the implied standards of performance are too loose. Every collection of data is a springboard for further analysis and constructive improvement, if the right questions are asked and answered. Often, accounting data properly handled can raise those questions which management ought to answer; the accountant's greatest contribution to management is in the preparation of reports which ask, rather than answer questions.

7. CONCLUSION

Too many people (and among them are some accountants) view the accounting process as a routine to collect stereotyped facts about business transactions, to be reported in general-purpose financial statements so that the financial "facts" of business may be portrayed. This is a narrow view, and one which prevents the use of accounting method in its real function, aiding management through measurements and data collection. Accounting contributes to the management process by providing a unified basis of expression and collection of diverse business data, enhancing the objectivity of this process by maintaining independence from other operations, localizing the effects of actions and decisions, yet insuring the completeness of data in its systematic routines. Applying these attributes of accounting method to the special and continuing problems of management, accounting methods analyze costs and revenues to separate the effects of different variables, and to report to management those data which ought to be examined and acted upon according to the principle of exceptions. In all of this the really basic function of accounting is to raise significant questions, rather than to present the answers.

However, the accounting method has no monopoly on data collection and analysis. Despite its long period of service, and its constant change to meet new conditions and problems, accounting is still capable of further development and growth. One direction in which such growth and added effectiveness may be achieved is to recognize that no one method of data collection and processing is a complete answer to the problems of management. Accounting should be combined with other techniques, to build a more efficient and more clearly integrated approach to the collection and processing of quantitative data. To this end, various groups interested in special techniques should combine their efforts to achieve better results. Accountants should use sampling and other statistical techniques more widely; data should be collected by combinations of techniques that will provide optimum service in meeting managerial needs. Those who are interested in data-processing and interpretation should work with accountants to improve the overall impact of quantitative methods in business. The combination of techniques and viewpoints can do much to assist management in meeting the ever-mounting difficulties of the business world.

QUESTIONS

1. What is responsibility accounting and why is it important in measuring management?

2. How is the "standard cost approach" useful in measuring management?

3. Should a budget director be complimented, ignored, or criticized when his company exactly achieves its budget?

4. According to Vatter, "incomplete data may be useful; in some cases, incomplete data are all that should be required." Why? What cases?

5. Why do accounting measurements have value even when nonquantitative judgments are to be made? Illustrate.

6. Is accounting more useful in evaluating the entire enterprise rather than a single department? Why (or why not)?

7. Why does Vatter argue that the separation of accounting from management is necessary for accounting to make one kind of contribution to the measurement of management? Do you agree?

8. Do you find any possible contradiction with (7) and Vatter's concern for "proper communication" between the accountant and management?

9. Is accounting most useful as a deterministic process or as a probabilistic process? Why?

20

Budgeting Business

John A. Prestbo

For EDWARD J. KANE, this is Judgment Day.

Today, his bosses will appraise his 1965 performance as a businessman in a highly competitive field, and question sharply his predictions of how well he will do next year, and why. Ed, 55 and a divisional vice president of Minnesota Mining & Manufacturing Co., has faced their inquisition before each of the past 15 Christmases, but he still can't take it calmly. He feels a butterfly in his stomach, and rubs his hands a little more often as the hour approaches for him to submit the 1966 budget of his printing products division.

Ed's moment of truth is being widely shared this month. At 3M alone, 44 other operating divisions and staff department heads are being called before the 17-man management committee this month to help nail down de-

From *The Wall Street Journal*, vol. CLXVI, no. 120 (December 20, 1965), p. 1. Reprinted by permission of the publisher. Mr. Prestbo is a staff reporter for *The Wall Street Journal*.

cisions on how much money the company can expect to make next year, and how much it ought to spend to reach that target.

A View of 1966

At thousands of other companies, other executives are going through the same procedure. Today, one corporate authority estimates, about 80% of all companies with sales of over $10 million a year, or with more than 500 employees, have some type of formal budget, up from only a handful in 1940. If all their documents could be scanned, a comprehensive view would emerge of how much corporate spending will contribute to the economy in 1966, in outlays for new plants and equipment, purchases of raw materials and hiring of men.

Each company has its own budgeting style, and they vary widely. Du Pont Co., at one extreme, doesn't have a company-wide budget. Each of its 12 industrial departments draws a 12-month budget quarterly, and Du Pont doesn't balance their claims against each other in the interests of an over-all plan.

The process at 3M, which in 1965 expects to sell $1 billion worth of such products as Scotch tape and Thermofax copiers, is more typical. It's winding up in a 14-story glass and steel administration building, flanked by research labs and a shallow pond, just outside St. Paul. But it has been under way since August in offices around the world.

Some 4,000 people, or 8% of 3M's work force, have had a hand in the forecasting, questioning, revising and "go" or "no-go" decisions that make the budget. Though not all figures are final, their labors have yielded a 15-inch stack of paper weighing 30 pounds. This pile of paper reveals that 3M in 1966 will spend about $46 million for research and about $70 million in capital outlays, and will buy, among other things, 60 million pounds of paper and 140,000 light bulbs.

What It Isn't

Still, 3M's budget, or that of any major company, isn't exactly a bigger version of the housewife's list of expenses subtracted from income. Nor does it pose quite the same problems that budget-makers of the Federal Government or a local hospital face in searching for ways to raise cash to meet spending commitments, or for ways to cut spending to bring it closer to anticipated revenue.

"We don't like the word budget," says 3M President Bert S. Cross. "It sounds as if we sit around and give each division so much money and the authority to spend it come hell or high water. Planning next year's operations is really a series of forecasts—what condition the economy will be in, how much our divisions can sell and how much profit we can make on those sales. If any of these conditions change, we have to revise our forecast of everything from sales volume to manufacturing costs."

The system for making these forecasts, which took its present form in the late 1940s, follows the pyramid-shaped 3M organization chart. Plans start at the plant-foreman level and filter up through narrowing layers of supervisors, managers and executives. At each major level—division, group of divisions, and total company—competing claims for each dollar are refereed and balanced.

The process pivots around the general managers, who run 3M divisions almost like independent companies, serving different markets and facing different competition. Minnesota Mining makes 35,000 products, including tape recorders, cameras, film, gift wrap, sandpaper and industrial adhesives, besides Scotch tape. It also operates the Mutual Broadcasting System, a billboard advertising concern, and a company producing TV commercials.

The Profit Yardstick

Despite these diversities, the general managers approach budgeting from a common angle: Profit. Each division is given a profit target—expressed both as a percentage of sales, which are expected to increase each year to maintain 3M's reputation as a growth company, and as a percentage of earnings on the division's invested capital. How to go about hitting these targets is left up to the general managers, provided they can convince management of the short and long range validity of their plans.

Thus, the general manager's chair is a two-way hot seat. He must work with his own management team to formulate a set of working plans that seem realistic to him. Then, he must sell the package to the upper echelon brass.

"Every division wants to at least triple its research and double its sales force," says 3M Controller Donald P. Selleck. "If we let them get away with it, we'd have the damndest profit and loss statements you ever saw." But, he explains, company ground rules head off a battle royal. "Profit is the game we're playing, and the profit target is the par for the course."

If it is to play at par, a division normally can't double its sales force—not even if it could get some other division's sales force cut in half. Thus, 3M says it avoids the back-stabbing and bloodletting that occur in some companies (and in Washington) when the irresistible force of expansion-minded department heads hits the immovable object of a limit on spending.

"Without a profit target, the only way we could settle differences would be by dictating who gets what," says Mr. Selleck. "And we don't like dictators."

A division, however, can balloon spending in one of its departments beyond the normal ratio to sales by short-changing other departments. This is frequently done, particularly to push new products. (3M, whose advertising slogan is "What Won't They Think of Next?" is getting about a fourth of its 1965 sales from products developed in the past five years).

Even then, the division head must show management that long-range opportunities in the department benefited outweigh short-range belt-tightening in the departments held down. If the extra spending will cause division profit to fall even slightly below target, he also must tell management how and when profits will again reach par, and back up his contention. And that's why Ed Kane is nervous today.

Ed, a tall, baldish man with a slow, broad smile, who always keeps his desk neat, joined the then new 3M printing products division as a salesman in 1944. Within a decade he rose to general manager of the rapidly growing division, which now sells over 30 products.

A Triple Budget

He draws three budgets. The biggest is an "operations budget," composed of a sales forecast, the basic strategy for achieving it, and the cost of carrying out that strategy. This budget covers both 1966 operations and those of the next five years.

Ed also must budget "cash flow," meaning he must correlate monthly expenses with income brought in by sales so that he isn't "overdrawn" at the 3M treasury. Finally, he must plan capital spending three years ahead, quarter by quarter.

Ed went over his plans with top aides for four hours Sept. 20. Believing that zooming sales will push output at one plant to capacity sooner than expected, the group moved construction of a new plant up one year in the capital budget. That finished the plans—but left a problem. For 1966, Ed is forecasting profit lower than in 1965.

The reason: Next fall, Ed plans to introduce a new product

aimed at a market almost wholly new to the division. Before then, he plans to spend $2 million for machinery, raw materials, advertising and other introductory expenses. The resulting drop in profit is expected to be small. But Ed knows it will raise management eyebrows today, because it will interrupt a steady profit growth in his division. So he has to justify it.

First Round Won

It took him only a half hour to win over his group vice president, Raymond H. Herzog of the graphic systems group (this comprises five divisions bringing in 13% of 3M's sales and profit). Mr. Herzog sliced some dollars off Ed's figure for product introduction costs, in part by reducing the number of hand-made prototypes for a test marketing program. But he believed Ed's estimate that the new product will be a solid money-maker in two or three years. Mr. Herzog vetoed a plan by another division to introduce a new product next year "because I'd grow old before I knew if it ever made a profit."

After Mr. Herzog and other group heads okayed division budgets, Controller Selleck consolidated them into a company-wide budget for the management committee. At 3M this is the court of last budgetary appeal; 9 of its members sit on the 15-man board of directors, making budget approval there a formality. (At some other companies it isn't. At Halliburton Co., corporate officers fill only 6 of the 16 board seats, and executives who had already approved a budget spent two hours last month justifying it before getting board approval.)

Until two years ago, each 3M division pleaded its case to the management committee before a company-wide budget took shape. So, says one officer, sessions dragged into January as the divisions "used every trick in the book to snow the brass into approving their requests." And the divisional trees blocked management's view of the budgetary forest. "How come I like each division but I don't like the total?" a vice president asked one year.

OK in General—Next . . .

Now the committee—President Cross, seven group vice presidents and nine vice presidents of staff departments such as finance—approves a 3M-wide budget before starting sessions with the division heads. On Dec. 8 it approved the 1966 budget as one that would meet the goals of keeping 3M sales rising about 10% a year, and of netting pre-tax profit of 20% to 25% on both sales and net worth. So division heads have had relatively easy sledding in their appearances before the committee.

Still, says Ed Kane, "it's like getting a physical checkup. You know you're healthy, but you imagine all sorts of ills you could have and don't know about."

The committee meets in a windowless, 40-by-70 foot room on the administration building's 14th floor. Members sit in soft, reddish-brown armchairs around a U-shaped arrangement of desks facing a podium and movie screen. Along the gray, cloth-paneled walls, in less comfortable chairs, sit division heads of the group being reviewed, and their aides.

The executives are convivial as they select chairs (cigar smokers clustering along one arm of the U). But when the heavy doors close precisely at 9 a.m., "Hiya, Bert," yields to "Yes, Mr. Cross."

Probing for "Weaknesses"

Division heads don't present their own budgets. Controller Selleck does, pointing out "weaknesses"—such as Ed Kane's forecast of a profit decline, perhaps—and he doesn't tell the divisions what he will say. The committee seeks not to review details but to ferret out problems from the rows of antiseptic figures.

"It's like trying to spot a swindle in an expense account," says Mr. Herzog, a committee member. "If you've done it yourself, you know where to look."

When Mr. Selleck's Midwestern twang stops, a division manager takes the podium and committee questions fly. At a session last week, members noted one division was forecasting a sales gain below the 10%-a-year target. Why?

Well, the division head replied, his already oversized research budget was being used up to improve existing products, just to stay ahead of competition. He didn't think he could ask for more to bring two promising new products out of laboratory. After all, he had his profit target to meet.

That's no excuse, committee members replied in effect. "We'll go along with a reduced profit margin for a couple of years if you can get out some new products that will bring your growth rate back in line," one summarized. "Come back with your product ideas. If they're as good as you say, we'll take your budget apart in the middle of the year and put it back together again if necessary."

Ed Kane to the Podium

Today, Ed Kane expects to be asked: Does the expected profit drop indicate your division's growth rate has peaked out? How fast do you expect to pick up sales on this new product? When do you expect profit to equal or better the 1965 level?

Ed has answers, illustrated by a bundle of transparencies of tables and charts to be flashed on the screen (with a 3M overhead projector, naturally) as he talks. "A little chuckle goes up from the committee when an old pro like Ed reaches for his transparencies," says one member. "It's as if he's saying: 'I'm glad you asked.'"

This readiness comes from three rehearsals by Ed and his aides. At these, Ed runs through his presentation and his aides, playing committee members, fire questions. If one stumps him, all search for an answer, which Ed notes in his "script." But for the toughest question—will this product sell?—he admits there is no answer. He thinks it will, and has a transparency showing his reasons. But he adds: "We really won't know until somebody pays hard cash for one of these things."

Ed won't be long in doubt about what impression he makes. Committee members shoot questions fairly rapidly, and since Ed is ready for them, he probably will be on the podium only 10 to 15 minutes.

Tension can build in these quick exchanges, but there are lighter moments, too. One year a division head brought in a sample of a product containing radioactive material. He insisted it wasn't radioactive, but President Cross still wouldn't let anybody touch it. "What a way to wipe us out at the top," he shuddered, as laughter exploded.

Round-the-World Budgeting

Other sessions end less happily for the men quizzed. In the last half of November eight committee members and international department executives set out to review the budgets of 3M's foreign units, which contribute 22% of 3M sales. Splitting into teams they traveled 88,000 miles, visiting factories in 16 countries and sales subsidiaries in 13, spread through Europe, the Far East, Latin America and Africa. At each stop they went through a budget review much like those in St. Paul, but with plant tours and product displays added.

This year the teams rejected four of the 29 foreign budgets. It one country a team member took a subsidiary's sales forecast, divided it by the number of salesmen, and came up with a volume-per-salesman figure far above anything the subsidiary had ever achieved. The team asked for a revised forecast.

Ed Kane's chances today? When considering a new product, says President Cross, "we frequently gamble on the man who's going to do the job. We take his word rather than rely entirely on statistics which might indicate the odds are against his selling as much of a new product as he forecasts. After all, he's putting his reputation as a businessman on the block when he commits himself to a forecast. And he knows we have good memories.

QUESTIONS

1. What is a "profit target" for a 3M division?

2. What are the three budgets prepared by a 3M division? Explain. What are the time dimensions of each budget?

3. How are the usual financial statements different from budgeted statements?

4. On the basis of the information presented in the article, prepare a summarized budget statement for Mr. Kane's use in appearing before the 3M management committee.

5

Financial Statement Analysis

21

18,000,000 Books Nobody Reads

Reynolds Girdler

ALONG WITH the singing of birds and the voice of the turtle
another vernal sound is being heard in the land this week.
It is the scrape, crunch, plod, and plop of the nation's
weary postmen, patiently delivering 18,000,000 copies of
corporate annual reports to the stockholders of 6,000 pub-
licly owned companies.

Some $9,000,000, countless hours of grueling and ex-
asperating work, and miles and miles of good intentions
have gone into the making of these many books. But for all
the cost, and for all the earnest endeavors of those who
wrote, edited and approved these publications, and for all
the importance of the subject matter, nobody—or almost
nobody—will read them.

Time was when the annual report of the average
American corporation was a brief and blunt affair indeed.

From *Saturday Review,* vol. 46, no. 15 (April 13, 1963), pp. 71, 78.
Reprinted by permission of publisher. Mr. Girdler is Vice President for
Public Relations and Advertising at the Sinclair Oil Company.

It was often four pages at best, and disclosed little more than the earnings for the year along with a congealed and restricted balance sheet.

But after the 1929–32 crash, there arose an outcry for full disclosure in all matters corporate and financial. The Securities and Exchange Act of 1934, as amended (the present law), commands every company with shares listed on a public stock exchange to make public a yearly accounting of its business and finances. The law even specifies the topics to be included in the report. The New York Stock Exchange also requires the companies whose shares it admits to trading to report regularly and in some detail to their shareholders. Few corporate executives of today find these requirements onerous. Indeed, the overwhelming majority of companies go far beyond the letter of the law. They genuinely want their stockholders to be well informed, and to have an intelligent grasp of the company's position and finances. They rightly consider their annual report to be the principal communication with their stockholders, and they hope mightily that all stockholders will read every word and study every figure.

But all the evidence clearly proves they are failing. Citing a study of stockholder readership of annual reports by Opinion Research Corporation, *The Wall Street Journal* says that stockholders find the reports a "confusing jumble." Some 37 of every 100 stockholders don't even try to read them.

A massive and detailed study made some years ago by the then Controllers Institute is even more dismaying. Commenting on its own dismal discoveries, the Institute said, "But when it comes to reading financial tables and forming his own conclusions about the soundness and prosperity of the company in which he owns stock, the typical stockholder loses interest—and his bearings!"

And then the Institute, elaborating on this point, chooses a curious word. "He [the stockholder] is *oppressed* by the complexity of financial data and frightened by what seems to him the incomprehensibility of accounting language. So, while he feels somewhat guilty about his lack of enterprise and in some instances tends to magnify the amount of attention he does devote to the subject, the typical reaction of the average stockholder to the fancy brochures he receives annually from companies, ranges from boredom to cursory interest."

So, say the controllers (who themselves have much to do with the contents of every report), the poor stockholder is not just baffled or puzzled or bewildered by the communication devices—he is "oppressed." He feels crushed, trampled down, and even burdened as by an abuse of power or authority. This is a sad plight indeed for the fellow who each year is asked to sign a proxy favorable to management.

What are the barriers that today separate management from a clear and complete understanding with the stockholder?

There are many. In the first place, few investors have ever learned even the ordinary words of the corporate world. Few, according to Opinion Research Corporation, can define the term "subsidiary." (Some even confuse it with that evil governmental practice, the subsidy.) Such terms as "deferred charges," "debentures," and "paid-in surplus" are, quite understandably, just pure Greek to the average investor, man or woman. So the corporate executive who wants to write intelligibly to his shareholders finds that he must use what seems to him a kind of babytalk, or include a glossary on every page.

Then too, there is the problem of the language described by Rudolph Flesch as the "special interest." By this term, Flesch means the language that builds up into a kind of shorthand in every trade. Thus, show people can read *Variety* with pleasure, though to others it is a flip kind of jabberwocky. It is natural for, say, a man in the steel business to think in terms created by the steel industry, and thus to express himself. If his writers try to describe a given situation in non-trade terms, the executive feels uncomfortable. Unconsciously, he wonders what his peers will think of him when they study his report and encounter this unsophisticated language. So he reverts to his shorthand and his women stockholders draw a blank.

But the most grievous wound inflicted on the annual report as a communications device between corporate management and corporate ownership was an "awards" promotion established some years ago by a financial magazine. * The motive in sponsoring judgments on the nation's annual reports was pure. An effort which would encourage companies to issue reports worthy of being judged "Best of Industry," and to receive in all humility an Oscar made of bronze and wood still appears entirely consonant with the trend toward full disclosure.

But the authors of the promotion made one serious mistake. In an understandable effort to avoid the complications that might ensue if the magazine personnel sat in judgment on General Motors or Ford, they went to the outside for their judges. And they selected, of all people, the security analysts of Wall Street. This was akin to asking Picasso to select the covers for the *Saturday Evening Post*.

Security analysts are a highly sophisticated and highly specialized

* EDITORS' NOTE: The reference is to the publication *Financial World*.

group of men. They want acres and acres of figures. And, once seated on the judge's benches, they set about getting them. It soon became known to company executives that they couldn't hope for Oscars unless they loaded their reports with figures in the most minute detail and related the activities of their various departments at greater and greater length. The ultimate reward for that company successful in accounting for the last paper clip of the fiscal year was the gold Oscar.

So the reports now seeping through the mails to 18,000,000 stockholders have, for the most part, been written not to the specifications of the stockholders, but to the specifications of a precious and unrepresentative group of men. The modern annual report, so hopefully launched as the bearer of vital and comprehensive information to Main Street, has been swerved from its course.

How can it regain its original true direction and serve its avowed purpose? It will take some doing. First, management must look with unblinking eyes on the facts established by competent readership studies. Second, it must break almost completely with the traditional form, and language of today's report, at the same time obeying the law. Third, it must give greater leeway to writers trained, preferably, in successful magazine writing and editing. And finally, it would help if writers, journalists, and communications experts, rather than security analysts, became the judges of what is to be said to the oppressed stockholder.

QUESTIONS

1. What are the characteristics of the "typical stockholder" whose case Mr. Girdler argues? If all the holdings of Mr. Girdler's typical stockholders were added together, how would the sum compare with the total value of stock held by all stockholders?

2. If, as has been asserted elsewhere, large institutional investors (insurance companies, pension funds, investment companies, foundation and endowment funds, mutual savings funds, and personal trust funds administered by banks), which employ professional financial analysts, hold an ever increasing proportion of stocks held, then how appropriate is Mr. Girdler's conception of the typical investor?

3. Suppose that a large portion of stock held (say nearly one-half) is held by a small number of institutional investors and that the remainder is held by a large number of small individual investors. Should the same annual report be sent to both groups? Discuss.

4. Mr. Girdler asserts that the complexities of business transactions can be stated in language that anyone can understand. He also asserts that reports can be shortened. Are the two assertions consistent? Explain.

5. Are the reporting objectives of public relations officials and certified public accountants compatible?

22

Forces Influencing Accounting: Employees

Nat Weinberg

MY ASSIGNMENT basically is to answer two questions. The first is: How has accounting been affected by the workers' needs for financial information? The second is: What should accountants do to meet those needs?

My answer to the first question is short and, unfortunately, largely negative. We have provided considerable additional work for accountants, but we have had only a negligible effect on accounting practice and, though not through any fault of our own, most of that effect, I am sorry to say, has been bad.

From the *Accounting Papers of The Seventeenth Annual Conference of Accountants,* The University of Tulsa, 1963. Reprinted by permission of the publisher. Mr. Weinberg is Director, Special Projects and Economic Analysis, United Auto Workers, and was a Visiting Professor at the University of California (Berkeley) during the spring of 1966.

The additional work and some new problems that have been created for accountants have risen in large part out of the necessity to keep account of the financial obligations arising out of union contracts, particularly in the fringe benefit area. An example is the problem of how to keep account of the liabilities and costs created by pension plans. The problem has grown enormously since we in the UAW pioneered the first collectively bargained pension plan in a major mass production industry back in September, 1949, when we negotiated an agreement with the Ford Motor Company. Now I know that pension plans and the accounting problems connected with them have created a very serious jurisdictional dispute between the accountants' union and the actuaries' union as to who should do what in relation to pension programs. (We are familiar, unfortunately, with jurisdictional disputes, although our union—the UAW—had done its best to avoid them and to develop mechanisms to settle them without strikes.)

The labor movement has also created a great deal of work for accountants through other fringe benefit plans: the necessity for keeping track of information on supplemental unemployment benefit plans; the various kinds of health and welfare plans; etc. With the negotiation of the American Motors profit sharing plan in 1961, and with the likelihood that that type of plan is going to spread, there is going to be considerable additional work for accountants which will be very, very important in the future.

Although we have provided you with additional work, our effect on your accounting practices, unfortunately, has been largely negative. We haven't been properly rewarded for the additional work we have made available for you. For example, the interest of unions in financial data for bargaining purposes has often put accountants under management pressure to approve practices designed to minimize or conceal profits. Some accountants—not all, I'm glad to say—but some accountants, regrettably have succumbed to that kind of pressure.

In other cases, corporations, with or without the collaboration of accountants, have used accounting data to prepare special financial reports for employees which were deliberately designed not to enlighten them but to mislead them. I have one in my briefcase which portrays the corporation in question as Old Mother Hubbard. She has an income from sales and she distributes this income—all of it. She distributes a good big chunk of it in the form of dividends, another big chunk of it in the form of retained profits. But when she is through distributing all of this, Old Mother Hubbard's cupboard is bare and so, the worker obviously is supposed to conclude, there is no room for a wage increase. On this basis, of course, there would never be any room for a wage increase in any corporation.

I might note in passing, because some of you may be interested, that I think it is fair to say that most financial reports prepared especially for employees tend to defeat the propaganda purposes for which they are intended. They are generally condescending and patronizing in their tone. The comic book versions, for example, are downright insulting to a worker's intelligence. They often arouse suspicion where none existed before. I do not hesitate to tell you that, if the workers themselves don't see through the propaganda, we in the labor movement are very happy to help them see through it.

Because my list of what accountants have done to meet workers' needs is short, the list of what they should do—of what remains for them to do—is quite long. I feel that we have a right to expect a great deal from the accounting profession. It seems to me that you cannot fulfill your professional responsibilities if you look upon yourselves as the servants of corporate managers and stockholders. Your proper role, as I see it, is to function as the eyes and ears of the entire public, including workers, in relation to corporate behavior. Corporations, as you know, are chartered by the state, created by the public, to serve a social purpose. The public must rely very heavily on accountants to provide the factual basis for evaluating the performance of corporations in relation to the social purposes for which they are created. We of the public, whether in labor or other segments of the public, depend upon accountants to give us the information that will enable us to answer such questions about corporate behavior as these: To what extent is the corporation making use of its capacity? How are the fruits of advancing technology shared by the corporation among management, stockholders, workers, and consumers? Is the corporation providing steady income for its workers? Is it wasting labor resources and causing human hardship by irresponsible pricing or production scheduling?

If accountants are to provide the kind of data needed for intelligent answers to these and many similar questions, accountants must see themselves as responsible primarily to society and only secondarily to their clients. They have to have a truly professional attitude and to adhere strictly to rigid professional standards. Among other things, I think accountants should act as the conscience of corporate management, requiring management to give the public the truth, the whole truth, and nothing but the truth with respect to every aspect of corporate behavior that impinges upon the public welfare.

Now truth, of course, is very often elusive and, in the field of accounting, a lot will depend upon the accounting conventions used. As accounting will probably always be to some degree an art rather than a science, we cannot ask for perfection. But we are troubled, as many accountants are troubled, by what Mr. Spacek of Arthur Andersen and Co. called the "wide range of alternatives now available" to accountants. This wide range of alternatives makes truth in any given case depend upon an accommodation between the wishes of management and the tolerance of the accounting firm involved. According to *Business Week* of January 26, 1963, Mr. Spacek said that it is absurd, for example, that his firm should certify the statements of three major oil companies as being in accord with generally accepted accounting practices when each accounts for drilling costs in a different manner, and each method can make millions of dollars of difference in the net income reported.*

This is a particularly serious problem for us in the labor movement because comparisons within an industry are very important to us. We are not concerned only with the single firm; we are concerned with a whole range of firms in any given industry. We would like to be able to see how the performance of one company stacks up against that of another. But if in the same industry the treatment of the same phenomenon varies from company to company, what do the comparisons mean? How can you make sense out of them? It is good, therefore, as far as we are concerned, to see the demand for the development of better accounting standards from within the profession. However, it is also deeply disturbing to see the resistance that must be overcome, even within the profession, if meaningful standards are to be developed and enforced.

It should be fairly evident that, in the absence of rigorous and enforced standards in the accounting profession, a kind of Gresham's law comes into operation. Gresham's law, as you may remember from economics, is the principle that bad money tends to drive out good money. In the absence of rigorous and enforced standards and as a result of competition among accounting firms for corporate clients and the pressures of corporate managements, there will be a tendency for bad accounting practice to drive out good accounting practice. I think

* EDITORS' NOTE: For further details, see pages 29–30 of "The Auditors Have Arrived" by T. A. Wise in this volume.

this is something with which all of us should be concerned. Accountants are human beings like all the rest of us. Not all human beings are equally capable of resisting pressures, but the temptation to succumb to pressure can be largely overcome by adoption of standards and vigorous policing to ensure the application of those standards. Experience in other fields should make it pretty clear that the alternative to the development and the policing of standards by the profession—the alternative to voluntary action and self-policing—is outside compulsion. Accounting may seem remote from the concerns of the average citizen, but so, under normal circumstances, is the testing of new drugs. Yet when the thalidomide scandal broke, Congress was galvanized into action and some new compulsions were applied to the drug industry. If standards and self-policing mechanisms are not established, it is not at all impossible that there could be an accounting scandal some day that would lead to similar action to impose rigid restrictions and severe penalties on accountants from outside.

And I might say that it does not seem to me sufficient to have standards that can be satisfied by fine-print footnotes relegated to the back of the book and often written in gobbledygook. It seems to me that the obligation of the accounting profession is to the layman who doesn't have his own batteries of clerks and computers to recompute the published financial statement on the basis of the footnotes.

I indicated before that accounting standards will become of particular importance to labor as profit-sharing plans of the American Motors type become more widespread. The success of the plans will depend in large part on the confidence of the workers in the accountants who audit the companies' books. Profit-sharing plans will break down and will create bitterness and hostility between workers and management if suspicions develop about the accounting methods used in implementing them. It would be an intolerable situation, as far as we are concerned, if the shares of workers in profits were allowed to vary from one company to another, or from time to time within the same company, depending upon the whims of management and what the accountants will tolerate in one situation compared to what they will tolerate in another.

As a general principle, I would consider it both necessary and proper that the accountants rather than management determine how financial data ought to be presented. Further, I believe that the accountants ought to determine this in accordance with standards developed by the profession and let management, if it so desires, insert the footnotes and take exception to the statements as prepared by the accountants in accordance with their own professional standards. Management, if it wants to make an additional presentation, can even recast the data in an entirely different form and give its reasons for doing so and why it disagrees with the way the accountants have chosen to present them.

The important thing, it seems to me, is to separate accounting facts, insofar as they can be determined, from management's self-serving arguments. If management, for example, would like to take extra depreciation based on replacement cost instead of actual cost in order to hide profits from the union or the public, management should do that on its own responsibility. The auditors should not sanction it even if it is consistent with the past practices of that management. If management wants to inflate profits in the stockholders' eyes by arbitrarily reducing its pension contributions in a given year, that should be presented clearly as a managerial action, not sanctioned by an accountant's certification. If management wants to show smaller profits by setting up needless reserves which are later quietly slipped into surplus without ever showing up on the books as profits, let management do that on its own responsibility, while the accountants blow the whistle to warn the public what is going on.

The accounting profession should be prepared to discipline any of its members who depart from its professional standards. As you know, other professions do this to some degree. It is done by lawyers, and it is done in other fields. It is not enough to establish advisory standards, because that does not provide the protection an accountant needs against improper pressure from a client.

As you know better than I, all kinds of inexcusable practices have appeared all too frequently in corporate reports without any notice in the auditor's certification. LIFO has been introduced in periods of inflation to conceal inventory profits. In some situations, corporations have simultaneously set up inventory reserves, which contemplate deflation, at the same time that they set up special reserves for depreciation, which anticipate inflation. I suppose this can be justified on the theory that consistency is the hobgoblin of small minds. Or, perhaps, it is consistent in the sense that both reserves have the effect of reducing reported profits.

In other instances, as you know, distinctions between capital expenditures and current expenses vary widely from company to company within the same industry, and from time to time within the same company. There has been some discussion recently of the treatment of research and development costs in that connection. We have found cases where companies found it convenient to charge off certain nonrecurring costs against profits in the last financial statements published before negotiation with the union, in order to support a plea of inability to pay higher wages.

I could go on indefinitely giving you examples of questionable accounting practices of this kind. As you know, I could document a great many of them from the official publications of the accounting profession.

I think that is why there is so much healthy soul-searching within your profession. But soul-searching is not enough. It has been going on for many years. It seems to me that the time is long past due for effective action.

Having indicated what bothers us about financial information as presently published, I now turn to what we need that is generally not published. Some of what we need arises out of the concern of workers as citizens—as part of the general public—and some of what we need arises out of the concern of workers in their role as workers and union members. Among the items that are most important from both standpoints is information on the break-even points and price policies of those corporations which are not subject to the forces of the competitive market place. I know that there are varying degrees of freedom in the market place. But in many industries, price decisions and break-even point decisions (which are related, of course, to price decisions) are made by a handful of executives and the competitive market has a very, very remote relationship to these decisions. In a very real sense the level of the break-even point is an index of the corporation's confidence in the economic system. In practical terms the break-even point can be a major influence in determining the level of sales, of production and of employment, and can even have an effect through the price route on the U.S. balance of payments. The break-even point has important bearing on the truth or falsity of widespread corporate allegations that union-won wage increases are a cause of inflation.

In part because of the failure of the accounting profession to insist upon disclosure of meaningful data on break-even points and price policies and costs, unions have been the victims of hit-and-run propaganda tactics.

Corporations repeatedly charge us with causing inflation and then refuse to make available the data necessary for an objective evaluation of their charges. Let me give you just one example. In our 1961 negotiations in the automobile industry, the corporations opened the negotiations with allegations that our demands would lead to inflation. Well, we called them on it. We said: We have a right under the Labor-Management Relations Act to information needed for intelligent bargaining. It is our policy not to insist upon demands that will lead to inflation, but, in order to know whether our demands are inflationary or not, we need certain facts. We addressed a number of questions to the General Motors Corporation about its price-profit formula. After some correspondence on the matter, General Motors refused to give us the data and we filed charges with the National Labor Relations Board. The General Counsel of the National Labor Relations Board issued a complaint and a statement saying that our charges raised an issue of major substance and importance. After we had filed our request for the pertinent data, we heard nothing further about the inflationary nature of our demands. Either they were inflationary, in which case the Corporation could have demonstrated it factually, or they were not inflationary. I think you can draw your own conclusions on the basis of what happened when we asked it to put up or shut up. It seems to me, although the case was never finally adjudicated and we withdrew the charge when we settled the contract, that we have a right to this kind of information. As the New York Labor Board noted on a similar point in a case on a somewhat different issue a long time ago, "Collective bargaining cannot exist if assertion is resorted to when documentation is readily available."

The old inability-to-pay argument of management now has a new facet—inflation—which really is a plea of inability to pay without raising prices. The NLRB has held in the past that workers are entitled to financial data when corporations plead inability to pay. I believe corporations are pleading a form of inability to pay when they say that union demands are inflationary.

In addition to material on break-even points and price policies, we very badly need, both as workers and as citizens, published data on changes in worker productivity. You know that the rate of productivity advance is urged upon us as one of the bases for determining whether or not our demands are inflationary. A favorite practice of corporations, you may have noticed, is to compare changes in the hourly wage rates of their workers with changes in the prices charged for their products, without reference to productivity. This, I am sure you will agree, is a half truth that creates a completely distorted impression because the relevant information in relation to prices and labor costs is not hourly labor costs but unit labor costs which, of course, are affected by productivity. Accountants, it seems to me, can make a very great contribution to the development of corporate productivity data which are badly needed both for public purposes and for collective bargaining purposes. The basic information that is needed for the computation of productivity is available in the books that accountants keep and examine. The data simply need reorganization to yield information on changes in productivity. In fact, the information is probably already computed in many cases. Corporations universally, in my experience, deny that they have productivity information when we ask them to give it to us. In spite of that, it is inconceivable to me that America's giant corporations are ignorant regarding the trend of their unit labor costs. And if they know the trends of their unit labor costs, they know the trends of productivity. If we are to bargain on the basis of economic facts as we are urged to do and as we would prefer to do, we have to have this information.

Historically, we in the UAW have taken the position that we want to make progress with the consumer, with the general public— with the community and not at the expense of the community. We have said that we want our gains in wages and fringe benefits to come out of profits and productivity, and not out of the pockets of consumers. In 1945–46, as some of you may remember, 200,000 General Motors workers struck for 113 days for wage increases without price increases. Repeatedly during the course of that strike they offered to reduce their demands to any extent necessary, even to zero, to avoid imposing on General Motors a need for a price increase. A presidential fact-finding board was appointed to hear the issues in that dispute. General Motors, which had claimed that it could not grant the workers' demands without raising its prices, when called upon to produce the evidence, simply walked out on the fact-finding board appointed by the President of the United States. How can we bargain on the basis of the facts if the facts are not available? How do we know whether our demands are actually inflationary and whether and to what extent they should be reduced to avoid inflationary consequences if the facts are not made available to us?

In addition to the kinds of things I have mentioned, bargaining on the basis of the facts means that we must have many other types of facts not presently available. We need better breakdowns, much more comprehensive breakdowns, of costs. We need data for wage and salary payments separately. We need data on hours worked by hourly workers and salary workers, respectively. We need breakdowns of hours worked and wages paid to direct and indirect production workers. We need data on average hourly, weekly, and annual wages of workers. We need data on fringe benefit costs—not propagandistic data, but hard, factual data. We need data on managerial salaries, bonuses, stock options, and other executive fringe benefits. The question of managerial salaries, for example, becomes extremely important in small firms where the profits, as you know, are frequently taken largely in the form of salaries. We need data on sales, distribution, and advertising costs, on research and development costs. We need clear separations of operating income or losses and other sources of income or loss.

We have reason to be highly dissatisfied with the way payroll and labor information is published today in those relatively rare cases where it is reported at all. Let me give you one example involving a major corporation, the Chrysler Corporation. In 1959, the Chrysler Corporation reported the cost of payrolls and employee benefits at $991,000,000. In 1960, when a comparison was made with 1959, payrolls and employee benefits were reported as $809,000,000 for 1959 —a difference of almost $200,000,000. What had happened? (Mind you, there was no indication of why the figure was changed. The 1960 report did not say a word about why the figure differed from that given in the 1959 report.) What had happened? Well, a simple error in transposition of figures had been made in computing the 1959 costs of materials, supplies, and services. In 1959 that figure was reported as $1,464,000,000. It turned out in the 1960 report that two of the digits had been reversed and instead of $1,464,000,000, it should have been $1,646,000,000. Thus, if you took the 1959 figure and the labor costs were calculated as a residual from total costs, then, as a result of the mistake in the materials, supplies, and service costs, payrolls and employee benefits amounted to 37.4% of total costs. However, according to the correct figures reported in 1960, they were only 30.5% of total costs. To treat a matter as important as payrolls and employee benefits as a residual to be obtained by subtraction of other figures, one of which was in error, seems to me hardly the way to provide the kind of information that is needed in the area of labor costs and payroll information. Needless to say, this was not in that part of the report certified by the auditors.

If any of you are familiar with General Motors annual reports, you will recognize what I have to say about the way that corporation reports employment and payrolls. They report hourly employment and payrolls for the United States only. They report their total employment—not broken down between hourly and salaries—for their world-wide operation. They report their profits on a world-wide basis with a percentage given for the proportion of the total profits made outside of the United States plus Canada. Now you try to find a basis on which to compare U.S. hourly workers' wages with U.S. profits. You have to resort to estimates to get meaningful comparisons for the U.S. General Motors sometimes complains about our estimates or the way we use the figures they publish, but they won't give us the figures that would make for a meaningful comparison.

Insofar as cost data are concerned, I do not think that too much stock can be placed in the plea that such data are competitive secrets. First, I think it must be recognized that cost information is important to the public which has chartered the corporations. The public interest is paramount. In order to evaluate the performance of a corporation in terms of the purposes for which it was created by society, you need to know something about its costs. Second, cost information cannot conceivably be a competitive secret in those industries where there is not price competition—where the price leader sets a price and all of the other corporations follow like sheep. The competitive secret argument often strikes us as the corporate equivalent of abuse of the fifth amendment privilege.

We need breakdowns of the financial picture for the separate operations of corporations engaged in various fields. Sometimes we need it on a plant basis where there is more than one union, each representing the workers at different plants of the corporation. We often run into the situation where Union A comes to the bargaining table and points to the corporation's profits and is told that those profits all originated in the plants represented by Union B. Union A is told that the plants that it represents suffered losses. And then Union B comes in and is told exactly the opposite. For this reason, a breakdown by plants is sometimes needed. For purposes of overall industry statistics on profits, there certainly needs to be a breakdown of the profits of the so-called conglomerate corporations that operate in a broad range of industries. The distortions of industry statistics on profits resulting from inclusion of operations outside the industry aggravate the distortions caused by the great variety of accounting practices.

Third, we need genuine consistency in financial reporting over extended periods of years so that we can evaluate, and the public can evaluate, the progress and prospects of corporations. In this connection, as you all know, there are special problems created by changes in the tax laws. For example, take changes in methods of charging depreciation. These changes emphasize the importance for workers, as well as stockholders, of cash flow data carried back on a consistent basis over a period of years. Cash flow data in these circumstances are much more meaningful than profit data.

In conclusion, I want to emphasize again that we think accountants have a major role to play in relation to the public in general and in relation to labor in particular—that accountants carry very heavy responsibilities in fulfilling that role. As big corporations increase their power, these responsibilities grow even heavier. The public must be informed in order to protect itself—it must know how that power is being used or being abused. We become increasingly dependent on the competence and integrity of the accounting profession and upon the development by the profession of sound and enforced professional standards. We therefore welcome the efforts being made by some members of the profession to develop such standards.

I do not think it is unreasonable to hope that, as progress is made in the development of standards, labor will be consulted in connection with the formulation of the standards. I have stressed the public obligation of accountants because I think that is their most important obligation. Wage and salary workers and their families, as you know, are the largest single group that makes up the total public. The interest of wage and salary workers, therefore, and their needs for information, have to be given great weight as the profession moves to meet its responsibility to the public through the development of standards—I hope enforceable standards.

QUESTIONS

1. List the information needs detailed by Mr. Weinberg. Which of these requests should be fulfilled by accountants? Why and how?

2. Identify the possible areas of agreement, if any, as to the possible nature and content of public financial reports as viewed by Mr. Girdler (see previous article) and Mr. Weinberg?

3. What difference should it make to the Certified Public Accountant as to how the user views his certified accounting reports? Do you consider that a trade union leader looks upon a firm's accounting reports for use in collective bargaining in the same way as an investor does who is considering purchasing stock of the company? As a creditor does who is thinking about making a loan to the firm? As the government or the general public? As the management of the firm does generally or in collective bargaining?

4. What kinds of costs and expenses are involved in divisional profit measurement?

5. Can the expenses of operating a plant or division be determined? Why?

6. How can the earnings for a single plant or division in a multi-plant firm or multi-division firm be computed? How, if the plant disposes of its entire product to another plant in the company?

7. What sort of measure of a firm's performance and activity might best fill the needs of a labor union? Can Net Income be the sole adequate measure of this? What other measures might be appropriate?

23

Cash Flow Is the New Fad

In wall street—where styles in investing change as often as they do for women's clothes on the Rue de la Paix—a new fad is appearing: "cash flow analysis." Increasingly, the market letters that pour from the major brokerages are talking about cash flow—defined by most analysts as a company's reported earnings plus such "non-cash" charges as depreciation and depletion—as the key to hidden value in stocks.

To take just one example, Schweickart & Co. recently published an analysis on Decca Records, Inc., which because it controls Universal Pictures is generally considered a motion picture company. Stanley A. Nabi, who heads Schweickart's research, recommended Decca because "reported earnings in the motion picture producing business are of secondary importance. Cash flow and depreciated films, are more important yardsticks since they actually represent hidden wealth with delayed income."

Some Wall Street firms—and corporate public relations men, who are beginning to highlight cash flow figures in company annual reports—are playing fast and loose with the cash flow concept. More and more market pundits are talking as though cash flow were synonymous with earnings, when of course, it is not. As one market man comments, "It's not the amount of cash flow that counts, it's the quality."

AVAILABLE MONEY. Actually, cash flow is a measure of the money available to corporate management—after out-of-pocket expenses—to keep a business running and pay a return to its owners. Whether the depreciation that a company is charging off against its income is excessive—which would give it a flavor of "hidden earnings" —or fails to cover capital exhaustion, will depend entirely on the company and industry in which it operates.

It's possible to trace the surge of interest in cash flow. The demand for growth stocks has declined rapidly as many companies that had been recommended because of their rapid rate of growth in earnings fell far short of projections. This has forced analysts to cast around for new concepts to use in selling stocks, and cash flow is providing a convenient and effective device.

Among other things, . . . stock prices look a lot more reasonable these days in relation to cash flow than in relation to earnings, though in both cases the market is historically high.

DEPRECIATION. Then, too, there's the fact that corporations are reporting a rapid increase in depreciation charges—from about $25-billion in 1954 to almost $40-billion in 1960. Some analysts say that this rapid growth of depreciation—largely resulting from the switch to the accelerated depreciation methods that were first recognized in the 1954 Tax Code—results in a progressive understating of corporate income.

There's not much argument about the growing role that depreciation is playing in corporate financing. But in view of Wall Street's attempt to popularize the cash flow concept, many market professionals are warning against indiscriminate use of cash flow in analyzing security values. For example, Moody's Investors Service points out that mounting depreciation charges today may simply be making up for inadequate depreciation in past years.

ANALYST'S GOAL. It's important for the investor to understand cash flow in making up his mind on which stocks to buy. A good starting point is to take a look at what the security analyst tries to do when he analyzes a common stock. In simplest terms, his aim is to decide whether the stock is selling too high or too low in relation to the securities of comparable companies.

Obviously, the outlook both for the general economy and the specific industry has a role to play. But from the analyst's point of view it's equally important to get at the company's basic earning power—to eliminate distortions in reported earnings caused by nonrecurring items, changes in accounting methods, and so forth. Similarly, since not all companies report their results on the same basis, they have to eliminate accounting differences between companies in order to get meaningful inter-company comparisons.

OIL PRACTICE. This is how the use of cash flow in security analysis got its start. In the oil industry, practices vary widely from company to company in accounting for exploration and development costs of oil finds. Most oil companies capitalize these costs, and then amortize the investment over the expected life of the well. However, a few companies—including Continental Oil Co. and to an extent Sun Oil Co. and Amerada Petroleum Corp.—charge exploration and development against current income.

This can make a substantial difference in the amount of reported net income. For example, in 1960 Amerada changed its accounting practice to charge to capital account the intangible drilling and development costs of productive wells in Libya. Previously, Amerada had charged all its development costs against current income. The effect of this change was to boost Amerada's net income per share in 1960 from $3.84 to $4.37.

VARIATIONS. Obviously, in comparing oil company earnings, allowance has to be made for such variations in accounting. An easy way to do this is simply to calculate cash flow for the companies being compared. In effect, this puts them all on the same footing.

This is what the managing partner of one small Wall Street firm calls a "legitimate" use of cash flow analysis—as one tool among many in the security analyst's kit. Indeed, most oil companies use cash flow analysis internally in making decisions on capital expenditures.

ACROSS THE BOARD. The application of cash flow analysis in the oil industry is clear cut, but its application across the board to all classes of securities is more questionable. In some industries it amounts to little more than a selling gimmick.

In the chemical industry, where plant and equipment generally become obsolete fairly quickly, a company is always spending for new facilities. So the chances are that heavy cash flow in a chemical company isn't going to make much difference from the investor's viewpoint.

On the other hand, in an industry where the rate of technological change is relatively slow—rayon, for example—a large amount of cash flow means that corporate management has the opportunity to invest surplus cash generation in improving the company's business. This is what happened at American Viscose Corp., which has parlayed a big cash flow into a $200-million, 13% stake in Monsanto Chemical Co., plus other profitable ventures in chemicals and paper.

CASE OF REALITY. In real estate—where assets tend to increase rather than decline in value—cash flow is generally equated directly with profit. In fact, most real estate companies pay at least part of their dividends from depreciation charges.

But the real estate outfits—which, in effect, traffic in depreciation by rolling over their investments whenever depreciation charges start to drop off—are a special case. There are few industrial companies where cash flow and profit are identical.

As one veteran Wall Street observer commented, "The fact that you have cash flow is no more important than the fact that you have research expenditures—neither means a thing until you accomplish something." *

QUESTIONS

1. How do you define "cash flow"?

2. For what purposes is cash flow a more useful measure than net income?

---

* EDITORS' NOTE: Since 1947, the American Institute of Certified Public Accountants publishes annually details of how 600 companies have prepared public financial statements. In its survey of corporate annual reports for 1964, the following trends are noted:

Some 65 percent of the companies included statements of source and application of funds in their 1964 reports, up from 45 percent in 1963.

"Cash flow," despite the campaign by the institute against this term, is increasingly used. Some 144 companies used this term in 1964 as against 101 in 1962 and 66 in 1960.

About 56 percent of the companies resorted to terms other than "surplus" on their 1964 balance sheets. This compares with 54 percent in 1963 and with 16 percent in 1948.

The number of firms restating or reclassifying previous years' figures grew to 206.

24

Stock Dividends: Boon or Bane?

A STOCK DIVIDEND is a pro-rata payment of additional shares to stockholders, sometimes in lieu of cash, sometimes in addition to it.

Back in 1920 the Supreme Court ruled that stock dividends were not income and not taxable as such. That started their modern vogue.

But, tax status aside, the value of stock dividends is still a matter of argument. Proponents call them a boon for growing companies, a tax-saver for stockholders. Critics, however, say they are mere pieces of paper—unnecessary, expensive and confusing.

PRO

To some, stock dividends are a snare and a delusion: mere paper-shuffling. But their defenders include Benjamin Graham and David L. Dodd, whose *Security Analysis* (now

From *Forbes*, vol. 91, no. 4 (February 15, 1963), pp. 34–35. Reprinted by permission of the publisher.

in its fourth edition) is the security analyst's bible. "Properly conceived and clearly understood," say the authors, "periodic stock dividends can contribute to sound corporate finance."

The main qualification Graham and Dodd make is that a stock dividend ought to represent recent earnings, reinvested for future profit. Thus they particularly recommend the use of stock dividends to utilities: Their need for new capital is steady and predictable. A growing utility that pays most of its earnings out in cash, Graham and Dodd argue, will merely have to turn around and ask stockholders to buy new shares with the money.

President E. J. Howe of smallish Rochester Gas & Electric Corp. agrees wholeheartedly with this thesis. "For us, paying nothing but cash dividends to stockholders means we just have to go out and get the money back after they have paid tax on it," says he. "That would be a vicious whirlpool." As things now stand, Rochester Gas won't have to issue new common (by way of direct sale) for from five to ten years.

Another enthusiastic user of stock dividends is Chicago's Commonwealth Edison Co. "Our stock dividend," says Executive Vice President Gordon R. Corey, "means that we can retain 50%, not 25%, of a year's earnings." That is one reason why Commonwealth won't be selling new common through 1967. Corey says that to issue new common worth the earnings retained would cost Commonwealth (in administration and bookkeeping) more than twice what the stock dividend does.

In the industrial field, Georgia-Pacific Corp. has been a leading user of stock dividends since 1955. The big plywood and paper concern keeps on paying them, says Chairman Owen R. Cheatham, "in part because the mail is overwhelmingly favorable." The stock dividend gives shareholders a choice, he adds. If they want, they can sell to supplement G-P's cash payout, paying only a small capital-gains tax. And if they don't sell, they hold a steadily increasing number of shares.

Cheatham claims that because stockholders like them, stock dividends have helped keep the price of G-P shares relatively high; thus he can issue fewer shares in making acquisitions. He also believes that the stock dividend appeals to the owners of acquired companies, which are quite often held closely by taxpayers in the higher brackets. In other words, says Cheatham, whatever the logic of the argument, stock dividends pass the pragmatic test: *They work.*

CON

Opponents have always objected that the stock dividend is a costly way to give stockholders something they already have. And if they sell their shares to obtain future earnings growth—is steadily diluted. There can also be unfortunate immediate results. Such was the case with the 10% stock dividend paid by Detroit Edison in 1947. Logically, the market price slipped. But employee stockholders did not understand, wondered why their shares lost so much in value.

The accounting complications bother C. Austin Barker, economist for Wall Street's Hornblower & Weeks. A company's earned surplus normally limits the dollar amont of a stock dividend; the New York Stock Exchange requires that the bookkeeping transfer from earned surplus to capital be based on market value per share—thus confronting management, he claims, "with an unpredictable and fluctuating yardstick."

"Falling prices," says he, "permit greater dilution on the same amount of surplus, when corporations least need it." Rising prices can force a cut in the percentage paid. That may confuse the public, who may think something is wrong. Such problems were encountered by International Business Machines, which, in the early fifties paid 5%; in the late fifties 2.5%. Even in paying the "reduced" dividend, IBM transferred (from retained earnings to capital) nearly $26 million more in 1958 than it netted in that year. Since 1959 IBM has paid no stock dividend.

Hornblower & Weeks' Barker has also sought to prove, through scholarly analysis, that stock dividends do little to help the market price of a company's shares. "For widely held, listed issues," says Barker, "stock dividends alone produce no lasting gains." A Barker backer is Vice President and Treasurer F. C. Eggerstedt Jr. of Long Island Lighting Co. "I don't believe," says he, "that you can jack yourself up by your bootstraps. After all, your stockholders own the same proportion, of the *same* company, that they did before." Unless they sell the extra stock, of course, in which case their proportion is reduced. Better to pay cash, Barker contends. Says he, earnings and cash dividends are what really count for stockholders in the final analysis.

And so the argument goes on. *A practical judgment on the situation probably boils down to this: So long as only a small minority of companies pay them, stock dividends probably do some good—possibly even helping the companies' shares attain a small premium in the mar-*

Paper-payers:
Each of these companies, over 50 in all,
pays a regular stock dividend.

INDUSTRIALS, MISC.*	RECENT PRICE	INDICATED CASH DIVIDEND	RECENT CASH YIELD	LATEST ANNUAL STOCK DIVIDEND
ABC Vending	13⅞	$0.50	3.6%	2.0%
Acme Markets	77¾	2.00	2.6	5.0
Aeroquip	24	0.40	1.7	5.0
Amerace	23	0.40	1.7	4.0
American Seal-Kap	13¼	0.25	1.9	3.0
Austin, Nichols	18½	0.40	2.2	5.0
Baker Oil Tools	13⅛	0.40	3.0	4.0
Beam, James B., Dist.	40½	0.80	2.0	2.0
Brown-Forman Dist.	26¼	0.40	1.5	3.0
Carnation Co.	90	1.85	2.1	3.0
Cerro Corp.	24⅛	1.10	4.6	6.0
Colonial Sand & Stone	17⅝	0.30	1.7	5.0
Columbia Broadcasting	47⅜	1.40	3.0	3.0
Elastic Stop Nut	34⅝	1.00	2.9	4.0
Firestone Tire & Rubber	35¼	1.00	2.8	2.0
Friden	32	0.40	1.3	2.0
General American Oil	38½	0.40	1.0	3.0
Georgia-Pacific	47⅞	1.00	2.1	4.0
Grace (W. R.)	40⅞	0.90	2.2	2.0
Grand Union	17⅛	0.60	3.5	3.0
Hunt Foods & Industries	32⅞	0.50	1.5	5.0
International Paper	29⅛	1.05	3.6	2.0
Interstate Dept. Stores	30½	0.50	1.6	2.0
Lear-Siegler	17¼	0.40	2.3	3.0
Mallory, P. R.	46¼	1.40	3.0	2.0
Masonite Corp.	38¾	1.20	3.1	4.0
McCall Corp.	19⅞	0.50	2.5	3.0
Monsanto Chemical	52¾	1.20	2.3	2.0

* Industries include only listed companies paying stock dividends of 10% or less for at least 4 consecutive years; utilities include unlisted securities.

Paper-payers (continued)

INDUSTRIALS, MISC.	RECENT PRICE	INDICATED CASH DIVIDEND	RECENT CASH YIELD	LATEST ANNUAL STOCK DIVIDEND
National Gypsum	44	$2.00	4.7%	2.0%
Philadelphia & Reading	38¼	1.00	2.6	2.0
Pittsburgh Plate Glass	57½	2.20	3.8	2.0
Pittston	59⅜	1.60	2.7	4.0
Rexall Drug & Chemical	32¼	0.50	1.6	3.0
Rohm & Haas	112½	1.00	0.9	4.0
Rubbermaid	12⅝	0.30	2.4	5.0
St. Regis Paper	30⅛	1.40	4.6	2.0
Sheraton Corp.	12⅜	0.60	4.8	2.0
Signod Steel Strapping	26	0.60	2.3	2.0
Stouffer Foods	28⅜	0.60	2.1	2.0
Sun Oil	47⅛	1.00	2.1	5.0
Tishman Realty	18⅝	0.55	3.0	3.0
Union Oil of Calif.	64	2.00	3.1	2.0
United Air Lines	34⅜	0.50	1.5	6.0
Walgreen	47¾	1.60	3.4	3.0
Wilcox Oil	28¼	0.60	2.1	2.5
Utilities				
Citizens Utilities, Class A *	24¼	none	—	3.45
Commonwealth Edison	48½	1.20	2.5	2.0
Michigan Gas & Electric *	89	2.00	2.2	4.0
Missouri Public Service	25⅛	0.72	2.9	2.0
New Jersey Natural Gas *	38¼	1.00	2.6	2.0
Phila. Suburban Water *	29⅞	0.85	2.8	3.0
Rochester Gas & Electric	29⅝	0.95	3.2	2.0

* Traded over-the-counter.

ket place. But if all companies used them, their practical effect would probably shrink to nothing but costly extra bookkeeping and administration.

QUESTIONS

1. What is a stock dividend? What is its effect on the balance sheet of the issuing company? What is its effect on the balance sheet of the stockholders receiving the dividend?

2. How can a stockholder be better off after a stock dividend than before a stock dividend?

25

Splitting Shares
Is a Complex Job

Gene Smith

SPLITTING A STOCK can be about as complicated as splitting an atom.

It is far more complex than the process envisioned by a stockholder of the American Telephone and Telegraph Company, who came to last year's annual meeting to see the room where they were going to split the stock. It entails far more than the soliciting of stockholders' proxies, their approving votes and the subsequent announcement that the split is to become effective on a specific date.

To persons such as the employees in corporate agency divisions of large banks and financial executives of companies listed on stock exchanges, the process is old hat. But, to the average investor, it is an unknown world. Once he

From *The New York Times*, vol. CIX, no. 37,360 (May 8, 1960), p. 1. Reprinted by permission of the publisher. Mr. Smith is on the staff of *The New York Times*.

casts his ballots for the action, the professionals take over and he awaits formal notification.

SPLIT APPROVED

So it was after the stockholders in the General Telephone and Electronics Corporation approved a three-for-one stock split at their annual meeting on April 20 at Tampa, Fla. Approval of the management-sponsored split provided that each stockholder of record of April 20 would receive two additional shares for each share held on that date.

This meant that the old stock certificates would continue valid, but that the stockholders would receive at a later date certificates covering the additional shares authorized by the split. The holder of one $10 par share would own three $3.33⅓ par shares for each of the older shares he owned on April 20.

As soon as the split had been authorized, the corporate agency division of the Bankers Trust Company, which is General Telephone's New York transfer agent, swung into action. The bank keeps stencil name plates for the more than 185,000 stockholders of General Telephone in twelve cabinets holding some 15,000 plates each.

Bank clerks were already working on updating shareowner records. The changes had been requested by management in the annual meeting announcements sent out prior to the meeting, plus change of address cards in the first quarter dividend mailing of March 30.

When this updating process was completed, new stockholder and work cards were prepared on Addressograph machines. The cards listed, in addition to names and addresses, the exact number of shares held on the record date. The work cards were then processed through a machine that calculated the amount of new shares due each stockholder. This machine also assigned new certificate numbers to the shareholder and provided the new share balance for the holder.

Next, the work cards were put into a 419 Tabulator of the International Business Machines Corporation (I. B. M.) for the printing of a tabular list that included names and addresses of each owner, the number of new shares to be sent and the new certificate number.

The work cards were then collated with the stockholder cards, processed through an IBM 557 Alphabetic Interpreter that transferred the information on the work cards to the stockholder cards and both sets of cards were separated once again.

At the same time, the new stock certificates are delivered to be inserted in an Addressograph machine that prints the name and address of the stockholder and embosses the number of shares held prior to the split.

Next, the stock certificates were separated into denominations. About 50 per cent of General Telephone's stock certificates are in five, ten, fifty or 100 shares. These certificates are then processed by denominations on a machine that prints on the certificates the number of new shares being issued and the date of issue.

In addition, a machine punch is used to punch into the certificate the exact number of shares.

The new certificates then go to the corporation's registrar. In the case of the General Telephone split, this was the Chase Manhattan Bank.

The registrar's duty is to check the denomination of each certificate and the certificate numbers. Then the authorized signature of the registrar is affixed. The certificates, complete with signatures of the corporate officers and the authorized signatures of both the transfer agent and the registrar are then mailed to holders.

The final step is for the transfer agent to revise the stencil plates to indicate the number of shares held after the split is effective. This must be done, in this instance, in time for the June 30 dividend mailing.

26

Key Business Ratios

HOW THE RATIOS ARE FIGURED

IN THE RATIO TABLES each group of ratios in each industry carries three sets of figures. The top figure is the upper quartile, the center figure is the median, and the bottom figure is the lower quartile. They are calculated as follows: Year-end financial statements are selected from a sampling of corporations whose tangible net worth, with few exceptions, exceed $35,000. The financial statements are those appearing in the Dun & Bradstreet credit reports on these businesses. Statement copies are referred to statisticians who compute each of the "14 Ratios" on each of the concerns. The ratios are then punched on data processing cards, and arranged into industry groups. After this, ratio figures are arranged so that the best ratio figure is at the top, the weakest at the bottom. The figure which falls just in the middle of this series becomes the median for that ratio in that line

Reproduced by permission, Dun & Bradstreet, Inc., 1964.

of business. The figure halfway between the median and the highest term of the series is the upper quartile; and the term halfway between the median and the bottom of the series is the lower quartile. The purpose of these interquartile ranges is to show an upper and lower limit area without reflecting the extremes either at the top or the bottom of the series. After the first of the "14 Ratios" has been compiled for a particular industry, the identical process is followed for the remaining 13 ratios in this industry group, and then for remaining industry groups.

CURRENT ASSETS TO CURRENT DEBT Current Assets are divided by total Current Debt. Current Assets are the sum of cash, notes and accounts receivable (less reserves for bad debt), advances on merchandise, merchandise inventories, and Listed, Federal, State and Municipal securities not in excess of market value. Current Debt is the total of all liabilities falling due within one year. This is one test of solvency.

NET PROFITS ON NET SALES Obtained by dividing the net earnings of the business, after taxes, by net sales (the dollar volume less returns, allowances, and cash discounts). This important yardstick in measuring profitability should be related to the ratio which follows.

NET PROFITS ON TANGIBLE NET WORTH Tangible Net Worth is the equity of stockholders in the business, as obtained by subtracting total liabilities from total assets, and then deducting intangibles. The ratio is obtained by dividing Net Profits after taxes by Tangible Net Worth. Tendency is to look increasingly to this ratio as a final criterion of profitability. Generally, a relationship of at least 10 per cent is regarded as a desirable objective for providing dividends plus funds for future growth.

NET PROFITS ON NET WORKING CAPITAL Net Working Capital represents the excess of Current Assets over Current Debt. This margin represents the cushion available to the business for carrying inventories and receivables, and for financing day-to-day operations. The ratio is obtained by dividing Net Profits, after taxes, by Net Working Capital.

NET SALES TO TANGIBLE NET WORTH Net Sales are divided by Tangible Net Worth. This gives a measure of relative turnover of invested capital.

NET SALES TO NET WORKING CAPITAL Net Sales are divided by Net Working Capital. This provides a guide as to the extent the company is turning its working capital and the margin of operating funds.

COLLECTION PERIOD Annual net sales are divided by 365 days to obtain average daily credit sales and then the average daily credit

LINE OF BUSINESS (AND NUMBER OF CONCERNS REPORTING)	CURRENT ASSETS TO CURRENT DEBT	NET PROFITS ON NET SALES	NET PROFITS ON TANGIBLE NET WORTH	NET PROFITS ON NET WORKING CAPITAL	NET SALES TO TANGIBLE NET WORTH	NET SALES TO NET WORKING CAPITAL
	TIMES	PER CENT	PER CENT	PER CENT	TIMES	TIMES
5511 †	2.37	2.26	21.54	29.53	15.73	21.83
Automobile Dealers (133)	1.78	1.28	13.12	18.02	9.88	14.70
	1.44	0.60	5.46	8.46	6.70	9.29
5212	4.33	4.04	12.16	17.10	5.17	8.54
Building Materials (110)	2.79	1.74	6.06	7.67	3.27	4.71
	1.74	0.23	0.46	1.26	2.17	3.13
5612	4.91	3.96	11.71	13.92	4.05	5.09
Clothing, Men's & Boys' (167)	2.77	2.34	6.05	7.37	2.81	3.43
	1.92	1.10	2.82	3.41	2.02	2.31
5651	5.16	4.06	15.54	16.68	4.54	5.27
Clothing, Men's & Women's (80)	3.13	2.20	6.44	7.77	2.93	3.38
	2.16	0.48	1.30	1.32	2.20	2.27
5311	5.30	2.50	9.26	11.32	5.22	6.17
Department Stores (266)	3.48	1.60	4.59	5.91	3.33	3.97
	2.26	0.53	1.96	2.60	2.18	2.90
Discount Stores (196)	2.18	2.19	19.09	24.79	12.31	17.08
	1.67	1.14	10.62	12.85	8.13	11.25
	1.41	0.39	3.51	4.52	5.90	6.99
Discount Stores	2.13	1.81	17.76	21.44	12.33	15.87
Leased Departments (49)	1.64	0.73	7.92	9.22	8.39	11.33
	1.31	0.26	2.93	4.25	5.83	6.57
5392	5.47	4.22	12.32	18.68	5.68	7.53
Dry Goods (88)	3.01	1.65	6.06	7.38	3.05	3.72
	1.86	0.37	0.99	1.45	1.87	2.40
5252	2.72	3.84	18.57	20.73	6.82	8.83
Farm Equipment (117)	1.94	1.63	8.10	10.70	5.04	6.71
	1.50	0.61	3.50	4.35	3.11	4.02
5969	6.41	4.90	15.65	25.57	4.33	8.18
Farm and Garden Supplies (75)	2.47	2.31	7.52	15.24	2.83	4.79
	1.49	0.80	3.01	5.75	2.07	2.88
5613	3.51	4.17	14.31	16.66	5.70	6.68
Furnishings, Men's (44)	2.51	2.14	6.48	6.60	3.96	4.49
	1.82	0.60	2.35	2.43	2.50	2.96
5712	4.92	4.88	13.25	14.33	4.43	6.22
Furniture (177)	3.03	2.06	5.99	6.42	2.57	2.74
	1.79	0.59	1.46	2.37	1.60	1.72

COLLECTION PERIOD	NET SALES TO INVENTORY	FIXED ASSETS TO TANGIBLE NET WORTH	CURRENT DEBT TO TANGIBLE NET WORTH	TOTAL DEBT TO TANGIBLE NET WORTH	INVENTORY TO NET WORKING CAPITAL	CURRENT DEBT TO INVENTORY	FUNDED DEBTS TO NET WORKING CAPITAL
DAYS	TIMES	PER CENT	PER CENT	PER CENT	PER CENT	PER CENT	PER CENT
*	12.2	11.5	49.1	80.7	95.8	63.2	11.9
*	9.4	22.8	91.2	132.2	160.3	84.2	26.3
*	7.8	42.9	153.8	167.9	234.9	102.9	66.3
38	10.7	13.0	21.7	59.6	44.8	53.6	24.8
51	6.4	26.9	36.7	84.1	65.7	87.7	43.7
82	4.9	53.9	73.8	136.7	93.2	141.1	87.8
*	5.0	5.4	22.1	65.4	67.9	30.5	3.6
*	3.4	10.7	43.6	93.7	92.1	57.6	19.6
*	2.5	20.9	90.2	148.1	137.9	95.3	39.2
*	5.4	5.0	19.7	48.1	63.3	27.9	12.0
*	3.8	10.3	43.9	100.4	94.8	54.8	31.6
*	2.9	20.5	73.6	150.9	121.7	85.7	48.1
*	6.9	11.6	18.1	37.9	54.5	38.6	13.1
*	5.4	25.9	31.8	63.2	75.2	61.1	30.8
*	3.9	46.6	63.6	113.5	107.5	85.2	53.3
*	8.0	15.1	67.1	107.7	114.9	60.5	21.6
*	6.1	27.3	115.6	160.1	165.4	83.7	45.0
*	4.4	49.8	182.5	256.3	250.2	108.7	77.3
*	7.8	13.4	78.9	128.9	117.4	75.9	18.6
*	6.2	22.6	122.2	184.9	167.2	90.6	40.2
*	3.6	38.9	226.1	284.3	258.5	122.2	55.3
*	5.7	6.5	22.4	37.6	68.6	29.4	7.3
*	4.2	12.8	40.4	57.7	99.9	62.4	32.5
*	2.9	24.3	90.7	119.7	156.5	88.9	73.2
*	6.2	9.7	47.4	91.2	89.3	56.5	19.0
*	4.2	16.5	88.0	138.4	149.2	74.8	28.1
*	2.8	35.3	146.8	240.1	239.1	95.1	56.4
*	17.1	17.3	13.7	34.3	35.5	36.4	18.5
*	10.9	32.3	32.4	54.2	54.9	103.1	61.7
*	6.2	68.3	80.4	125.4	90.2	229.3	122.6
*	5.0	2.2	27.7	49.7	94.2	32.9	12.1
*	3.4	7.4	50.8	78.5	135.3	49.2	28.5
*	2.5	21.9	100.2	113.5	166.1	78.2	64.9
39	7.1	4.4	20.3	63.7	35.3	50.0	11.3
81	4.9	10.6	48.0	97.6	63.0	86.8	23.8
184	3.6	25.8	104.4	184.6	111.7	143.1	51.6

LINE OF BUSINESS (AND NUMBER OF CONCERNS REPORTING)	CURRENT ASSETS TO CURRENT DEBT	NET PROFITS ON NET SALES	NET PROFITS ON TANGIBLE NET WORTH	NET PROFITS ON NET WORKING CAPITAL	NET SALES TO TANGIBLE NET WORTH	NET SALES TO NET WORKING CAPITAL
	TIMES	PER CENT	PER CENT	PER CENT	TIMES	TIMES
5541	4.45	5.90	17.89	45.77	5.79	11.97
Gasoline Service Stations (105)	2.26	2.97	9.93	25.42	3.53	7.14
	1.62	0.87	4.50	8.65	2.25	4.71
5411	2.67	1.94	19.56	58.88	13.41	43.51
Groceries and Meats (154)	1.83	1.16	10.36	28.65	8.65	20.31
	1.22	0.54	4.19	9.23	6.18	12.03
5251	8.48	3.16	7.61	10.91	3.16	4.13
Hardware (115)	3.71	1.97	3.63	5.26	2.23	2.72
	2.28	0.21	0.26	0.34	1.57	2.16
5722	3.75	3.35	13.38	21.34	6.32	11.66
Household Appliances (126)	2.36	1.45	7.08	9.44	3.89	5.02
	1.54	0.42	2.05	2.31	2.50	3.19
5641	5.06	2.74	8.53	12.67	4.96	6.65
Infants' & Children's Wear (38)	2.91	1.09	3.94	4.15	3.62	4.23
	1.93	0.18	0.65	0.71	2.14	2.65
5971	4.91	4.53	9.67	11.29	2.83	3.21
Jewelers (62)	2.61	2.78	5.88	5.92	2.07	2.36
	1.79	0.69	1.93	2.00	1.52	1.55
5211	7.85	4.09	10.59	15.38	3.87	5.49
Lumber Yards (127)	4.28	2.07	5.24	6.86	2.29	2.84
	2.31	0.71	1.94	2.41	1.64	2.05
5231	4.54	3.09	11.59	18.84	4.84	5.69
Paint, Glass and Wallpaper (29)	2.60	1.21	4.35	7.42	3.23	4.02
	1.95	0.34	0.75	0.98	2.14	3.20
566-	6.04	3.39	13.06	15.57	4.29	4.97
Shoes, Men's, Women's & Children's (107)	3.21	1.69	5.66	6.88	2.88	3.33
	2.25	0.42	0.91	0.93	2.09	2.49
5531	3.11	4.00	14.68	22.60	5.46	8.80
Tires, Batteries & Accessories (85)	2.05	1.77	5.49	7.88	3.80	5.55
	1.55	0.61	2.20	3.30	2.55	3.44
5331	4.33	4.31	17.78	21.26	4.54	5.79
Variety Stores (57)	2.68	2.03	7.68	11.31	3.03	4.63
	2.01	1.24	4.21	5.84	2.15	3.37
5621	4.65	3.83	13.97	18.15	5.52	8.87
Women's Specialty Shops (216)	2.46	1.86	6.90	8.65	3.71	4.75
	1.72	0.45	1.70	1.81	2.44	3.09

* Not computed; necessary information as to the division between cash sales and credit sales was available in too few cases to obtain an average collection period usable as a broad guide.

† SIC (Standard Industrial Classification) categories.

COLLEC-TION PERIOD	NET SALES TO INVENTORY	FIXED ASSETS TO TANGIBLE NET WORTH	CURRENT DEBT TO TANGIBLE NET WORTH	TOTAL DEBT TO TANGIBLE NET WORTH	INVENTORY TO NET WORKING CAPITAL	CURRENT DEBT TO INVENTORY	FUNDED DEBTS TO NET WORKING CAPITAL
DAYS	TIMES	PER CENT	PER CENT	PER CENT	PER CENT	PER CENT	PER CENT
*	22.3	21.1	16.1	39.3	36.9	55.7	14.5
*	10.8	38.1	35.8	77.3	65.0	102.4	40.6
*	6.9	63.4	80.2	133.2	125.6	207.4	114.8
*	27.3	35.9	26.6	57.2	72.4	66.7	25.3
*	18.6	59.1	49.5	85.3	111.6	94.8	58.3
*	13.0	93.4	76.6	118.2	191.5	135.5	165.7
*	4.9	6.7	10.4	39.2	62.3	17.5	10.9
*	3.4	18.4	28.6	71.0	80.2	41.8	30.9
*	2.6	33.9	52.5	107.9	109.6	84.6	65.6
25	7.4	6.7	29.0	47.9	52.6	54.8	14.8
47	5.3	16.5	53.9	112.3	93.8	83.1	31.1
63	3.7	37.6	114.2	159.6	168.1	118.3	52.9
*	6.9	9.8	21.1	69.6	60.6	30.9	5.7
*	4.6	16.0	48.3	98.4	108.9	56.6	19.6
*	3.2	30.5	65.7	118.9	146.1	78.0	49.2
*	3.7	1.9	30.4	57.3	64.2	42.2	10.3
*	2.6	5.7	56.3	91.5	97.0	64.1	28.5
*	1.9	11.2	86.8	157.6	131.9	106.4	44.1
42	6.7	8.4	11.8	41.6	47.3	25.9	9.1
57	4.9	16.6	24.0	70.7	64.2	49.5	25.5
82	3.4	32.5	62.6	124.0	85.5	93.4	38.2
*	6.7	7.8	17.9	25.9	62.5	41.5	4.2
*	5.6	22.8	48.1	95.7	74.3	73.2	46.0
*	4.3	33.5	83.9	144.0	102.5	101.3	75.1
*	4.2	3.8	16.8	58.8	86.6	23.3	14.5
*	3.1	8.3	40.9	91.7	110.2	41.6	24.9
*	2.4	17.7	74.4	137.6	148.0	60.5	53.8
*	10.1	9.5	36.3	65.7	55.2	56.1	7.9
*	6.7	26.8	66.2	113.4	99.1	108.9	46.7
*	4.7	59.7	107.1	171.6	141.2	187.5	114.9
*	5.4	13.1	19.4	61.7	80.1	25.4	25.5
*	4.5	26.8	37.2	83.8	102.3	47.8	37.2
*	2.9	39.2	69.7	112.0	155.2	69.7	62.6
*	8.9	6.8	22.5	72.2	51.6	51.6	16.8
*	6.2	17.5	55.4	111.6	83.1	85.3	36.3
*	4.3	31.7	98.5	158.1	133.3	115.3	65.8

LINE OF BUSINESS (AND NUMBER OF CONCERNS REPORTING)	CURRENT ASSETS TO CURRENT DEBT	NET PROFITS ON NET SALES	NET PROF- ITS ON TANGIBLE NET WORTH	NET PROFITS ON NET WORKING CAPITAL	NET SALES TO TANGIBLE NET WORTH	NET SALES TO NET WORKING CAPITAL
	TIMES	PER CENT	PER CENT	PER CENT	TIMES	TIMES
3522 *	3.53	4.70	16.32	28.56	4.53	6.36
Agricultural Implements	2.42	3.40	10.00	14.73	3.06	4.55
& Machinery (61)	1.62	1.48	5.79	7.12	2.05	3.23
3722-23-29	3.08	4.48	17.29	29.23	5.39	7.58
Airplane Parts &	2.01	2.64	8.10	14.58	3.88	5.15
Accessories (55)	1.52	1.26	3.46	5.83	2.47	3.98
3714	3.91	6.08	20.33	28.09	4.05	6.53
Automobile Parts	2.97	3.63	11.15	16.68	2.96	4.41
& Accessories (89)	2.20	2.16	5.94	9.61	2.33	3.43
205	2.92	3.10	13.74	44.07	5.87	28.03
Bakers (65)	1.85	1.89	8.88	26.15	4.65	16.44
	1.35	0.60	3.45	7.87	3.09	8.74
2515	5.63	2.02	8.38	10.39	5.29	8.45
Bedsprings &	3.23	1.09	3.09	4.35	2.85	5.14
Mattresses (52)	1.97	0.30	0.77	1.41	2.22	3.10
2331	2.17	1.57	13.69	19.87	13.74	15.83
Blouses &	1.78	0.70	8.08	8.82	9.00	10.57
Waists (32)	1.40	0.25	2.50	3.15	6.83	7.60
3712-13	4.24	4.33	11.63	24.18	5.55	10.13
Bodies: Auto,	2.50	2.61	7.74	14.17	3.97	6.21
Bus & Truck (40)	1.66	1.27	4.79	6.35	2.62	4.22
345	3.54	4.36	14.72	35.33	4.72	13.31
Bolts, Screws,	2.45	2.73	8.79	16.58	2.92	5.28
Nuts & Nails (67)	1.32	1.74	5.21	7.94	1.88	3.15
273	4.04	7.66	19.02	24.48	3.32	5.29
Books, Pubshg.	2.97	4.95	12.49	14.53	2.23	3.14
& Printing (36)	2.05	1.66	4.40	7.11	1.95	2.43
2082	4.26	4.77	10.85	32.59	2.73	9.27
Breweries (36)	3.02	3.12	6.34	17.52	2.24	6.62
	2.09	0.82	2.18	6.54	1.85	4.29
287	4.22	3.20	11.43	27.13	4.92	13.92
Chemicals,	2.63	2.39	5.90	12.20	2.90	6.56
Agricultural (30)	1.36	0.47	1.95	2.27	1.66	2.23
281	4.12	7.37	12.26	34.78	3.08	7.36
Chemicals,	2.91	4.61	9.03	21.98	1.78	3.95
Industrial (62)	1.82	2.67	5.79	8.02	1.32	2.80

COLLECTION PERIOD	NET SALES TO INVENTORY	FIXED ASSETS TO TANGIBLE NET WORTH	CURRENT DEBT TO TANGIBLE NET WORTH	TOTAL DEBT TO TANGIBLE NET WORTH	INVENTORY TO NET WORKING CAPITAL	CURRENT DEBT TO INVENTORY	FUNDED DEBTS TO NET WORKING CAPITAL
DAYS	TIMES	PER CENT	PER CENT	PER CENT	PER CENT	PER CENT	PER CENT
24	6.7	24.8	27.8	61.3	66.9	45.0	23.2
37	4.8	38.6	48.9	92.7	99.3	73.9	43.6
48	3.1	59.2	89.1	149.2	134.3	106.8	62.2
26	11.1	27.7	34.0	56.5	53.8	76.9	24.7
43	7.1	49.9	54.9	112.4	74.9	122.0	45.5
66	5.3	75.6	105.7	142.9	133.5	215.2	83.0
31	9.3	22.5	23.4	45.3	46.8	57.0	5.0
42	6.6	32.4	36.3	69.5	71.7	85.5	23.9
51	4.7	45.0	57.8	91.7	96.7	114.4	42.9
12	35.7	59.8	19.1	31.2	39.0	116.9	18.1
16	29.4	71.6	30.5	59.1	63.4	191.3	66.2
22	19.3	101.5	46.5	102.2	124.8	269.3	165.1
24	10.2	16.3	15.1	38.5	49.2	39.0	9.9
41	6.9	26.1	24.5	53.3	68.0	75.7	24.8
49	5.8	47.6	68.9	107.7	88.2	113.0	60.2
25	26.4	3.3	72.4	—	61.3	105.5	—
32	13.2	7.5	106.5	—	90.3	132.2	—
45	7.5	11.3	200.4	—	126.8	250.7	—
36	9.4	25.7	24.3	69.1	58.5	63.9	20.7
44	6.5	38.8	46.9	105.2	88.5	90.9	31.4
57	4.8	58.1	78.4	147.9	132.2	139.2	65.8
25	20.2	41.1	19.9	36.0	41.2	57.0	8.3
32	10.4	60.3	31.1	59.9	71.1	123.4	40.5
40	5.2	94.6	69.3	131.6	112.6	235.8	139.4
42	7.9	9.1	25.2	41.4	44.4	56.6	11.4
66	6.5	25.8	45.0	62.1	60.8	83.0	17.4
93	3.3	46.3	62.5	76.3	81.1	161.9	57.9
10	22.4	42.8	11.5	20.4	30.2	81.0	7.6
17	14.1	56.2	15.9	28.4	43.1	123.7	35.0
21	12.2	77.2	26.9	47.4	68.9	192.4	96.1
26	14.8	24.0	17.1	73.6	37.1	63.4	34.6
49	7.1	51.6	39.8	99.5	64.3	100.8	73.6
97	5.4	87.5	89.6	204.2	117.0	239.5	198.5
37	8.9	41.8	18.3	40.7	46.3	55.1	40.8
48	5.9	72.4	26.1	67.0	66.1	93.1	89.4
62	4.5	99.4	60.3	108.5	95.0	145.2	135.5

LINE OF BUSINESS (AND NUMBER OF CONCERNS REPORTING)	CURRENT ASSETS TO CURRENT DEBT	NET PROFITS ON NET SALES	NET PROF-ITS ON TANGIBLE NET WORTH	NET PROFITS ON NET WORKING CAPITAL	NET SALES TO TANGIBLE NET WORTH	NET SALES TO NET WORKING CAPITAL
	TIMES	PER CENT	PER CENT	PER CENT	TIMES	TIMES
236	2.00	1.58	16.47	26.59	13.23	18.40
Child. & Infants	1.53	0.89	6.80	7.58	10.34	13.25
Outerwear (62)	1.27	0.15	1.62	1.77	7.72	8.71
2311	2.67	1.98	9.48	11.71	7.99	10.61
Coats & Suits,	1.89	0.88	5.68	7.23	5.35	5.70
Men's & Boys' (131)	1.43	0.41	1.69	1.82	3.38	4.03
2337	2.31	1.77	14.79	18.50	11.83	13.97
Coats & Suits,	1.76	0.65	8.17	9.52	7.75	10.36
Women's (100)	1.40	0.28	1.59	2.10	4.82	6.31
366	3.70	6.08	22.61	31.68	4.75	6.20
Communication	2.34	2.87	9.49	12.45	3.33	4.30
Equipment (61)	1.77	1.13	3.64	4.95	2.15	2.80
327	3.95	5.32	13.69	37.12	3.55	8.99
Concrete, Gypsum	2.14	3.35	9.03	18.34	2.49	5.75
& Plaster Prod. (81)	1.58	1.59	4.32	9.37	1.76	3.67
207	4.06	4.98	16.58	30.81	5.50	17.19
Confectionery (43)	2.52	2.35	10.03	16.42	3.88	6.40
	1.57	0.18	0.74	2.14	2.45	4.39
353	3.86	5.32	14.77	23.60	4.21	7.21
Construction	2.75	2.70	8.08	11.70	2.50	3.93
Machinery (78)	1.89	1.19	3.12	4.37	1.75	2.63
1511	2.22	2.98	20.11	41.54	12.19	22.44
Contractors,	1.53	1.48	11.50	18.76	7.52	12.60
Bldg. Constr. (164)	1.22	0.85	5.66	8.38	4.37	6.55
1731	3.70	4.33	19.43	28.03	7.42	11.36
Contractors,	2.42	1.88	10.32	13.06	4.73	6.19
Electrical (100)	1.57	0.83	3.69	5.20	3.12	4.51
1621	3.72	4.84	20.04	45.10	5.80	11.27
Contractors,	2.15	2.70	10.44	18.62	3.97	6.70
Heavy Constr. (85)	1.31	1.31	5.02	10.42	2.55	4.30
1711	2.56	4.04	23.95	30.75	8.88	13.19
Contractors, Plumbing,	1.79	1.70	10.79	13.90	6.71	8.52
Heating & Air Cond. (75)	1.39	0.65	4.50	4.96	3.63	4.74

* SIC Categories.
* * Building trades contractors have no inventories in the credit sense of the term. As a general rule, they have no customary selling terms, each contract being a special job for which individual terms are arranged.

COLLEC-TION PERIOD	NET SALES TO INVENTORY	FIXED ASSETS TO TANGIBLE NET WORTH	CURRENT DEBT TO TANGIBLE NET WORTH	TOTAL DEBT TO TANGIBLE NET WORTH	INVENTORY TO NET WORKING CAPITAL	CURRENT DEBT TO INVENTORY	FUNDED DEBTS TO NET WORKING CAPITAL
DAYS	TIMES	PER CENT	PER CENT	PER CENT	PER CENT	PER CENT	PER CENT
26	17.2	6.0	81.2	106.9	61.7	103.7	29.9
35	8.8	9.9	159.0	204.4	100.6	137.6	41.4
52	6.0	20.8	281.5	354.9	213.2	197.1	55.9
28	8.7	2.7	48.3	91.3	63.3	68.8	8.3
54	5.8	7.7	92.7	140.4	98.9	97.4	23.3
90	4.2	18.6	164.0	242.2	164.5	146.6	36.8
26	25.6	2.9	47.5	56.4	44.1	93.3	9.8
36	12.1	6.2	96.4	169.2	90.0	153.7	30.2
52	6.4	14.8	177.6	248.9	136.4	239.5	56.9
43	9.8	24.9	31.8	67.6	42.5	68.9	15.0
56	5.5	42.1	55.2	99.6	76.6	99.5	43.3
70	3.7	70.1	95.1	165.5	113.8	170.1	78.9
40	19.4	44.3	19.9	51.6	34.1	73.1	19.5
57	11.5	60.3	33.8	77.8	51.2	166.6	49.1
75	6.1	81.5	59.3	121.6	77.6	322.0	101.4
14	11.8	29.2	22.5	34.6	45.5	66.5	7.9
20	8.8	39.5	37.8	73.9	81.0	87.8	39.8
31	6.2	59.8	69.6	158.9	147.4	127.7	144.0
39	9.7	22.7	25.9	46.6	59.5	50.2	17.8
54	4.9	32.4	42.0	81.4	74.5	79.4	38.4
66	3.1	51.0	70.7	136.4	108.8	141.9	88.3
**	**	11.6	54.9	103.9	**	**	14.9
**	**	26.3	107.6	143.8	**	**	44.9
**	**	49.8	147.6	262.0	**	**	93.9
**	**	10.3	29.0	48.9	**	**	12.4
**	**	21.3	52.2	76.7	**	**	33.4
**	**	34.5	107.3	137.6	**	**	54.3
**	**	30.3	21.8	58.6	**	**	40.0
**	**	46.5	55.6	103.0	**	**	52.9
**	**	87.9	110.8	217.9	**	**	134.7
**	**	11.4	44.1	77.9	**	**	8.8
**	**	20.8	80.4	110.8	**	**	16.4
**	**	40.8	167.6	231.9	**	**	79.5

sales are divided into notes and accounts receivable, including any discounted. This ratio is helpful in analyzing the collectibility of receivables. Many feel the collection period should not exceed the net maturity indicated by selling terms by more than 10 to 15 days. When comparing the collection period of one concern with that of another, allowances should be made for possible variations in selling terms.

NET SALES TO INVENTORY   Dividing annual Net Sales by Merchandise Inventory as carried on the balance sheet. This quotient does not yield an actual physical turnover. It provides a yardstick for comparing stock-to-sales ratios of one concern with another or with those for the industry.

FIXED ASSETS TO TANGIBLE NET WORTH   Fixed assets are divided by Tangible Net Worth. Fixed Assets represent depreciated book values of building, leasehold improvements, machinery, furniture, fixtures, tools, and other physical equipment, plus land, if any, and valued at cost or appraised market value. Ordinarily, this relationship should not exceed 100 per cent for a manufacturer, and 75 per cent for a wholesaler or retailer.

CURRENT DEBT TO TANGIBLE NET WORTH   Derived by dividing Current Debt by Tangible Net Worth. Ordinarily, a business begins to pile up trouble when this relationship exceeds 80 per cent.

TOTAL DEBT TO TANGIBLE NET WORTH   Obtained by dividing Total Current plus Long-term Debts by Tangible Net Worth. When this relationship exceeds 100 per cent, the equity of creditors in the assets of the business exceeds that of owners.

INVENTORY TO NET WORKING CAPITAL   Merchandise Inventory is divided by Net Working Capital. This is an additional measure of inventory balance. Ordinarily, the relationship should not exceed 80 per cent.

CURRENT DEBT TO INVENTORY   Dividing the Current Debt by Inventory yields yet another indication of the extent to which the business relies on funds from disposal of unsold inventories to meet its debts.

FUNDED DEBTS TO NET WORKING CAPITAL   Funded Debts are all long-term obligations, as represented by mortgages, bonds, debentures, term loans, serial notes, and other types of liabilities maturing more than one year from statement date. This ratio is obtained by dividing Funded Debt by Net Working Capital. Analysts tend to compare Funded Debts with Net Working Capital in determining whether or not long-term debts are in proper proportion. Ordinarily, this relationship should not exceed 100 per cent.

QUESTIONS

1. Are there any differences between the ratios discussed in your text and those presented by Dun & Bradstreet, Inc.? Consider both the ratios computed and how they are computed. Discuss the significance of these differences.

2. In what industries do you find the largest variance between the high and low ratios? The smallest? What explanation can you offer and how is the amount of the variance of significance in evaluating the ratios for a particular firm?

HOW TO SUCCEED AT AT&T:
START WITH A's IN COLLEGE

NEW YORK—If you get good grades in college, you'll rise faster as a corporate executive.

At least that appears to be the situation at American Telephone & Telegraph Co. The communications concern recently compared the academic records of 17,000 of its executives with their present salaries. The findings were disclosed by Frederick R. Kappel, chairman, in a speech at Westminster College in Fulton, Mo.

The figures, Mr. Kappel said, show that a man's college standing is the "single most reliable predictive indicator" of his later success at AT&T. Of the men who were in the top third of their classes, 45% also are in the top third in salary he said. Of the bottom scholastic third, on the other hand, only 26% made the top pay bracket.

Extracurricular activities and the fact that a man worked his way through college—traditionally regarded as omens of a successful career—appear to be poor indicators of an executive's future paycheck. According to Mr. Kappel, men who were campus leaders reached the top pay third only in "slightly greater" proportion than those who were not. As for working one's way through college, he said, "the facts show that this by itself is not a significant yardstick."

Despite these findings, Mr. Kappel said, AT&T has no intention of "hiring according to marks alone." But, he asked rhetorically, "As we look for career managers, why should we spend a large part of our effort searching among men who have made a career of just getting by?"

From *The Wall Street Journal*, vol. CLIX, no. 69 (April 9, 1962), p. 8. Reprinted by permission of the publisher.

27

Those "Special Items"

ONE DAY several months ago the stock of U.S. Industries, Inc., which is listed on the New York Stock Exchange, was hit by a flood of sell orders. After a delayed opening, the stock fell rapidly to 9⅞, down from an 11⅜ closing price the day before; the loss represented a market value of $3,800,000. U.S.I. has since recovered part of this loss (the stock was around 10½ early last month), but it is clear that stockholders have not entirely recovered from a piece of overnight news that triggered the sell orders originally.

The news concerned the accounting treatment of some "special" or "extraordinary" items in the company's financial statements. The U.S.I. episode, along with others recently, suggests that stockholders are often uncertain what to make of such items.

Special items are those relatively large gains, losses, charges, or credits that derive from some untypical opera-

Reprinted from the August, 1964, issue of *Fortune* Magazine by special permission; © 1964 Time, Inc.

tion and are therefore set apart in some way on the financial statements. Accountants have always had two schools of thought on this subject. One school maintains that, while these items of profit and loss may indeed be "special," they are nevertheless important; accordingly, they deserve maximum exposure and should be carried on the income statement, to be reflected in the net income or loss for the year. The other school holds that such a procedure misleads stockholders as to the true operating results and earning power of the business; therefore, they say, most special items should be carried on the statement of retained earnings, or surplus.

For investors, this professional disagreement has meant a lack of comparability between reports of different companies, and sometimes even between successive reports of the same company. For example, in its 1962 annual report Colorado Fuel & Iron showed on its income statement a special item of $3,882,000 for "loss in connection with closing of plants." In 1963 the company suffered exactly the same kind of loss—but this time for a whopping $26,428,000. And this time the loss was shown on the retained-earnings statement. Recently the treasurer of Colorado Fuel was asked where he would put a $3-million or $4-million loss if one were again incurred this year; he said he probably would put it back on the income statement. Accepted accounting practice permits this kind of inconsistency (although Colorado Fuel's auditor felt obliged to call attention to it).

A Push from Washington

Both the SEC and the New York Stock Exchange have been increasingly disturbed about the wide latitude allowed companies in handling special items, and have tried hard to get the accounting profession to put more special items on the income statements. The SEC has also induced the American Institute of Certified Public Accountants to undertake a study that will ascertain whether, as the commission suspects, more and more companies are simply choosing whichever method makes their income statements look better—i.e., they are putting special *credits* on the income statement and special *charges* on the surplus statement. The study will be completed this fall, and the institute's Accounting Principles Board has agreed that, if the SEC turns out to be right, the rules must be clarified so as to give companies less latitude.

In the meantime the SEC has already adopted a rule that seems likely to exert a corrective influence. This rule requires that when

Statements of Consolidated Income

U.S. INDUSTRIES, INC. AND CONSOLIDATED SUBSIDIARIES Years Ended December 31, 1963 and 1962			U.S. INDUSTRIES, INC. AND CONSOLIDATED SUBSIDIARIES Year Ended December 31, 1963	
	1963	1962 (Note D)	Statement of Consolidated Income	
Income:			Income:	
Net sales	$95,963,076	$97,423,983	Net sales	$95,963,076
Other income	1,178,604	1,086,625	Other income	1,178,604
	$97,141,680	$98,510,608		$97,141,680
Deductions:			Deductions:	
Cost of products sold	$74,051,772	$76,808,632	Cost of products sold	$74,051,772
Depreciation and amortization of properties	1,476,827	1,517,258	Depreciation and amortization of properties	1,476,827
Selling, administrative, and general expenses	16,502,419	15,589,547	Selling, administrative, and general expenses	16,502,419
Interest	2,064,976	1,600,039	Interest	2,064,976
Miscellaneous	541,841	473,015	Miscellaneous	541,841
Income taxes (principally foreign)—Note D.	687,573	806,272	Income taxes (principally foreign)—Note D	687,573
	$95,325,408	$96,794,763		$95,325,408

there are material differences between the accounting principles and practices used in a published annual report and those used in the official 10-K report to the SEC, these differences must be explained or reconciled. Since the 10-K rules require that practically *all* special items must go on the income statement, it would appear that any annual report carrying these items in the surplus statement must also carry some sort of reconciliation. The probable effect of the SEC rule will be to encourage a trend toward making the annual report conform more closely to 10-K standards in the first place.

The background of the U.S. Industries case is itself an argument

U.S. INDUSTRIES, INC. AND CONSOLIDATED SUBSIDIARIES Years Ended December 31, 1963 and 1962			U.S. INDUSTRIES, INC. AND CONSOLIDATED SUBSIDIARIES Year Ended December 31, 1963	
Net Income— exclusive of items charged to earnings retained in the business—			Net Income— before Separate Charge	
			below	$ 1,816,272
			Separate Charge incident to products and operations discontinued or to be discontinued, etc.—	
Note H	$ 1,816,272	$ 1,715,845	Note H	7,269,106
			Net Loss (after Separate Charge)	$5,452,834

After the New York Stock Exchange forced U.S. Industries to make its published 1963 financial statements (left) acceptable to the company's auditor, there was a considerable change at the bottom of the income statement: instead of a $1,816,272 profit, the revised figures (right) showed a $5,452,834 loss.

for conformity in accounting. The company's annual report, which appeared in late March, had two interesting items. The first, at the bottom of the income statement, was a line reading, "Net Income—exclusive of items charged to earnings retained in the business" (see statement above). The second interesting feature of the report was an "excepted" auditor's certificate from Ernst & Ernst, indicating that the firm felt the treatment of those "items" to be improper.

It was astonishing that this report had ever got into print at all, since it obviously collided head on with a long-standing New York Stock Exchange policy prohibiting "excepted" reports. Within days after the report had appeared, the Exchange had sternly told U.S. Industries to come up with a financial statement that the auditor would approve.

U.S.I. executives say they were surprised and shocked by the Exchange's demands, and they have argued strenuously that the company was victimized by the accounting profession's indecisiveness. The methods it had used to report its special items, U.S.I. argued, conformed to "generally accepted accounting principles," even if Ernst & Ernst believed otherwise; other equally reputable auditors, the company held, might even have found the company's procedures to be preferable to those advocated by Ernst & Ernst.

The Stock Exchange replied that it was taking no position itself as to the propriety of U.S.I.'s accounting methods, and that it did not matter in the least what any other accounting firm thought. What did matter, the Exchange said, was that Ernst & Ernst was the company's accountant and that it had found the statements unsatisfactory.

The "Cleanup"

The Exchange, of course, prevailed. If U.S. Industries had refused to make the changes, its stock would probably have been delisted. On April 13, U.S.I. sent to its stockholders a four-page report by John I. Snyder, Jr., chairman and president, referring to the discussions with the Exchange. "As a result of such discussions," Snyder said, "the company has elected to adopt the treatment recommended by our accountants." His statement was followed by three pages of amended financial statements and a new, "clean" auditor's certificate. It was the first time in at least two decades that the Stock Exchange had forced a company to make major changes in its published annual report.

There were two big changes in the new financial statements. The first involved a credit of $6,750,000, originally added to retained earnings and attributable to a gain realized on the sale of certain facilities, which were subsequently leased back. Ernst & Ernst had maintained that this credit should not be taken in a lump sum at all, but should be spread over the ten-year life of the lease. On the amended statements the credit disappeared from retained earnings, appearing instead as a deferred credit on the balance sheet; the effect was to wipe out the company's retained earnings, leaving a deficit of $5,643,000.

The second change seems to have caused the company even more anguish. It involved the disposition of a charge of $7,269,000 for "losses incident to products and operations discontinued or to be discontinued, etc." This charge too had originally shown up in the retained earnings statement, and Ernst & Ernst contended it did not belong there either. In the amended report the charge was shifted to the income statement. The effect was to change sharply the "bottom line" from the previously reported net income of $1,816,272 to a "Net Loss (after Separate Charge)" of $5,452,834.

A Peculiar Position

Two points about this case are worth noting. One is that the *location* of U.S.I.'s special charge of $7,269,000 seems to have made a difference to investors. Many seem to have read the news to mean that the company had been forced to acknowledge a loss that had not previously shown up on its books. In reality, of course, the loss had been there all the time and had merely shifted its position.

The second point is the peculiarity of the Stock Exchange's stance in such accounting controversies. The Exchange is in the position of forcing from its companies strict compliance to the rules of auditors, even though it admits auditors cannot agree on the rules. The Exchange's central difficulty is that, in taking action, it was in effect saying that it believed the auditor to be right in withholding approval. What, then, if U.S.I. turns out to have been right in arguing that some other auditor might have found the company's accounts to be perfectly acceptable? Suppose, in fact, that U.S.I. were now to change auditors, were to charge off on its 1964 retained earnings statement the same kind of losses on discontinued operations that it had in 1963, and were this time given a "clean" certificate by its new auditor. Presumably the company's accounts would then be considered satisfactory by the Exchange.

Could such a scenario actually develop? It appears possible. To be sure, the American Institute of Certified Public Accountants' guidelines, laid down in a 1953 research bulletin,* seem to indicate that Ernst & Ernst was correct in insisting that the special charge had to go on the income statement. However, a look at the financial statements of some other companies suggests that not all auditors have been interpreting the guidelines in the same way.

Drawing the Line

In any event, the background of the U.S.I. case suggests that there is room for argument within the guidelines. In the years before 1963, U.S.I. had accumulated considerable experience in charging off huge amounts in its surplus statement. From 1960 through 1962 these charges —none of which were reflected in the income statements—totaled $18,112,000, while reported net income totaled $5,418,000. These ac-

* EDITORS' NOTE: Reference is to *Accounting Research and Terminology Bulletins Final Edition* (New York: American Institute of Certified Public Accountants, 1961), p. 63.

counting practices were passed by Ernst & Ernst, although the firm has always been a strong believer in the all-inclusive income statement and, privately, may well have objected to U.S.I.'s method of presenting the figures.

When the 1963 special charge came up for consideration, however, Ernst & Ernst drew the line. This charge, the firm noted, included losses on *operations* of divisions the company had discontinued or was planning to discontinue. And the institute's bulletin says plainly that the only kinds of items that can legitimately be excluded from the determination of *net income* are those which are "material" and which "are clearly not identifiable with or do not result from the usual or typical business operations of the period." Examples of such items, the bulletin says, would include adjustments of taxes for prior years, write-offs of intangibles, losses on such calamities as wars, riots, and earth-quakes, and profits or losses on the sale of assets.

But the management of U.S.I. can point to the financial statements of several other companies that, with their auditor's approval, are charging losses on discontinued operations to retained earnings. One such is A. O. Smith Corp. Its 1963 report shows a $3,900,000 charge to retained earnings for "costs related to discontinuance of Process Equipment business." Of this amount, $1,081,643 was for operating losses and expenses sustained in 1963, after the decision to discontinue the business was made, the remainder for losses expected to be incurred before the business is completely phased out.

Profits in Milwaukee

The inclusion of even the 1963 losses in the 1963 income statement would have dropped profits below those for 1962; as it was, profits were up. A. O. Smith's auditor is Arthur Young & Co.; it gave the company's 1963 statement a clean certificate.

In determining how it would handle its special charge, furthermore, A. O. Smith took note of the example set by another Milwaukee company, Allis-Chalmers. In 1962, A-C had shown a profit of $6,478,000 —not including, however, an extraordinary charge of $20,850,000 to retained earnings for "discontinuing certain products and facilities." Of this amount, about $500,000 was for costs and expenses incurred in 1962 and $16,810,000 was for costs and expenses expected to be incurred as the company completed its sales order backlog (the remaining $3,500,000 was for anticipated losses on disposal facilities). None of these expenses, of course, will ever get onto the income statement. Allis-

Chalmers' auditor, Price, Waterhouse & Co., gave the 1962 financial statements a clean certificate.

Both Arthur Young and Price, Waterhouse say that they believe the matter of timing in these cases is important. They point out that the only operating losses they allowed to be charged to retained earnings were those incurred *after* a decision to discontinue a business had been made. But from a stockholder's point of view it is hard to see that this argument is relevant—i.e., to the question of where the special charges should properly be placed on the statement.*

QUESTIONS

1. How is materiality relevant to the accounting treatment of some "special" or "extraordinary" items on the income statement according to the AICPA?

2. What evidence exists that investors do regard the location of a special item as significant?

3. In view of (2), is it possible to argue that the location of a special item is really part of a more general issue, namely, to what extent is an accountant responsible for preparing analysis beyond that of presenting information? State your position.

* EDITORS' NOTE: Since 1947, the American Institute of Certified Public Accountants publishes annually details of how 600 companies have prepared public financial statements. In its survey of corporate annual reports for 1964, it notes that 252 extraordinary items, such as large and unusual sales of assets, were disclosed by 187 companies. Of these, 152 were treated in the income account, including footnotes, and 100 in the retained earnings account.

28

The Accounting Unit

H. S. Hendrickson and T. J. Burns

BROADLY CONCEIVED, accounting includes all areas where the accumulation, reporting, and analysis of financial data are significant factors. However, not everyone, not even every accountant, appreciates that the complete array of accounting units logically extends from those of the individual or household to those of international organizations and includes eleemosynary institutions, "non-profit" enterprises, and the many governmental units and agencies. Somewhere within this range are the so-called private business enterprises which are usually classified as either a sole proprietorship, a partnership, or a corporation.

Special permission to publish was granted by the authors. The authors, the editors of this book, are, respectively, Assistant Professor of Accounting and Management Science at the State University of New York and Associate Professor of Accounting at the Ohio State University.

VARIOUS CONCEPTS OF THE ACCOUNTING UNIT
FOR THE BUSINESS ENTERPRISE

Regardless of whether it is a corporation, a partnership, or a sole proprietorship the business enterprise is viewed by the accountant as a distinct unit with its activities and affairs reflected in a set of accounts that are separate from those of its owners.

This distinction is widely accepted and usually creates no serious difficulties. Beyond this, however, the corporation in particular poses some additional, interesting problems for the accountant because of the many ways in which he might define the unit on which he should focus his attention. Should he be concerned with the institution itself which was formed under the laws of the state—the legal unit (or entity)? Should he concentrate on one or more of the various internal groups (cost or profit centers, branches, departments, divisions) which are often very important to the corporate enterprise and its management? Or, should he center his attention on a group of two or more interrelated corporations—separate, legal units which may form an economic unit?

The accountant must consider the corporation's responsibility for providing status and performance reports to owners, creditors, income tax authorities, and other interested parties. For these external reports, the legal concept of the corporation is relevant, but it is not necessarily the most important accounting unit.

On the other hand, when considering the needs of management in planning, organizing, and controlling the activities of the business enterprise the legal unit may be of little relevance. Instead, the accountant must study the various internal groups and their interrelationships to determine the combination of accounting units which will best aid management in attaining its goals. The set might include a hierarchy of accounting units with the basic one being a very small area of individual responsibility—a cost or profit center—which in turn is combined with other areas into a larger unit such as a branch, department, or division, one or more of which in turn will be combined to form the entire enterprise.

Occasionally, one reads that a single unit (such as a division) of a multi-unit corporation has been organized into a separate corporation, or that two or more separate corporations are operated as divisions or departments of another corporation. Thus, for many purposes an accounting unit which is the separate, legal unit may be less meaningful or useful than one which is based on the economic unity of a group of associated corporations—for which consolidated statements may be prepared.

One need not conduct an extensive survey of the annual reports of large corporations to discover the dominant role of consolidated statements. Such statements minimize the legal distinctions and emphasize the essential economic unity of the group of companies—which means that the group should be centrally controlled and have closely integrated operations. Thus, financial reports for such managerial groups are prepared as if the companies were united in a legal as well as an economic sense.[1] This position has been so widely accepted that sometimes such statements are prepared for groups which are not economic units.

This was not always the case. A story is told of a company which several decades ago prepared only parent company statements. Anyone seeking information regarding any of its *eight hundred* subsidiaries was invited to inspect the annual reports of these companies in a room where they were used as wallpaper. This situation, as contrasted to current practices, indicates that the concept of the corporation as applied by the accountant to integrated groups of business corporations appears to have evolved from a legal-oriented unit to an economic-oriented one.

Accounting practice, however, occasionally fails to include all parts of an economic unit in the consolidated group. Examples of this can be found in the automobile industry where the manufacturing company has organized a subsidiary company to handle the financing of its receivables and then has failed to include the subsidiary in its consolidated statements.

Thus the appropriate accounting units for internal, managerial purposes could be a cost or profit center, a division, a branch, a department, or some combination of these; and for external reporting purposes it might be the legal, or a combination of legal entities, namely, the economic unit.

ENTITY VIEWPOINT AND THE
INTERPRETATION OF NET INCOME

After selecting the appropriate accounting unit(s) for external reporting, the problem remains of selecting the appropriate viewpoint(s) from which the entity might be viewed in interpreting

[1] For example, see Maurice Moonitz, *The Entity Theory of Consolidated Statements* (Brooklyn: Foundation Press, 1951).

its net income. The problem is one of distinguishing between the determinants of net income (expenses) and the distributions of net income. The major items which might change from one classification to the other as the viewpoint is changed are interest charges, income taxes, and cash (or property) dividends declared on preferred and common stock.

Probably there are as many viewpoints of the entity as there are kinds of entities. These are classified in various ways and reflect various stages of entity and social development. Some of these have been identified or defined fairly carefully; others are yet to be developed or recognized as the nature of accounting units evolves.

The accounting unit (or corporation) is generally considered to be an entity or institution in its own right and has been viewed variously as a fictitious legal person, a creature of the state, or a real legal unit.[2] From this viewpoint interest charges, income taxes, and dividends declared are expenses—costs incurred to permit continuance in business (income taxes) or to compensate for the furnishing of services to the entity (the use of debt and equity capital in the case of interest charges and dividends).

From the most popular viewpoint of the unit (or corporation) as a separate and distinct entity operating for the benefit of the owner equity (the preferred and common stockholders), interest charges and income taxes are expenses, but dividends are a voluntary (or contractual) distribution of income to preferred and common stockholders.[3]

From the viewpoint of the unit as a separate and distinct entity operating for the benefit of all long-term equity, only income taxes are an expense and both interest charges (contractual obligations to bondholders) and dividends are distributions of income.

It is possible that the unit might also be viewed as operating for the benefit of employees as well as all long-term equity.[4] From this

---

[2] The entity theory of accounting is generally considered to be based upon the legal concept of the corporation. For a further discussion of this and other legal concepts see Robert T. Sprouse, "Legal Concepts of the Corporation," XXXIII, *The Accounting Review*, no. 1, January 1958, pp. 37–49.

[3] This, the basis for the proprietary theory of accounting, is also a legal view of the corporation as being merely an association of individuals (common and preferred stockholders) united for a common purpose and permitted by law to use a common name—for a more extensive discussion of this, see *Ibid.*, pp. 41–44.

[4] This is based on the thesis that employees may have some sort of property right in their jobs and this has some validity when one considers the separation of management from ownership in the large corporation, the extensive development of pension

viewpoint, only income taxes are expenses and employment costs (wages, salaries, and related costs) join interest charges and dividends as distributions of income.

Three other common viewpoints of the unit (which classify income taxes as distributions of income) are those of operating management, the Internal Revenue Service and the general public or society.

For operating management, interest charges, income taxes, and dividends become distributions of income. Policy-making management (the board of directors) and the tax authorities (or government levying the tax) would tend to have prior authority for these items; thus, the ideas of responsibility accounting dictate that these items should not be deducted from an income figure which is to be used in evaluating the operating managers.[5]

For the Internal Revenue Service, following its income tax laws would result in the classification of interest charges as expenses and income taxes and dividends as distributions of income.

For the general public or society, the viewpoint follows from the social objectives expressed for many units (or corporations) such as growth, development, and survival in the interests of society. It would be difficult or impossible to measure and record these social conscience considerations in the accounts of an entity—one usually reads of these only in the "President's Letter" of corporate annual reports—nevertheless, a socially responsible institution would imply that the stewardship should be to the general public. Under this viewpoint, interest charges and dividends are expenses and income taxes (assuming that the tax incidence is not shifted) are a distribution of income to society through the medium of the federal and state governments. This position can be most successfully defended on the grounds that society benefits from governmental activity; that the corporation exists to furnish products at cost (total costs as defined by the economist); and that income taxes are merely a substitute for government regulation (as in the case of public utility companies) and, therefore, are a distribution of income to society through its agents, the federal and state governments.

The seven viewpoints presented are summarized below:

---

funds and other employee benefit plans, and the seniority and related security clauses of most employment contracts.

[5] For an extended discussion of this viewpoint, see Mason, Davidson and Schindler, *Fundamentals of Accounting*, Fourth Edition (New York: Holt, Rinehart and Winston, Inc., 1959), pp. 281–291.

	WAGES		INTEREST		INCOME TAXES		DIVIDENDS	
	EXP.	DISTR.	EXP.	DISTR.	EXP.	DISTR.	EXP.	DISTR.
1. Entity	x		x		x		x	
2. Proprietary	x		x		x			x
3. Long-term equity	x			x	x			x
4. Employees & Long-term Equity		x		x	x			x
5. Operating Management	x			x		x		x
6. Internal Revenue	x		x			x		x
7. Social	x		x			x	x	

OTHER ENTITY IDEAS

Still another aspect of the problem is one of determining whether accounting costs are associated with a particular asset, with a particular accounting unit, or with an entity which may consist of many units. Examples of such systems are those prescribed by the Federal Power Commission (regulating interstate aspects of electric and gas utility firms) and the Federal Communications Commission (regulating interstate aspects of radio, telephone, telegraph, and television firms) which define *"original cost"* of an asset as the cost "to the person first devoting it to public service." This unusual concept (of a timeless social institution) when applied to property acquired by one utility from another conflicts with the basic valuation idea of accounting that cost is measured by the amount of cash or equivalent (the fair market value of non-cash items) given or to be given in exchange by the present, acquiring accounting unit.

Procedures such as this magnify rather than reduce the inherent limitations of accounting by requiring the use of old, irrelevant costs in the accounts rather than more meaningful current costs. In addition, these procedures ignore the economic aspects of accounting costs and units—which may vary not only with place, form, and circumstance, but also with time.

The problem of the accounting unit is also highlighted in those changes in corporate structure which involve the transfer of property from one corporation to another as in the case of consolidations and mergers. In some situations it is impossible for the accountant to differentiate sharply between significant and merely nominal changes in the corporate entity. For example, the accounting tests used to distinguish a purchase (of one or more corporations by another) from a pooling of interests (of two or more corporations) are not sufficiently well defined to properly evaluate whether a change is merely in the legal form or whether it is an economic, substantive one.

In conclusion, one must have a concept of society before one can conclusively arrive at a concept of an accounting unit—and as concepts of society change, so do concepts of the corporation, of accounting, and of costs. The Ford Motor Company of Henry Ford was not the same one as that of Henry Ford II, especially when the Ford Foundation is brought into consideration. Similarly, one must recognize that we should not expect to have a single concept of the accounting unit which can be adjusted to fit perfectly the many purposes of the diverse private, semi-private, and public agencies and institutions. However, this should not be construed as an excuse for not attempting to improve accounting unit concepts in both theory and practice.

QUESTIONS

1. If a company has period revenues of $1 million, period wages of $500,000, period interest charges of $150,000, period income taxes of $125,000 and period dividends declared of $110,000, compute the company's period net income from seven different viewpoints.

2. Which of these viewpoints, in your judgment, is least useful from an accounting standpoint and why?

3. In his book *The Securities Markets,* Professor Sidney Robbins of Columbia's Graduate School of Business notes that "the lawyer is more concerned with standards of conduct of the participants in an industry; the economist with the economic impact of their actions." What is the concern of the accountant?

6

Accounting Principles

29

Some Critical Areas in the Development of Accounting Principles

Maurice Moonitz

CONFLICT OVER THE NATURE OF THE INCOME CONCEPT

ACCORDING TO ONE GROUP, as exemplified in the writings of George O. May, income is an economic and political concept. According to another group, as exemplified by R. H. Montgomery, income is a business and accounting concept. As an immediate consequence of this difference in views as

From *The Florida CPA,* vol. 3, no. 11 (November, 1963), pp. 15–21. Reprinted by permission of the publisher. Mr. Moonitz is Professor of Accounting at the University of California (Berkeley) and a former Director of Research for the American Institute of Certified Public Accountants.

to the nature of income, we find a related conflict over the source of authority for whatever principles are set forth. For example, the group represented by Mr. May would and has taken the position that accounting principles should be determined in cooperation with those who use accounting reports and financial statements. The group represented by Mr. Montgomery, on the other hand, asserts that accounting principles should be determined by accountants on behalf of the business community.

As examples of what they have in mind, the proponents of the first view or position, point to the success of two or three projects. The first of these was the preparation in 1917 by the American Institute of Accountants at the request of the Federal Trade Commission of "A Memorandum on Balance Sheet Audits," which the Commission approved and transmitted to the Federal Reserve Board for its consideration. The Federal Board published it in the *Federal Reserve Bulletin* of April, 1917. Reprints of this memorandum were widely disseminated under the name of "Uniform Accounting: A Tentative Proposal Submitted by the Federal Reserve Board." In 1918, it was reissued under the same sponsorship with very little change but under the title "Approved Methods for the Presentation of Balance Sheet Statements." A decade or so later, in 1929, the American Institute of Accountants undertook the revision of this earlier pamphlet and, with the experience gained during the intervening ten years, issued a considerably improved booklet called "Verification of Financial Statements," again under the auspices of the Federal Reserve Board. The significance of this particular project for our purposes is that the accountants served simply as technical experts to supply the commercial bankers with a set of standards which the bankers themselves then imposed upon applicants for loans.

Another example of this type of sponsorship occurred in 1932 when a special committee on cooperation with stock exchanges was set up by the American Institute of Accountants. This committee entered into correspondence with the New York Stock Exchange. The exchange of views resulted in the promulgation of five principles of accounting, dealing with the treatment of unrealized profit, capital surplus, earned surplus of subsidiaries prior to acquisition, treasury stock, and notes and accounts receivable due to officers, employees, and other affiliates. Again we can see the same pattern as before, namely, that the accountants served as technical experts assisting the stock exchange in forming a group of principles which were then enforced, in effect, by the stock exchange, standing as representatives of investors in stocks and bonds. A final example of this type of co-operative effort is found in the deliberations of the Study Group on Business Income which issued its report in 1951 under the title "Changing Concepts of Business Income." The Study Group was composed of representatives drawn from business, Government, and labor, and included professional accountants, economists, and lawyers. The findings and recommendations of the Study Group never attained the same acceptance accorded those of the Federal Reserve Board and the New York Stock Exchange in the earlier examples, but the effort of the Study Group is still illustrative of the point being made here.

With respect to the other attitude, namely, that accounting principles should be determined by accountants on behalf of the business community, the principal exhibit is the committee on accounting procedure, formed in 1938 and terminated in 1959 when the new research program of the Institute went into effect and the Accounting Principles Board was created. This committee on accounting procedure, as we all know, issued a series of accounting research bulletins, some 51 in all, many of which have served as guidelines and standards for accountants and businessmen in the preparation of their financial statements. The committee was composed entirely of members of the Institute. Its recommendations were never submitted to other groups for formal adoption. One result of this pattern of operation was the widespread adoption of some of the committee's recommendations and the ignoring of others.

THE SELECTION OF THE
PRINCIPLES OF ACCOUNTING

Who is to determine what principle or principles of accounting are applicable in a given concrete business situation? In the English-speaking world, the dominant point of view certainly is that expressed in the British legislation on company law and company accounting. This view stems from the widely accepted notion that the financial statements are the primary responsibility of the management of the business issuing the statements and that as a corollary each management should be free to choose those principles, standards, rules and procedures of accounting which best serve its needs in issuing fair and complete financial statements reporting on the results of its operations and its financial position. A further requirement under this view is that each company must disclose what principles it is following, and must follow them consistently. As a result, the function of the independent accountant is rather clearly defined. He determines whether or not the company is in fact following the principles which it announces it is following and the accountant then reports his findings to the reader of the financial statements.

In the United States, this particular point of view was not adopted in its literal form because it was pointed out that to do so would leave business management with too much discretion to pick its own accounting principles. This attitude led to the adoption of the notion of a range of accepted principles, within which management would be free to choose those principles applicable to its own situation. This approach is summed up in the standard phrase used in this country: "generally accepted accounting principles."

A contrary view has gained some adherents in recent years. Under this contrary view it is the function of the accountant as an independent technical specialist to determine what the appropriate principles are in specific circumstances. Management should have no discretion at this level. In other words, management should manage and the accountant should determine what the results are and express his findings in terms of the results of operations and the financial position of the company. Under this view, the concept of "generally accepted accounting principles" loses its relevance and a different conception, such as "sound accounting principles," takes its place.

ARE ACCOUNTING PRINCIPLES THE SAME FOR ALL TYPES OF ENTERPRISES?

Specifically, are accounting principles the same in the case of regulated companies, such as the electric and gas utilities, as they are in the case of nonregulated companies, such as manufacturing or retailing generally? A similar question relates to the nonprofit areas. One other phase of the broad question is whether or not accounting principles applicable to listed companies (that is, those whose shares are widely held) are the same as the principles applicable to private or closely held companies. The answers to these questions depend upon a fairly precise definition of what we mean by "principles." If the term is used in a broad sense to encompass such things as accrual accounting or financial statements couched in monetary terms, then principles such as these are applicable to all of these areas without distinction. If, on the other hand, "principles" refers perhaps to rules to fit specific concrete situations, then some differences are to be expected. In general, I hold to the belief that broad principles, properly conceived, must be relevant to all economic units of the type under discussion. To this end, we need to pay close attention to the identification and statement of these basic propositions, somewhat along the lines of the American Institute of Certified Public Accountants' research studies No. 1 and No. 3 on basic postulates and broad principles.* In terms of expediting developments in particular areas, however, it might be wise at the same time to accelerate the formulation of sets of rules specific to particular specialized areas such as hospitals, electric utilities, or companies with widely held capital stock. These sets of specific rules would highlight the issues that are common to more than one area and those that are different. At the same time their relationship to the broad principles could be delineated. Any contradictions or inconsistencies among these specialized sets of rules would have to be ironed out and eliminated, but ultimately we would emerge with a set of broad principles applicable across the board.

LACK OF COMMON BACKGROUND OF ACCOUNTANTS

One of the major difficulties standing in the way of a more rapid development of accounting principles is the heterogeneous background of the members of the accounting profession. The profession is clearly not unified in this respect. The key issue here is one of communication. It is extraordinarily difficult to know at what level to pitch a particular analysis or a particular report. Many of the members of the accounting profession know the requirements of a logical method of analysis and can follow, appreciate, and react critically to highly sophisticated studies. Others, however, have learned their skills mainly by experience of a specialized and limited type and do not find it easy to absorb a sophisticated discussion. As a result, anyone who tries to formulate a set of postulates or principles must reconcile himself to the fact that he is not going to be able to communicate effectively with a large segment of the audience that ought to be listening to him and reacting critically to what he has to say. As the years go by, how-

* EDITORS' NOTE: The monograph on postulates, "The Basic Postulates of Accounting" by Maurice Moonitz, was published as Accounting Research Study No. 1 in 1961 by the AICPA. The monograph on principles, "A Tentative Set of Broad Accounting Principles" by Robert T. Sprouse and Maurice Moonitz, was published as Accounting Research Study No. 3 in 1962. In a statement issued April 13, 1962, the AICPA Accounting Principles Board commissioned its new research director, Mr. Paul Grady, to prepare an "Inventory of Generally Accepted Accounting Principles for Business Enterprises" in June, 1963. This 469 page monograph was issued as Accounting Research Study No. 7 in March, 1965.

ever, this problem will undoubtedly become less difficult because of
(a) increasing educational requirements for entrance to the profession,
(b) improvement in education at the collegiate level, especially in
schools of business, and (c) a sustained effort on the part of the profession to describe the "common body of knowledge" that all certified
public accountants should possess.

NEED FOR RESEARCH ON ACCOUNTING MEASUREMENTS

How accurate are the estimates that are actually made in connection with accounting data and financial reports? In a cost or market
adjustment, for example, were the market prices subsequently realized
equal to, greater than, or less than the estimates used in making the
writedown? In depreciation calculations, were the estimated lives used
equal to, greater than, or less than the actual experienced lives for
major items or major classes of property? Financial ratios of various
types are used to measure certain qualities of a business. How good a
predicter are these ratios in specific cases? Why were they good or bad
predicters in specific instances?

How can we measure the investment (asset) in research and
development costs, in goodwill, or in other types of intangibles? What
about the accretion of timber or other kinds of natural resources
where growth is a factor? What about the whole problem of appreciation of plant and equipment? Here is a vast area where investigation
and research in accounting has for all practical purposes been at a
standstill for many years. The reason probably lies in the fact that
several decades ago accountants decided that some current practices
in these areas were not satisfactory and that, accordingly, we should
not classify research and development costs or other similar outlays as
assets. Instead these types of costs were and are usually charged off as
incurred. We also inhibited or stopped development with respect to
cases such as the accretion of a stand of timber by simply denying that
accretion had any status in financial reporting. A similar situation
exists with respect to appreciation in the value or market price of
plant and equipment generally. In an important sense, accountants
came to a decision much too quickly. As a result of the decisions
reached, either to ignore these events altogether or to deny them
recognition as assets, practically no one bothered to push inquiries
further into these most intriguing and exceptionally important areas.
We now have numerous cases where these "non-assets" constitute the
most important resources of the enterprise.

INFLUENCE OF INCOME TAXES
ON ACCOUNTING PRINCIPLES

The reference here is not to the influence of taxes on the financial statements themselves. I am not at this point and in this place concerned with the problem of tax allocation or deferred tax accounting, important as that subject is, nor am I concerned with the situations in which the tax rules tell us explicitly to treat an item in one way and business accounting tells us, just as explicitly, to treat the same item in another way. These items, and other similar ones, are of importance but they do not pose a new and continuing influence on accounting principles. I have in mind the interaction between tax rules on the one hand and the development or formation of accounting principles on the other. This interaction was clearly evident in the adoption of the last-in, first-out method of inventory pricing. In this case, certain provisions of the Internal Revenue Code were used as the basis for an accounting dictum that LIFO is a cost method when in fact it is no such thing, and would be virtually nonexistent in practice, if the Internal Revenue Code were amended slightly. It has also been evident in the accounting dictum that the costs of pension plans are being accounted for on the accrual basis in financial statements when in fact they are on a cash-outlay basis to conform to the tax requirements for qualifying a pension plan for optimum tax benefits. As a further example, the emergence of a distinction between a pooling and purchase in accounting for the merger of two or more companies is closely related to a conflict between accounting principles with respects to the proper basis for property accounting and the tax rules for dealing with the same property in so-called "tax-free" exchanges. These three cases are the more obvious ones. There may be others that are more subtle and therefore more difficult to detect. I do not wish to leave the impression that I believe that this interaction between tax and business accounting is necessarily bad and always leads to undesirable results. Certainly the income tax laws have aided immeasurably in raising the level of accounting and the adequacy of accounting records; the acceptance of ideas such as depreciation accounting and the need for appropriately classified expense and revenue data has been speeded up by the requirements of tax law. What I do want to leave is the impression that accountants have lost the initiative to the U.S. Treasury and to Congress in several important areas in the formation of certain accounting principles, whether those principles are good, bad, or indifferent in and of themselves. But as long as tax rates remain at high levels, this interaction will continue, and accountants may lose the initiative even more in the future.

NEW FORMS OF FINANCIAL STATEMENTS

There has been a persistent questioning of traditional forms of financial statements in recent years on the grounds that these forms prove inadequate in many situations. Among some of the manifestations of this trend, I refer you to the development of the so-called "New look" in financial reporting which stems from the immediate postwar period. In this revised form, the balance sheet is rearranged to show current assets minus current liabilities, with a subtotal for net working capital. After the subtotal, noncurrent assets are added and noncurrent liabilities deducted to arrive at a figure for stockholders equity. Immediately below this total figure the details of stockholders equity are given, frequently preceded by a caption such as "represented by."

Another manifestation of this trend is the increasing reference and inclusion in financial reports of a statement of source and application of funds. There is a tendency to minimize the importance of these funds statements, but their significance is great. They represent the first breach in the professional accountant's preoccupation with income measurement as the basis for financial reporting. More recently we have had the introduction of a concept known as "cash flow" which in and of itself is probably mischievous, but does reflect a certain underlying deep dissatisfaction with conventional reporting forms.

Also in the picture, but probably not as widely known, are the forms prescribed by the Securities and Exchange Commission in Article 5a of Regulation SX, "Commercial, Industrial, and Mining Companies in the Promotional, Exploratory, or Developmental Stage." To companies of this type, the Securities and Exchange Commission says, in effect— Do not file a balance sheet and an income statement but, instead, file five separate statements, as follows:

1. Assets and unrecovered promotional, exploratory, and development costs;
2. Liabilities;
3. Capital shares;

4. Other securities;

5. Cash receipts and disbursements.

As we can see, the SEC takes the sensible position that companies in this situation are in no position to prepare a statement of financial position that is at all meaningful or a statement of results of operations in the form of a conventional income statement. These companies can, however, supply a considerable amount of other information which would be useful in assessing their status. I have also recently heard suggestions for a fragmented kind of balance sheet for companies which are past the exploratory or developmental stage. These suggestions arise mainly out of the notorious difficulties of getting reliable figures as a basis for including plant and equipment in present-day balance sheets. As a consequence, a statement of current assets and current liabilities, and changes therein, would be given special prominence. To them would be appended "statements of unrecovered costs" with respect to the fixed assets generally. Other data of a purely financial nature, such as the existence of long-term debt, and of preferred and of common stock, would also be provided.

One fairly recent development, namely, the rapid emergence of private pension plans on a large scale, has raised the question whether the conventional balance sheet is capable of conveying all of the information that is necessary to a proper portrayal of financial position. What is happening in this area is that employees are building up an equity in the business, along with or coordinate with the equities of the creditors, of the stockholders, and of the Government. As usually occurs, the developments in the economic and social fields come first; then after a period of time the financial forms begin to adapt to the changed circumstances.

WHO SHOULD FORMULATE "ACCOUNTING PRINCIPLES"?

Within the framework of the American Institute of CPAs, statements on accounting principles have come from committees, principally from the committee on accounting procedure, and in the future from the Accounting Principles Board. These bodies are, however, concerned more with policy prescriptions than they are with principles in the strict sense. It is even questionable whether the committee on accounting procedure was actually concerned with "principles." At least at its inception, there is evidence to indicate that the founders had in mind the formulation of specific rules for application in well-defined cases. This, you will note, is a fairly satisfactory explanation of why the committee was called a committee on accounting *procedure* and not a committee on accounting *principles*. Incidentally, the Institute did have a committee on accounting principles in the 1930's under the chairmanship of George O. May, but in the late 1930's, during the administration of R. H. Montgomery, this committee's name was changed to the committee on accounting procedure and reconstituted in its function.

The American Accounting Association has also used the committee route. Over the years since 1936 its statements of principles or of standards have been prepared and presented by the Executive Committee or by the Committee on Concepts and Standards.

Both the Institute and the American Accounting Association have sponsored statements of principles by individuals. The Institute, working through the Haskins & Sells Foundation published the Sanders, Hatfield, and Moore "Statement of Accounting Principles" in the late thirties. More recently, we have the Institute sponsoring and financing within its own organization a Division of Accounting Research which produces studies published, not in the name of a committee or of a board, but in the name of the individuals who actually conducted the research. The American Accounting Association has a monograph series, the most prominent of the items being the Paton and Littleton monograph "An Introduction to Corporate Accounting Standards." More recently, the Financial Executives Institute has been wrestling with the problem of the extent of their responsibility in formulating principles. So far they have not resolved the problem, even to their own satisfaction, but they do know that if they want a voice in formulating principles they will have to participate actively, in brief, become involved, in the whole process of research and committee activity. They will also have to face squarely the hard fact that whatever they do will not be popular with some of their members or with influential groups outside their own ranks.

QUESTIONS

1. What are "principles"?

2. What historical examples do we have of accounting principles established by those who use accounting reports and financial statements?

3. Do we have any evidence of accounting principles determined by accountants on behalf of the business community?

4. What is the distinction between "generally accepted accounting principles" and "sound accounting principles"?

30

Showdown on
Accounting Principles

Robert N. Anthony

WHO WILL DEVELOP accounting principles? One answer to
this question—although an unpalatable one—is: the Securities and Exchange Commission. Unpalatable, yes, but is
it unreasonable? So that the reader may arrive at his own
answer to this question, I am here setting forth the case
that can be made for SEC action. It is, I think, a strong
case. Probably the reader does not relish the thought of
having accounting principles prescribed by a government
agency any more than I do. But this is no time for wishful
thinking. If the danger exists, we should be aware of it,

From *Harvard Business Review,* vol. 41, no. 3 (May–June, 1963), pp.
99–106. Reprinted by permission of the publisher. Mr. Anthony is on
leave as Ross Graham Walker Professor of Management Controls at
Harvard University to serve as an Assistant Secretary of Defense
(Comptroller) under President Johnson.

and with this awareness see to it that steps are taken to prevent this possibility from becoming an actuality.

The argument that accounting principles may end up eventually being prescribed by the SEC rests on two propositions:

1. If the American Institute of Certified Public Accountants fails in its present program for developing accounting principles, the Securities and Exchange Commission will act to develop these principles.

2. The AICPA effort is likely to fail.

Most informed people would agree that in this country there are at present only two bodies capable of formulating a set of accounting principles which can gain general acceptance:

In the *private* sector, there is no organized group comparable to the American Institute of Certified Public Accountants in prestige, in resources, and in ability to obtain general acceptance of its views. (The only other organized private effort in recent years has been that of the American Accounting Association. But the reports of its Committee on Concepts and Standards are regarded at best as statements of long-run objectives, rather than as principles to which the profession is expected to adhere currently. The AAA has almost no financial resources and not one full-time staff member. And because it is dominated by teachers, practitioners tend to suspect the practicality of AAA statements.)

In the *public* sector, the SEC is generally regarded as the agency responsible for matters of financial reporting.

Theoretically, an organization such as the New York Stock Exchange might be a possibility in the private sector. Also, theoretically, common law doctrine as evolved in the courts might be a possibility in the public sector. As a practical matter, however, these possibilities are so remote that we need not discuss them here.

NEED, AUTHORITY, WILL

In order to support the first proposition—that if the AICPA fails, the SEC will take over—one must demonstrate the validity of three statements:

(1) That a *need* for established accounting principles exists.

(2) That the SEC has the *authority* to meet this need.

(3) That the SEC has the *will* to meet the need.

This is the same line of argument used in military strategy where the corresponding breakdown is (1) objectives, (2) capability, and (3) intentions. The principle involved is analogous to the physical principle that nature abhors a vacuum. If a need exists, and if there is an agency with the authority to meet this need and the desire to do so, then it will do so.

Need for Principles

I use the word "principle" in the sense of "a general guide to action." Principles are broad, general statements which serve as guides for solving specific problems; they are not detailed instructions. All accountants abhor the idea that any person or organization should prescribe a detailed manual of rules for handling every type of transaction. No responsible agency would attempt to do this, and the reader should understand that no part of this article is meant to suggest such a possibility.

Currently, a comprehensive, consistent, and generally accepted body of accounting principles does not exist in the United States. This is a flat statement. Many businessmen may find difficulty in accepting it, especially when they read on most auditors' certificates that the certified statements were prepared "in conformity with generally accepted accounting principles." It is, nevertheless, a statement that most professional accountants will support. There are some principles which are followed, but there is no comprehensive, consistent set of principles.

Such a body of principles should consist, first, of a few fundamental concepts. Probably only three concepts are necessary, specifically those dealing with:

The nature of assets and liabilities.
The measurement of assets and liabilities.
Net income.

These three concepts are interrelated, so they must be developed concurrently. Secondly, on this foundation a set of guides must be erected for the solution of more specific accounting problems.

Those who have the impression that an adequate body of principles does exist probably have in mind the series of *Accounting Research Bulletins* and *Accounting Terminology Bulletins* which are issued by the AICPA. But these bulletins contain only fragmentary statements on selected topics, not a coherent set of principles. Scattered throughout these bulletins are some statements that relate to the three fundamental concepts, but they are fuzzy and ambiguous. And the "guides" for many of the specific topics are not very helpful to a person who genuinely asks for guidance. For example:

"Balance sheet" is defined by the tautology, "a list of balances in the asset, liability and net worth accounts."

For inventory valuation, *Accounting Research Bulletin No. 43* permits use of FIFO cost, average cost, or LIFO cost, whichever "most clearly reflects periodic income," but it does not say on what basis someone should decide which of these three methods does, in fact, reflect periodic income in a given set of circumstances.

Perhaps the best indication of the profession's agreement that the present accounting situation is unsatisfactory are the events leading up to the establishment of the AICPA Accounting Principles Board in 1959 and the statements which were made at the time this board was established. The long list of gaps and inconsistencies as well as the absence of standards cited in the article by Carman G. Blough in the *Journal of Accountancy* [1] (and the evidence given in some of Leonard Spacek's articles and addresses [2]) should be enough to convince almost anyone. As Blough, Spacek, and others point out, there are a variety of "equally convincing" opinions and "equally acceptable" practices with respect to accounting for such matters as pension funds, income tax allocation, research and development costs, exploration costs, stock options, mergers, inventory valuation, depreciation, revenue from long-term contracts, stock dividends, installment revenue, treasury stock transactions, bond discount, depreciation methods, and so on.

Comparing the financial status or performance of several companies is an extremely difficult task under the best of circumstances. But when the figures for the several companies are prepared under different ground rules, the task is made even more frustrating. (It should be noted that the problem relates primarily to comparisons between companies since the principle of consistency gives adequate assurance that the data for a single company follow the same principle from one year to another.)

A few people, however, see no need for generally accepted accounting principles. They argue that each management should be free to choose the principles that it thinks are best. In effect, they support

[1] "Challenge to the Accounting Profession in the U.S.," December 1959, p. 37.

[2] "Are Accounting Principles Generally Accepted?" *Journal of Accountancy,* April 1961, p. 41; and *Business Success Requires an Understanding of Unsolved Problems of Accounting and Financial Reporting* (New York, Arthur Andersen & Co., 1959).

Humpty Dumpty's philosophy: "A word . . . means just what I choose it to mean—neither more nor less." This may be appropriate for Wonderland, but it would lead to chaos in the real world.

There are a few others who, although admitting the need for principles, believe that these should "evolve" rather than be decided by an Accounting Principles Board. The nature of this evolutionary process is left vague. Sometimes these people say that the process is analogous to the common law. But when it is pointed out that the foundation of the common law is precedent, that a precedent is binding, and that such a process would therefore sharply reduce management's freedom of choice, they say, "No, that isn't what we mean at all." What they really want is laissez faire which is the antithesis of the litigation, adjudication, and enforced judgments and rulings that are the essence of the common law process.

Laissez faire is not the same as flexibility. Maurice E. Peloubet, who advocates the latter, argues for different treatments when these are justified by differences in the underlying facts of the situations being recorded.[3] This, then, is an argument for flexibility in the *application* of principles, not an argument that denies the desirability of setting principles.

It is certainly conceivable that the gain on the sale of a capital asset under certain circumstances should be credited to net income, and under other circumstances should be credited directly to owners' equity. But this difference in practice should be consistent with some principle which gives a guide to the action that is appropriate. By contrast, the current situation is illustrated by the following example:

General Motors and Standard Oil of New Jersey each recently sold its half ownership in Ethyl Corp. at a book gain of many millions of dollars. GM reported its 50% of the gain as a part of its net income for the year. Standard Oil left net income unaffected, crediting its 50% directly to surplus.

In an art, or at best an inexact science, such as accounting, any generalization, if at all operational (in the sense that it serves as a guide for action), is fraught with dangers—unless it is used wisely. Since a generalization can never specify all the circumstances which govern its application, judgment is called for. Even the pure art of painting has discipline. Although a statement of sound and internally consistent principles suggests the appropriate treatment under a

[3] "Is Further Uniformity Desirable or Possible?" *Journal of Accountancy*, April 1961, p. 35.

given set of circumstances, it does not forbid another treatment under a different set of circumstances.

Ideally, accounting principles should be clear and definite enough so that intelligent, well-informed professionals, when given a description of the facts about a given transaction and the environment in which it occurs, will agree, reasonably closely with one another, as to how the transaction should be recorded. If they differ, it should be because they interpret the facts differently, not because they are applying different principles. This goal is not easily or quickly attainable, but it should *be* the goal, and accountants should be dissatisfied if continued progress is not being made toward it.

SEC's Power

The fact that the SEC already possesses the authority to meet the need in question is perhaps not generally known. It does have this authority, through the Securities Act of 1933, the Securities Exchange Act of 1934, the Public Utility Holding Company Act of 1935, and the Investment Company Act of 1949. Section 19(a) of the Securities Act of 1933 reads:

> The Commission shall have authority from time to time to make, amend, and rescind such rules and regulations governing registration statements and prospectuses for various classes of securities and issuers, and defining accounting, technical, and trade terms used in this title. Among other things, the Commission shall have authority . . . to prescribe the form or forms in which required information shall be set forth, the items or details to be shown in the balance sheet and earning statement, and the methods to be followed in the preparation of accounts, in the appraisal or valuation of assets and liabilities, in the determination of depreciation and depletion, in the differentiation of recurring and nonrecurring income, in the differentiation of investment and operating income, and in the preparation, where the Commission deems it necessary or desirable, of consolidated balance sheets or income accounts. . . .[4]

Similar power is given to the commission over the companies subject to the Public Utility Holding Company Act of 1935. The SEC may prescribe, for companies subject thereto, "uniform methods for keeping accounts . . . , including, among other things, the manner in which the cost of all assets, whenever determinable, shall be shown,

[4] 48 Stat. 85 (1933), as amended, 15 U.S. Code 77s (1958 edition).

the methods of classifying and segregating accounts, and the manner in which cost-accounting procedures shall be maintained." [5]

Similarly, under the Investment Company Act of 1949, "the commission may . . . issue rules and regulations providing for a reasonable degree of uniformity in the accounting policies and principles to be followed by registered investment companies in maintaining their accounting records and in preparing financial statements. . . ." [6]

How difficult would it be for the SEC actually to take the steps that are needed to exercise this authority? William L. Cary, SEC chairman, need only say to his chief accountant, Andrew Barr, "Six months from now, the commissioners would like to see a tentative draft of a statement of accounting principles." Barr can produce such a statement. Presumably, a period of three or four months would then be allowed for public exposure and perhaps for SEC hearings. At the end of that time the commission could vote whether to adopt the revised document.

Although technically these SEC principles would be binding only on registrants, as a practical matter other companies would probably have to fall in line. This follows from the fact that registrants comprise such a large fraction of U.S. business. How could an auditor certify that the financial statement of a nonregistrant conformed to "generally accepted principles" if it was at variance with the practice of this large fraction?

Hope vs. Action

So far the SEC has not had the will to act. The commissioners have hoped all along that the accounting profession itself would take the necessary action. Indeed, the commission has done everything it could to encourage the development of principles through mechanisms created by the profession. Although the SEC has been forced to make a few pronouncements on principles so as to meet urgent problems on which the profession was unwilling to take any action whatsoever, it has done so reluctantly and only after giving the profession full opportunity to carry the ball. Andrew Barr himself has made it abundantly clear that he dislikes the thought of having accounting principles prescribed by a government agency.

The fact remains, however, that the SEC is responsible for safeguarding the public interest. It cannot tolerate indefinitely a situa-

[5] 49 Stat. 827 (1935), 15 U.S. Code 790(i) (1958).

[6] 54 Stat. 836 (1940), 15 U.S. Code 80a–30(c) (1958).

tion in which the accounting reports submitted to it have less meaning than they should have because they are not constructed on a solid foundation of generally accepted accounting principles. The SEC has looked to the AICPA to fill this need; but if it concludes that the AICPA is not going to do so, then it presumably must take action on its own. Under these circumstances, for the SEC to refuse to act would be to abrogate its statutory responsibility to the public.

As a former president of the AICPA, John W. Queenan, said:

> The American Institute's research program brings CPAs to a crossroad in the development of their profession. . . . If it should . . . become abortive, it is not inconceivable that the latitude CPAs have enjoyed to develop accounting principles within the profession might give way to government regulations. In short, we have probably passed the point of no return with our research program; we must see that it becomes a genuine success.[7]

Except that the phrase "it is likely" fits the situation better than "it is not inconceivable," this is a reasonable size-up.

WILL AICPA FAIL?

This brings us to the second proposition. Is it now possible to make a reasonable judgment about the likelihood of success or failure of the AICPA effort?

Admittedly, it is early to attempt such a judgment. The Accounting Principles Board began work only in September 1959. No one expects, or should expect, that the board will act hastily to overcome a weakness that has existed for so many years. The problem is an extremely complicated one. For this reason it is important that the effort be started in the right direction and, particularly, that a well-thought-out conceptual foundation be agreed on before much is done to erect a superstructure of decisions relating to specific issues.

The board's predecessor, the Accounting Procedures Committee, did not devise a body of principles. Indeed, it was never charged with the job of doing so. It had practically no research staff; it had no adequate mechanism for obtaining the views of interested parties on topics under discussion; and, most important of all, it did not even attempt to codify and adopt an underlying rationale for the whole body of accounting into which pronouncements on specific topics could be fitted.

---

[7] "Postulates: Their Place in Accounting Research," *Journal of Accountancy*, August 1962, p. 32.

The new board was set up in a way that was deliberately intended to overcome these weaknesses,[8] and its effort began in as promising a manner as anyone could hope. The board was provided with adequate funds; it was given a full-time, capable research staff, which could prepare research studies, either itself or through contract, on each of the topics to be considered; it was supplied with a set of advisory committees to bring professional opinions to bear on accounting topics; and it had the entire profession to draw on for advice (indeed, it has publicized widely—and sincerely—its requests for comments from the profession).

The founders of the board recognized the need for an underlying rationale, and the first research projects were designed to construct one. The men appointed to the Accounting Principles Board, moreover, are unquestionably leaders in their profession, and they had taken their responsibility seriously. In short, the intentions, the organization, the staffing, and the general procedure of the AICPA effort are fine.

But now we are starting to see the results of this program, and there is little evidence to date that the tree, however well-germinated, planted, and watered, is bringing forth fruit. Let us look at the facts.

Since its inception in 1959, the board has approved the following projects for its research division:

Basic postulates and broad principles of accounting.
Cash-flow analysis and the funds statement.
Accounting for leases.
Accounting for income taxes.
Accounting for business combinations.
Accounting for nonprofit organizations.
Accounting for pension costs.
Intercorporate investments.
Accounting for foreign operations.
Price-level changes.

Of these, research reports have been received and published on three of the ten items: (1) postulates and principles, (2) funds-flow analysis, and (3) leasing.* It has also taken some action of a "putting out brush fires" nature.

[8] For a summary of the purpose, authority, and organization of the board, see "News Report," *Journal of Accountancy* (December 1958), p. 62; see also Weldon Powell, "The Challenge to Research," *Journal of Accountancy*, February 1960, p. 34.

* EDITORS' NOTE: Since this article was written, research reports have been published on business combinations, pension costs, price-level changes, an inventory of general accounting principles and income taxes.

Postulates & Principles

The research study on postulates was published in the spring of 1961 and the one on principles in the spring of 1962. Following its April 13, 1962, meeting, the board issued a statement about these studies that read, in part, as follows:

> The Board is therefore treating these two studies (the one on 'Postulates' and the other on 'Principles') as conscientious attempts by the accounting research staff to resolve major accounting issues which, however, contain inferences and recommendations in part of a speculative and tentative nature. It hopes the studies will stimulate constructive comment and discussion in the areas of the basic postulates and the broad principles of accounting.
>
> . . . the Board believes, however, that while these studies are a valuable contribution to accounting thinking, they are too radically different from present generally accepted accounting principles for acceptance at this time.
>
> After a period of exposure and consideration, some of the specific recommendations in these studies may prove acceptable to the Board while others may not. The Board therefore will await the results of this exposure and consideration before taking further action on these studies.[9]

The board has "awaited the results of this exposure" for a year now. The statement that the proposals in these studies are "too radically different from present generally accepted accounting principles for acceptance at this time" certainly suggests that these proposals are *not* to be the conceptual foundation that everyone agrees is necessary. If this is so, then the board has (and has had since April 1962) an inescapable responsibility to prepare and adopt some alternative. It has not done so. In fact, it has authorized neither a new study to make an alternative proposal, nor even a study of what the "present generally accepted accounting principles" are.

Funds-Flow Analysis

The board has discussed this topic, and it may well take action on it in the near future. It should be noted, however, that the proposal here is for an additional financial statement that describes the flow of

[9] "News Report," *Journal of Accountancy,* May 1962, p. 10.

funds. Such a statement would in no way affect the principles governing the preparation of the balance sheet and the income statement. In
considering this proposal, therefore, the board does not actually have
to come to grips with any of the fundamental issues in accounting.

Leases

The research report about leases was submitted in the spring
of 1962; there was some discussion of it in the board meeting of December 1962 but, again, no action. The board's failure to recommend
any principle at all to govern the treatment of leases is especially
indicative of its reluctance to act on fundamentals. Few, if any, members of the board believe that the present situation with respect to
accounting for leases is satisfactory. Yet the members have been unable
to agree (and they show no evidence of ever being able to agree) on
some alternative procedure.

The leasing problem is a relatively easy one. It involves only
the first of the three fundamental concepts—the nature of assets and
liabilities—whereas the principal differences of opinion among accountants relate to the second and third concepts—the measurement
of assets and liabilities and the concept of net income; therefore,
resolution of the differences of opinion with respect to the second and
third concepts is not necessary in order to arrive at a decision on the
leasing question.

In short, here is a clear-cut situation where a problem exists,
where the present accounting treatment is unsatisfactory, where no
factual information needed as a basis for making a decision is missing,
and where the arguments pro and con have been thoroughly listed;
yet the board is unwilling to act.

The board *may* act on this issue by the time this article is published. If it does, and if the action is the adoption of a genuine principle, then this part of the argument becomes void. If, instead, the board
fails to make a clear statement of the circumstances, if any, under
which lease agreements give rise to assets, then it will again have
demonstrated its unwillingness to face decisively the real accounting
issues.

Income Tax

The board has acted on two accounting problems created by
changes in the income tax regulations and statutes:

1. In November 1962 it issued a noncontroversial statement explaining the accounting impact of the new depreciation guidelines. No issue of principle was remotely involved in this.

2. In December 1962 the board issued a statement on the treatment of the investment credit. The statement itself makes clear that it deals with an *application* of accounting principles to a new problem; it does not involve a new principle or a re-examination of old principles.

Moreover there are some aspects of the decision on the investment credit which should be noted. The board discussed this relatively insignificant issue for most of its October 1962 meeting and also for the entire two days of its next meeting in December 1962. Also the board members spent many additional hours reading the flood of correspondence that was received on the subject. If this much time is required to settle one *application* of one principle, then how long can we estimate it will take to decide on the whole body of principles? Furthermore, three of the eight major accounting firms, all of whom have members on the board, have indicated they will not adhere to the board's final decision. If they persist, how can anyone say that the board's actions are "generally accepted"? *

Price-Level Changes

The board has considered this topic briefly, but it has not yet adopted a principle. It seems likely that at the very most the board will suggest a *supplementary* statement showing the effect of price-level changes. Again, the board will avoid the problem of the principles which govern the basic financial statements.

Implications

What does this record add up to? The board has shown an inclination to deal with matters involving *supplements* to the balance

---

* EDITORS' NOTE: Subsequently in 1964 the Federal government eliminated the Revenue Act's requirement that the credit be treated for tax purposes as a reduction on the basis of the property. The AICPA Accounting Principles Board issued in the same year Opinion No. 4 which called the flow-through approach acceptable, in addition to the productive life method which it previously advocated in Opinion No. 2. The AICPA reported in its survey of 600 corporate annual reports for 1964 that a majority of the companies used the 7% investment credit as a reduction of their 1964 Federal income taxes (flow-through method) rather than spreading it over the productive life of the property acquired. Many of them converted from the productive life method which was most common in the previous year.

sheet and income statement. It has spent a large fraction of its time deciding on the application of one principle (the "tax allocation" principle) to new and relatively insignificant problems. It has taken no action whatsoever on any matter involving new principles or a re-examination of old principles governing the preparation of the balance sheet and income statement, despite its recognition of the need to do so. It has concluded that the research reports proposing a set of basic postulates and principles are "too radically different" to be acceptable, but in the year that has elapsed since these were submitted it has taken no action to have an alternative set prepared.

This evidence does not necessarily indicate that the AICPA effort will fail. It is possible to say: "Granted that not much has happened so far . . . three years is a relatively short time. It is premature to make a judgment now. Let's be patient and see what develops, especially since the investment credit controversy is finally behind us. Evolution is a slow process." Yes, this is possible.

But it is also possible that the SEC's patience is nearing an end. And, no matter how sincerely the accounting profession may believe in the necessity for careful, rather than hasty, action, if the SEC decides to act, it can act.

EFFECT OF SEC CONTROL

As already stated, I do not like the idea of government action. The consequences of SEC take-over could be quite unpleasant. My greatest worries are that:

(1) The SEC will go beyond the stage of principles and prescribe detailed rules.

(2) Once it has set such rules, it will freeze them and thus stultify progress.

(3) Having started with prescribing principles, the SEC will next move to enforce its principles by taking over the auditing function now performed by the accounting profession.

Experience, both here and abroad, gives support to these fears. In this country, accounting systems prescribed for railroads by the Interstate Commerce Commission and for public utilities by certain state regulatory bodies are (with considerable justification) described as cumbersome, restrictive, unduly expensive, uninformative, and inflexible. Likewise, the government-prescribed systems in France and West Germany have been criticized on the same grounds. In particular, inflexibility seems to be a characteristic of most government regulatory efforts, whereas accounting principles *must* change as the business environment changes.

On the other hand, there is some evidence from government experience that is less discouraging. The present Federal Power Commission requirements seem to be considered reasonable by many public utility people. The accounting principles prescribed by the Department of Defense for use in government contracts apparently do not work a great hardship on contractors. Indeed, there is even some feeling that the Defense Department principles are not tight enough to accomplish their legitimate purpose of assuring that contractors are paid adequately, but not lavishly, for the work they do.

Furthermore, the SEC commissioners and the accounting staff are intelligent, reasonable people. It is unfair to assume that they would act precipitously or that they would intentionally repeat the mistakes of history. Undoubtedly, if the SEC decides to act, it will first set up an advisory committee. Some members of this committee might be members of the present Accounting Principles Board. The chief difference between the two might only be that, whereas the Accounting Principles Board can refuse to act indefinitely, the advisory committee could not delay action beyond a time limit dictated by the patience of the commissioners.

The SEC staff, which is larger than and probably as competent as the AICPA staff, would prepare draft statements for discussion with the advisory committee. In due course, the SEC would undoubtedly give wide public exposure to revisions of these draft statements and seek public opinion on them, just as it does now for proposed changes in SEC regulations. Also, it would probably arrange public hearings, and only after a thorough airing of all points of view would it make its final determination and publish its principles.

These favorable signs do not really allay my worries, however. Action by the accounting profession would surely be preferable to action by the SEC. But, to be realistic, we must admit that SEC action is preferable to no action at all.

AN ALTERNATIVE

If the SEC were convinced that the Accounting Principles Board would act reasonably, and promptly, and decisively, then there would be reason to believe—in view of its long-standing philosophy—that it would refrain from taking over. But what sort of indication would be convincing? Although it would be presumptuous of me to attempt a detailed prescription, some general observations seem evident from the foregoing analysis.

As a beginning, the board will have to make a statement covering the three fundamental concepts listed earlier. This need not be a lengthy document, nor is extensive research (in the sense of "obtaining evidence") needed in order to formulate it. All the likely possibilities have been set forth and discussed in the literature for years. A small group of well-informed and well-intentioned people could write the first draft of such a statement in short order. It would be strenuous, irritating, brain-wearying work, but it could be done. Then would follow the process of inviting public comment, evaluating this comment, and reaching a decision—not a decision that would remain immutable, but one which would serve for the present as a guide for resolving specific issues.

Possibly, there should be two such statements of fundamental principles. The first would be, essentially, an explicit formulation of the accounting principles that implicitly govern the best current practice and would serve as a bench mark for resolving pressing current issues. The second would be a statement of the direction in which accounting should move in, say, the next five to ten years. It is possible that there would be no difference between these two statements. That is, it is possible that the current formulation would also be the best long-run formulation, but, at first, separation of the current problems from the long-run problems would permit many decisions to be made without waiting for the long-run answers.

The most clear-cut example of a difference between current principles and possible long-run principles relates to asset valuation. There are various proposals for modifying the principle that assets are valued essentially at unexpired historical cost. Perhaps one of these proposals should be adopted, perhaps not; but if one *is* adopted, a transition period of some years will probably be necessary. Thus, there is no point in considering such proposals as a way of solving current problems. . . .

Even without waiting for the formal adoption of the first set of fundamental principles, the AICPA can take action on certain pressing issues—issues which are unlikely to be affected by whatever wording is eventually agreed to. Two such issues have been referred to already: accounting for leases and the funds-flow statement. There are others included in the research studies now underway, and still others implicit in the list of topics given before on which different treatments are equally acceptable.

All of this requires a sense of urgency, a feeling that this is the eleventh hour, and it would indeed be presumptuous of me to suggest how such a feeling might be created.

QUESTIONS

1. What authority does the SEC have for establishing accounting principles?

2. What three concepts does Anthony contend should probably constitute the body of accounting principles?

3. Devise a body of principles based upon Anthony's concepts which you think would be acceptable to your textbook authors.

4. If you accept Anthony's proposal that there might be two sets of principles, one for use now and one to become applicable within a limited number of years, how would you revise your answer to (3)?

5. What objections do you think might be raised against the proposal in (4)?

6. There are three acceptable procedures for the handling of oil drilling costs on published statements (see page 29): (1) Deduct drilling costs as expense in the year in which the costs are incurred; (2) Deduct drilling costs as expense over the useful life of the wells with which they are associated; (3) Deduct drilling costs as expense in the year in which the associated well runs dry.

   a. Why do oil drilling costs encourage a multiplicity of handling procedures?

   b. Phrase a general principle that would secure uniformity and that would not conflict with our usual handling of other assets. Do not refer to oil drilling costs specifically.

   c. What difficulties do you foresee in the application of the general principle in (b) above to the handling of oil drilling costs?

7. If a company purchases an asset for $1 million on which it receives the 7% investment credit, calculate the difference for financial statement purposes if (a) the productive life method or (b) the flow-through method is used. Other data: 5-year life. Straight-line depreciation. No salvage.

31

Accounting Reform

Frederick C Klein

PRESSURED FROM within and without, the accounting frater-
nity is likely to adopt important reforms soon—producing
some handsome dividends for stockholders everywhere.

The benefits won't be in cash, but in the form of
clearer and more copious information in company financial
reports. Some of the changes the public accountants en-
vision will arbitrarily settle honest differences of opinion
on technical accounting principles. Others may rule out
practices that now tempt some managements to manipulate
figures in such a way as to mislead investors. Still other
changes could help prevent outright fraud.

Basically, the accountants will try to give more meaning to the standard declaration included in annual reports.
In all but those very few cases where the auditors take
serious exception to the financial data as presented by the

From *The Wall Street Journal,* vol. XLVI, no. 151 (May 16, 1966),
p. 2. Reprinted by permission of the publisher. Mr. Klein is a staff
reporter for *The Wall Street Journal.*

company, these declarations have an identical and reassuring ring; they attest that the auditors find the financial statements "present fairly" in company's condition "in accordance with generally accepted accounting principles."

"A Roulette Wheel"

But these "generally accepted" principles are so varied, and can be applied so flexibly, that investors can hardly be blamed for sometimes throwing up their hands in confusion when trying to compare a company's current results with past performance, or with the results of a competitor. Some leading accountants feel it's high time that the investor got a better break. Leonard Spacek, senior partner of Arthur Andersen & Co., a major accounting firm, declares: "My profession appears to regard a set of financial statements as a roulette wheel for investors—and it's their tough luck if they don't understand the risk that's involved in interpreting any accounting report."

Some certified public accountants (CPAs) are arguing for a go-slow approach to new rule-making, but the pressures for change appear so strong that their objections will go unheeded in part because the profession is feeling the heat of outside criticism as well as demand for reforms by its own practitioners.

Banks want to see some changes made, and fast. Recently J. Howard Laeri, vice chairman of giant First National City Bank of New York, coupled a plea for more accountant-banker cooperation with an attack on what he called "the audit gap." Under present accounting procedures he said "the investor or lender . . . is very much like the navigator who would have to pilot" by a drifting beacon.

Under Legal Fire

The accounting profession has also been hit with a rash of lawsuits (some filed by banks) charging that accounting firms have permitted dissemination of misleading information about companies' financial condition. The American Institute of Certified Public Accountants (AICPA) doesn't know precisely how many such suits are outstanding but estimates that about 50 "cases" (several suits may be filed under a single case) may now be up for litigation. This is a sharp increase from prior years, and the AICPA last year set up a special committee on accountants' liability to study the problem.

Last year the Securities and Exchange Commission initiated a major change in accounting procedure on its own, without prior action by the profession—the first time in years such a step had been taken. The commission ruled that companies which list the uncollected portion of instalment receivables as a current asset must also list the resulting deferred tax as a current liability. The ruling was designed to halt the spreading practice of listing the deferred tax as a noncurrent item. This artificially inflated "working capital" (current assets minus current liabilities), a key credit rating factor.

Board Rulings Expected

Thus prodded from several directions, the AICPA now is ready to act through its accounting principles board, a body known principally for its lethargy during the six years since its formation. It has issued only six opinions on specific matters, and "none of these . . . served to narrow the areas of difference and inconsistency in practice," according to one board member.

This year, however, it's considered almost certain that a revitalized board will take steps to bring about more conformity in at least two areas—accounting for pension costs and for the reporting of "special items" affecting earnings. In the latter case, it's expected the board will require a two-part income statement—one part dealing with operating earnings only, and the other with items of non-recurring gain or loss.

This would be a radical departure from past practice for many companies. A recent AICPA survey of a sample of 600 companies revealed that 60% of 252 "unusual" items of income and expense they reported in 1964 were lumped into the reported net income figure for the year, which in turn was used to compute earnings per share. Only 16% of these special items were reported as such and listed separately after the net income figure. The remaining 25% were taken directly to retained earnings and did not show up in the year's profit statement at all.

This lack of consistent treatment of nonoperating items of gain and loss is a prime source of stockholder confusion. Companies sometimes highlight these special items one year and ignore them the next, making comparisons of year-to-year performance difficult for those without a practiced eye.

Consider Firth Sterling, Inc., a maker of specialty steels and tungsten carbide based in McKeesport, Pa. In 1964, when earnings from operations dipped to 19 cents a share from 32 cents the previous year, the company featured prominently in its annual report an additional special profit of 8 cents a share realized from investment tax credits. This gain was mentioned in five separate places in the report, including a "highlights" table and the president's letter to stockholders.

In 1965, however, Firth Sterling's earnings from operations bounced back to 31 cents a share—and readers of this annual report had to search hard to find any reference to the 1964 special gain. It was recognized only once—in a source-and-use-of-funds table deep in the report—and the source of the gain wasn't spelled out anywhere. All this, of course, made Firth Sterling's earnings compare more favorably year to year than would otherwise have been the case.

Varying accounting practices among different companies in the same industry also create confusion. Last year, for example, reported net income of Inland Steel Co. dropped 4% from 1964. But unlike most of its competitors, Inland prorates its 7% investment tax credit over the depreciable life of new equipment. If Inland had emulated other steelmakers and taken the full credit each year, its 1965 net income would have shown a gain of 7% over 1964 instead of a 4% drop, says Chairman Joseph L. Block.

Similar confusion has arisen over the handling of damage suit payouts by General Electric Co. and Westinghouse Electric Corp.; GE has reduced its profits by the amount of the payouts in the years they were made, but Westinghouse has elected to write them off against retained earnings, not current profits.

The current state of accounting for pension costs is described as "chaotic" by Clifford B. Heimbucher, a San Francisco CPA and current chairman of the accounting principles board of AICPA. Companies currently use at least three widely divergent methods of accounting for these costs, and auditors can take exception to them only if a company changes from one to another in the midst of a year.

"Everyone Won't Like It"

To clear up the chaos, the board is expected to establish a single method of accounting for pension costs. "Everyone won't like it, but it's an area where we must take a stand," says Mr. Heimbucher.

The principles board has other thorny items on its docket, including measures to bring more conformity to accounting for the allocation of some taxes, the handling of treasury stock, changes in price levels, and research and development cost. The latter is an area where particularly divergent practices now exist.

Any decisions the board comes to will undoubtedly be widely followed by companies and accounting firms. Before 1964, board rulings were only one source of "authoritative support" for a given accounting procedure. Others included textbooks, opinions of leading CPAs or simply widespread use of a method. In 1964, however, the governing council of the AICPA resolved that effective with statements for fiscal years beginning after Dec. 31, 1965, departures from board opinions would have to be disclosed in footnotes to financial statements or in the standard auditor's opinion at the back of annual reports. Also, the effect of such departures on per-share earnings would have to be stated.

Compliance by member accounting firms is now voluntary, but the AICPA expects that few, if any, will choose to disregard the council's resolution. If that should occur, however, the AICPA could insert the resolution in its code of ethics; a member firm breaking this code could be subject to expulsion from the AICPA.

Encouraging Conformity

This ruling on exceptions "makes the board more a judicial than an educational body," says John L. Carey, executive director of AICPA. Corporation executives agree it can only encourage greater accounting conformity. "The last thing any company wants is an auditor's exception," says the president of a big Eastern manufacturing concern. "It guarantees a lively annual meeting."

In addition to the board's work, the AICPA itself is deep in study of the internal auditing methods of public warehouses; the data gathered could be used to help prevent the type of manipulations involved in the Allied Crude Vegetable Oil Refining Corp. salad oil scandal. Guidelines to be used by auditors in checking warehouse inventories are expected to result from the study.

More often now, individual accounting firms are amplifying their written opinions when they feel a company's report requires further interpretation. Last year, for example, Price Waterhouse & Co. included a clarification of per-share earnings of Unexcelled Chemical Corp. in the auditor's statement in that company's annual report. Unexcelled Chemical had listed separately both a charge and a credit affecting profit, and Price Warehouse apparently felt this might confuse some stockholders. Says the AICPA's Mr. Carey: "There's a growing feeling in the profession that the auditor should give his opinion when he feels something needs to be said."

The Liability Question

Though the accountants won't say so outright, it's understood that the current rash of lawsuits against them has helped speed reform. Broadly speaking, accountants are liable for damages when company statements come up wrong if they are found to have participated in a fraud, or if they are judged negligent in exercising normal professional care in approving a company's statements.

CPAs are quick to point out that their statements are no guarantee against fraud; their checks are made on a sample basis, and they must rely heavily on company representations of the facts. This was brought home recently when Frank G. Shattuck Co., New York, disclosed that its earnings from 1965 and 1964 were overstated by a total of about $600,000, primarily because of "collusive fabrication of fictitious invoices" and other accounting records by certain department heads of the company's W. F. Schrafft & Sons Corp. subsidiary in Boston.

Peat, Marwick, Mitchell & Co. was the auditor. Walter E. Hansen, senior partner, calls the case "a perfect example of what can happen when top people in a company or division operate collusively" to falsify records. Discrepancies resulting from such collusion "come out sooner or later when figures get out of line," says Mr. Hansen, but they are "virtually impossible" to detect immediately in the course of a normal audit.

"Absolutely Blameless"

Edward E. Butler, group vice president of Shattuck, says his company feels Peat-Marwick is "absolutely blameless" in the matter. The firm was of "great assistance" in uncovering the collusion, he declares, and adds that "in the light of all the circumstances, the auditors had no way of knowing what had taken place" in time to prevent the misstatements.

Such arguments evidently cut no ice with plaintiffs in the many suits filed against accountants. As it happens, Peat-Marwick has been charged in some of the larger, more publicized actions. In San Francisco, four banks are suing the firm for more than $6 million in connection with the 1963 bankruptcy of Otis, McAllister & Co., a coffee importer. The suits charge that financial statements of the company from 1958 through 1960, audited by Peat-Marwick, were "misleading." A Peat-Marwick spokesman says his firm refused an offer from the banks calling for an out-of-court settlement for $1.3 million, and will "have the matter litigated on its merits."

Peat-Marwick is also the target of more than a dozen suits filed in connection with the 1965 bankruptcy of Yale Express System, Inc. The accounting firm claims that information was withheld by accounting personnel of Yale Express and that under assets the company listed receivables it never got around to collecting.*

QUESTIONS

1. What events have occurred recently to cause the AICPA to consider more favorably greater accounting uniformity?

2. Under what circumstances, may a CPA use any accounting practice that is different from those approved by the AICPA Accounting Principles Board?

3. "CPA's are quick to point out that their statements are no guarantee against fraud; checks are made on a sample basis, and they must rely heavily on company representations of the facts." Why do you think that these arguments are invalid (or valid)?

THE HARDSHIP OF ACCOUNTING
ROBERT FROST

> Never ask of money spent
> Where the spender thinks it went
> Nobody was ever meant
> To remember or invent
> What he did with every cent.

From *Complete Poems of Robert Frost.* Copyright 1936 by Robert Frost. Copyright © 1964 by Lesley Frost Ballantine. Reprinted by permission of Holt, Rinehart and Winston, Inc.

* EDITORS' NOTE: For further details, see Richard J. Whalen, "The Big Skid at Yale Express," *Fortune* (November, 1965).

YOUNG MAN, BE AN ACCOUNTANT
CAROLINE BIRD

ELBERT HUBBARD, the writer who went down with the *Lusitania* in 1915, described the typical auditor as "a man past middle age, spare, wrinkled, intelligent, cold, passive, noncommittal, with eyes like a codfish, polite in contact, but at the same time unresponsive, calm and damnably composed as a concrete post or a plaster-of-Paris cast; a human petrifaction with a heart of feldspar and without charm of the friendly germ, minus bowels, passion or a sense of humor. Happily, they never reproduce and all of them finally go to Hell."

All of a sudden, however, the accountant has changed. No longer is genius alone enough to run a business; today it takes a man with a knowledge of numbers. Nobody could run General Motors by hunch. By no particular accident, it happens to be run at the moment by Chairman of the Board Frederic G. Donner, a numbers man from way back. At Ford, two recent top men have been accountants: Ernest Breech, Chairman of the Board; and President Robert McNamara, formerly of Price Waterhouse & Co., who went on to the even bigger job of running the U.S. Department of Defense. As for Chrysler, the administrative vice-president who is favored to emerge as the next president of that troubled company is Lynn Townsend, a former partner of Chrysler's national auditing firm: Touche, Ross, Bailey & Smart.*

The whole profession makes good money. Doctors are the only professional men who clearly top the $15,000 median income estimated for established C.P.A.'s, but the sky is the limit for accountants. A doctor, for instance, would not dare to charge the $30,000 the late George O. May, architect of the Federal Reserve Board's audit standards, is supposed to have been paid by U.S. Steel for a twenty-minute consultation. Senior partners of the big auditing firms draw salaries and participation in six figures. And, according to a recent survey of seventeen hundred chief executives of listed companies, more of them started in finance and accounting than in any other department. . . .

From the September, 1961, issue of *Esquire* Magazine. Reprinted by permission of *Esquire* Magazine © 1961 by Esquire, Inc.

* EDITORS' NOTE: Subsequently Mr. Townsend was appointed President of the Chrysler Corporation.

7

The New Accounting

32

CPA Invasion

Ed Cony

WHEN LOCKHEED AIRCRAFT CORP. set out to slash costs in its white collar departments, it called in an outside consultant. With this aid, new work standards were set up for office employes and a more efficient flow of paper-work assignments was achieved. Result: $3 million was saved in the first year under the program.

Similarly, Pittsburgh & West Virginia Railway turned to outside help in launching a general company-wide cost cutting program which is expected to pare expenses $1,038,000 this year.

In neither case were conventional management consulting firms employed. Lockheed called on Arthur Young & Co., its regular accounting firm. And Pittsburgh & West Virginia also used the firm that audits its books, Price Waterhouse & Co.

From *The Wall Street Journal*, vol. 1, CLVIII, no. 84 (October 30, 1961), p. 1. Reprinted by permission of the publisher. Mr. Cony is a staff reporter for *The Wall Street Journal*.

Help Plan Products

Much to the distress of management consultants, an increasing volume of consulting work of all sorts is now flowing to the accountants. Some of this advice-giving is far removed from matters directly related to the corporate balance sheet. Accounting firms now stand ready to help their clients plan the layout of a new factory, develop new products and work out marketing programs. In some cases, they may even sit in on labor negotiations.

Ernst & Ernst has "over 250" staff men in its "management services" division, which on a manpower basis puts it on a par with all except the very largest conventional management consulting firms. In 1952 Peat, Marwick, Mitchell & Co. had a dozen people in its then new "management controls" department; today it has 200 professional people in this department. Arthur Young & Co.'s consulting staff has spiraled from about 12 in 1954 to "well over 100" today, according to an official of the firm. A fourth member of the "Big Eight," as the largest CPA firms are called, says income from its management consulting department has "grown tenfold in a matter of eight years."

"The future of management consulting belongs to the accounting firms because of our continuing, close, confidential relationship with our clients," declared Kenneth S. Axelson, a Peat, Marwick, Mitchell partner who heads his firm's management consulting department.

No Corporate Secrets

He explains: "We know things about a company that perhaps only one or two company executives know. There can't be any secrets from us—or we won't sign the financial statement."

Mr. Axelson's confident prediction of the eventual dominance of accountants in the consulting field, of course, would be hotly disputed by many management consultants. In similar fashion, a "boundary dispute" has been simmering for years between lawyers and accountants over the giving of tax advice.*

A few of the older partners of accounting firms, it must be said, also look askance at a good deal of the non-accounting consultant work being conducted by members of their profession. In their view, such

* EDITORS' NOTE: For a similar "boundary dispute" between actuaries and accountants, see "Those Uncertain Actuaries" by T. A. Wise in the December, 1965, and January, 1966, issues of *Fortune.*

work raises some rather delicate ethical questions about the propriety of an accounting firm wearing two hats: As a supposedly independent auditor or reviewer of a company management's financial practices while at the same time becoming closely involved with the same management by advising it how to run the business.

Nevertheless, there seems little likelihood of the accounting firms pulling out of the lucrative consulting business. In fact, the buildup of their staffs to include marketing and production specialists, psychologists for personnel work and others with skills outside of accounting points to greater consulting activity as time goes on. Some of the old-line auditing firms are even taking on executive recruiters to find top management talent for their clients.

CPA firms are chary about giving the precise amount of business they now derive from consulting, but one partner in a Big Eight firm makes this "educated guess": "Among the Big Eight, management consulting now accounts for from 5% to 30% of the firms' total revenues."

Taking a Plunge

Smaller CPA firms are taking the plunge too. One medium-sized firm is now said to get over 50% of its revenues from management consulting. "Right here in New York we have some small CPA firms which won't take any audit work at all now," says Robert Ettlinger of the American Institute of Certified Public Accountants. These firms—usually one, two or three man operations—normally specialize "in one or two areas of management services such as electronic data processing," he explains.

The Institute employs Mr. Ettlinger, a former controller of the Papermate Division of Gillette Co., to stimulate smaller CPA firms to get into, as Mr. Ettlinger phrases it, "this hifalutin field of management advisory services."

A few examples of work being done by accounting firms suggests the broad scope of their "management services" work.

Lybrand, Ross Brothers & Montgomery is deep into operations research, a system which borrows from the disciplines of many sciences, including physics and higher mathematics, to solve management problems. One client is confronted with this situation: It has a multiple product line of more than 200 products, manufactured in 12 plants and eventually shipped to about 20 warehouses. Each plant has different costs for each product and each factory can produce a variety of products. Currently, Lybrand is trying to minimize the cost of producing and transporting everyone of the 20-odd products, by using operations research.

A Million Possibilities

Says Felix Kaufman of the accounting firm's management consulting services: "The range of possibilities in allocating production and distribution is in the range of one million. We think we've conjured up a technique, using computers, which will give us the answers." Mr. Kaufman says costs could be cut "by millions of dollars" as a result of the current study.

The computer field is a rich one for accountants giving advice to companies. Peat, Marwick, Mitchell is currently working with a client to help him use his computer to forecast sales much more accurately than he could in the past. "Already—and we aren't nearly through yet—the company thinks it can reduce its inventory by as much as 75%," says an official of Peat, Marwick.

Price Waterhouse recently worked closely with a client's own personnel to "revitalize the company's financial department," says Arthur Toan, senior partner in charge of Price Waterhouse's management advisory services department. He describes the results: "The company replaced people, changed the organization of the department, came up with a whole new approach to providing financial information to top executives. They're getting fewer figures, more highlights. They now report, for instance, the percentage of the market which the company enjoys." He adds that in the process the company has "made very substantial clerical savings—hundreds of thousands of dollars annually."

White-Collar Costs

White-collar costs are a prime target of accountants turned consultants. Establishing work standards for white-collar workers accounts for about 40% of Arthur Young's work in management services, says Ralph Lewis, who heads the department. For years manufacturers have had good performance standards in production lines, he says, "but typically we find the white-collar worker is working at 60% of capacity —mostly because of bad loading assignments from his immediate supervisor."

After Arthur Young helped Lockheed set up work standards for its white-collar workers, a Lockheed accounting official reported: "Many of our (clerical) organizations which were operating at between 60% and 70% (of capacity), today are operating close to or at 100%." Among others with whom Arthur Young has worked in this field are: Sinclair Oil Corp., Continental Baking Co., and Encyclopaedia Britannica, Inc.

Manufacturing costs occupy CPAs also. Fred Sengstacke, a partner of Scovell, Wellington & Co., tells of this case: "We had one client in a heavy industry who was very enthusiastic about sales of a new product. We went in and found that actually they were losing money on it, because they had incorrectly analyzed the costs involved. The last we heard, they'd pretty much decided to discontinue the product."

Head-Hunting for Executives

Analyzing costs is not a big departure from traditional accounting. But some new CPA activities are considered "far out." Arthur Young, for instance, now employs four full-time executive recruiters, or "head-hunters." Recently they found an administrative vice president for a top company, a position which commands $50,000 a year, plus stock options.

Ernst & Ernst does a variety of personnel work for clients. "Professional trained psychologists" on E&E's staff interview clients' employes, give them batteries of tests and make "appraisals" of the individuals which E&E says "are designed for constructive guidance in matching the man and his abilities with the requirements of a particular job."

Actually, CPAs insist they have been giving management advice, on a limited scale, for a good many years. Mr. Toan of Price Waterhouse says he has in his files a consulting job dated in 1898. "And you could lift out some of our recommendations and use them today," he adds.

Peat, Marwick, Mitchell did some consulting work at the birth of General Electric "when several companies were put together," says Mr. Axelson. Scovell Wellington participated in a massive "systems and procedures" study for U.S. Steel in the 1930s, says Mr. Sengstacke. And Ralph Kent, managing partner of Arthur Young, says: "We've always had calls to help clients with budget services and accounting systems. The partner in charge of the audit used to handle such chores himself. But after World War II, we set up a separate department of experts in the management services field."

A Postwar Phenomenon

Most accountants agree the spurt in their consulting work has been a post-World War II phenomenon. They cite a variety of reasons for the rapid growth and for their expectation it will continue. Since the war business has become more complex, more highly mechanized and more competitive, say the CPAs. All these factors have contributed to management's increasing interest in "how to run a business scientifically," says Mr. Ettlinger of the CPA institute.

One prominent member of a Big Eight firm says with candor: "After World War II, we saw management consultants putting in cost accounting, budgeting systems, even general accounting systems for our clients. We saw them collecting big fees on the order of $100,000 when perhaps our clients were paying us only $10,000 for auditing the books. Our partners were upset by this invasion of a field we regarded ourselves as particularly qualified in."

The CPA firms, while careful not to knock the ability or work of outside management consulting firms, are fond of talking about the high quality of the work CPA firms do. A typical comment: "The client knows we'll do as good a management consultant job as we can. With us, it's not a one-shot proposition. We'll be coming back next year for an audit exam. We have a continuing stake in the company."

Older Men Worry

But this is just the point that worries some of the older, more conservative audit partners. They fear that a management consultant job may turn sour and cause the client to turn over his auditing and accounting work to a rival CPA firm.

Another problem: "If an auditing partner has been auditing a firm 15 or 20 years and we're going in to make an organizational study, some of the people he has come to know in the company may get hurt. So he worries about the good relations he's built up over the years," says a senior man in one accounting firm.

Some old-line partners also worry that the consulting business endangers the independence of the accounting firm. One man states this point of view as follows: "We are supposed to audit the books at arm's length, but aren't we auditing our own work in some cases a year or two after our consulting people have reorganized a department?"

Some management consultants believe the accounting firms may be stretching their available talents a bit thin when they venture far from "financial facts and figures work." Says one consultant: "One of the Big Eight CPA firms has done some pretty bad work in production planning and control. I know of several instances where companies had to call in a management consulting firm to undo the damage."

QUESTIONS

1. What kinds of "new" activities are now being undertaken by CPAs?

2. Do you foresee any conflict of interest for a CPA firm undertaking these additional activities?

3. Would you suppose that a similar expansion of activities might be feasible for an accountant employed by a single business firm? Why?

4. What educational implications, if any, do you think that these "new" activities might have for accounting students?

33

Company Watchdogs

George Melloan

THE COMPANY AUDITOR, whose job once was confined to poring over financial ledgers, is now becoming a combination private detective, credit sleuth, cost-cutter and all-round trouble shooter.

Auditors who work for corporations still check books for errors or signs of chicanery. But they also are moving into new areas of responsibility that bear little relation to their traditional tasks. They are reviewing price policies for possible antitrust violations, investigating outside activities of company officers to spot conflicts of interest, checking credit of suppliers, customers and potential merger partners and roaming plants and offices in search of inefficiency.

Thus an auditor from Pacific Telephone & Telegraph Co. visited a San Francisco couple to inquire about the quality of service when a phone was installed recently. And

From *The Wall Street Journal*, vol. CLXIV, no. 83 (October 26, 1964), p. 1. Reprinted by permission of the publisher. Mr. Melloan is a reporter for *The Wall Street Journal*.

at the Louisville works of International Harvester Co. two auditors in white shirts and ties poke into piles of rusty scrap and surplus parts, looking for waste.

Harvester's Savings

There's evidence that the new look in auditing pays off. Harvester auditor John D. Bergerson, for example, spotted the fact that two different size bolts were used on one of the company's disc harrows. He asked if the smaller bolt could be used exclusively. Engineers decided it could, saving Harvester $19,000 a year. Another sharp-eyed Harvester auditor touring a plant suggested that, in view of capabilities of new steel rolling mills, steel sheets could be ordered by Harvester to closer thickness tolerances. Such orders, which insure that the company now gets the maximum number of sheets per ton, save over $200,000 a year at one plant and could save up to $1 million a year if all Harvester divisions adopt the practice, an official says.

This broadening role of the auditor as the eyes and ears of top management is a relatively new one. It comes about largely because many U.S. companies have grown so complex and far-flung that the people who run them can never be wholly certain that they know about important things that are happening at lower levels. These managers often find it highly useful to have a reasonable objective and independent branch to look into situations that other subordinates might be reluctant to report, or the significance of which they might not understand.

Auditors can expand their role because office automation is freeing them from much of their traditional routine paper work. Edward A. Johnson, assistant general auditor for Minnesota Mining & Manufacturing Co., notes that a computer can scan through credit accounts in a few hours in search of any that are dangerously overdue. Before automation the job required several hundred man-hours of auditing department time.

"Operational Auditing"

Lockheed Aircraft Corp. has expanded its auditing staff to 112 persons today from 14 in 1949, says Frederic E. Mints, resident internal auditor at the Lockheed-California division. But only about 30% of the man-hours of the department today are expended on financial auditing, he says. The rest are devoted to broader "operational" auditing, involving such things as surveying the efficiency of aircraft assembly lines.

A survey of auditing practices by the National Industrial Conference Board (NICB), a non-profit business research institution, confirms this trend. Over 60% of the 177 companies checked had made a significant move toward broadening auditors' duties in the last five years.

As auditors tackle new jobs, many concerns are drawing recruits for their auditing departments from fields other than accounting. John M. Schulz, general auditor at Atlantic Refining Co., started his career as a chemical engineer and has never had any formal training in accountancy.

"A few years ago most people were drawn from accounting but today we just look for brains," says Robert L. Richmond, general auditor at B. F. Goodrich Co. At Shell Oil Co., promising men are given two or three years in internal auditing as a means to train them for top management posts. Since auditors see all phases of a corporation, some executives think it is an ideal training ground.

Demand and Pay Are Up

Demand for company auditors who can fill more "sophisticated" jobs is growing and salaries are rising, says Robert C. Zabor, vice president of Heidrick & Struggles, a New York executive recruiting and management counseling firm. Managers of internal auditing now can command salaries ranging from $20,000 to $30,000 a year, he notes. Four or five years ago the range was more likely to be $18,000 to $22,000, he says. "There's a general upgrading of the field," says Mr. Zabor. "The man who goes into it is required not only to be a good auditor but a potential executive."

Archie McGhee, managing director of the Institute of Internal Auditors, a professional association, says one large company now hires new auditors at $10,000 a year or more, compared with about $8,000 a few years ago. The Institute also reports a higher turnover in auditing jobs; 14% of jobs changed hands last year, according to a survey, compared with a "normal" level of 11%. Mr. McGhee says higher turnover often reflects higher salaries that induce auditors to change jobs.

Broader assignments for auditors often reflect the concern of management over dangers of fraud and overextended credit. The well-publicized "salad oil scandal," in which perhaps $150 million in edible oils proved to be fictitious, spurred the auditor of one petroleum pipeline company to study his own firm's techniques of checking what is in its storage tanks.

At another large concern, the president recently called in auditors and asked them to give credit checking procedures a close scrutiny. The move was prompted by word that a finance subsidiary of Whirlpool Corp. had been forced to set up a $21,376,000 reserve to cover uncollectible receivables, which resulted partly, according to Whirlpool, from inadequate checking of credit. "Fortunately, we found our control systems were working well," says the auditor.

A large Midwest concern not long ago took a loss of some $1 million when a customer that owed it that sum went broke. According to the concern's auditor, the report of a public accounting firm erroneously showed that the customer was in sound condition with net assets of nearly $2 million just before it collapsed. The Midwest company now has its own auditors check over the books of its big credit customers, making it clear to the customers that this is one of the conditions of obtaining credit.

About one-third of the companies surveyed by the NICB now have their own auditors investigate other companies they deal with. These include organizations being considered for acquisition, concessionaries, licensees, subcontractors, sole suppliers of a vital material, dealers and advertising agencies.

About half of the 151 companies in the NICB survey that engage in operational auditing have their auditors check whether their respective companies are complying with Federal, state and local laws and rules of regulatory bodies. This ranges from determining if a refinery is complying with local fire ordinances to checking whether branch offices are violating the Robinson-Patman Act by making price concessions to some customers and not others, says a major oil company auditor. Checking for collusion that might run the company afoul of antitrust laws is one of the toughest jobs he says. "What you are really dealing with there is collusion among salesmen and that can be very difficult to detect," he says.

Smoking Out Conflicts of Interest

According to the NICB study, conflicts of interest, in which some company executives "may have outside business interests that adversely affect the fulfillment of their obligations to their principal employers," are another concern which managers are turning over to their auditors. "At times the auditors go so far as to obtain retail credit reports and

Dun & Bradstreet reports on individuals who appear to be living be
yond their company salaries," the report says.

A general auditor at a big chemicals producer recently made his
first report to the board of directors on possible conflicts of interest in
his company. Though neither the auditor nor the directors have rea
son to suspect any wrongdoing, the new policy was begun as a precau
tionary step.

In a few companies the general auditor reports to the board at
all times. Such is the arrangement at New York Life Insurance Co., a
mutual insurance firm with assets of some $7 billion. New York Life's
general auditor has authority to make audits and examinations of company affairs on his own initiative and report directly to the board.
The company says it believes it is necessary for the auditor to report
to a level beyond that of the executives whose activities are audited.

"Play Golf With Sales Manager"

As their authority broadens, auditors find new demands being
made upon them to develop outgoing personalities, as well as to show
considerable tact. At the annual convention of the Institute of Internal
Auditors in Houston this summer, Clyde Skeen, executive vice president of Ling-Temco-Vought, Inc., urged auditors to unbend a bit in
dealing with other company workers so that management won't be
faced with protests from sales managers and engineering department
heads about second-guessing from the auditors. "Put on a sports shirt
and go out and play golf with the sales manager—it won't hurt you,"
Mr. Skeen advised.

An auditor for Vickers division of Sperry-Rand Corp., Robert
M. Miller, suggests that auditors avoid disagreeing with a manager
"when he (the manager) is feeling depressed, irascible or ill." Mr.
Miller, in an article in an auditing journal, adds, "Train yourself to
be sensitive to storm signals of facial expression, posture, tone and
voice" and don't press a manager "for an unmistakable statement that
he has reversed himself."

Most auditors contend they try to sell themselves to the people
whose activities they're inspecting. For one thing, says one auditor, a
friendly, relaxed approach often allows the auditor to pick up gripes
or information that might be important to his investigation. But
another remarks, "You can't be out trying to make yourself popular.
In the final analysis we have to be on management's side and we have
to deal with some very hard questions."

QUESTIONS

1. Why has the role of the internal auditor been broadened?

2. Of the various activities now being undertaken by company auditors, do you feel that there are any that they should not undertake? Why?

3. It has been said that an accountant is like the Lord in the Bible, where it is written that "a thousand years are in His sight as yesterday," in the sense that every figure is equally important to him. What implications do you see in this observation for a company auditor?

34

Automation and the Future of Accounting

Arthur E. Carlson

THE VALUE of a business reporting system is closely related to its capacity to produce information needed by management. In this regard, it is helpful to distinguish between data and information.

Any collection of symbols or characters arranged in an orderly manner can be called data. However, only data from which meaning can be derived should be thought of as information.

The value of information is largely in its contribution to managerial decision-making. It increases with timeliness up to a point, but information can be made available to management too soon as well as too late.

From the NAA Bulletin, vol. XLV, no. 12 (August, 1964), pp. 46–48. Mr. Carlson is a Professor of Accounting at Washington University (St. Louis).

In an automated system, the point-of-sale or immediate record assumes much more importance than ever before. Information captured at the source in machine language can be reproduced as many times and in as many forms as management may desire without human recopying. The adoption of this "write-it-once" principle removes the need for journals as temporary storage devices.

If desired, debit and credit elements of journal entries can still be recorded on cards or tape and preserved in card or tape "libraries." "Library" information may be printed out in English language if management wishes to have access to a complete journal entry.

The ledger account will occupy the center of the stage in the modern accounting system. Posting will be completed by electronic transfers of dollar amounts from cards or tape to storage facilities connected to the computer. Each active account will be served by an assigned storage location. The most recent account balance will be developed automatically for any account by instructing the computer to add or subtract, whichever may be appropriate.

Numerical designations of active account locations (known as storage addresses) will be the equivalent of account numbers in a conventional chart of accounts. The accounts in these locations will not reflect individual transactions, because the account balances will be updated currently. Entries will be made by referring dollar amounts to proper storage addresses. Reference information, such as dates of transactions and coded business paper data, will be kept on tape or cards. Access to reference information of this sort will require printout of cards or tape on high-speed printing machines.

Microfilm will be widely used to preserve invoices, receipts, cancelled checks, and other memoranda. Large retail stores do this now, and it will spread to other areas. Also, equipment will be utilized to reproduce previously microfilmed punched-card information on new punched cards.

The treatment of adjustments will continue to be a periodic process. The closing process will consist of electronic transfers of revenues and expenses from temporary storage addresses to permanent storage addresses. Assets, liabilities and owner's equity account balances will occupy permanent storage locations. Revenue and expense account balances may be stored on cards or tape if permanent storage capacity is limited.

Trial balances will be prepared by printing out amounts from individual storage locations on tabulating machines or high-speed printers. Stored ledger information can be used to print out income statements, balance sheets and retained earnings statements. Coded alphabetical information will be used to print statement captions, account titles and amounts from storage. Captions and titles will also come from stored information.

Controlling accounts will be part of the stored general ledger. Subsidiary ledger accounts will be stored on cards or tape, because of the frequent updating and rearrangement that they require. By summing up card or tape entries, storing the result, and comparing this result with the stored balances of the related controlling account, subsidiary ledgers can be proved to their respective controlling accounts. If an inequality exists, it will be necessary to print out subsidiary ledger information for comparison with another print-out of related transaction information since the last proof.

A system may be completely redesigned, simplified, or merely mechanized. Complete redesign changes the entire structure of the system. Simplification removes limited amounts of unnecessary complexity. Mechanization merely changes the techniques of systems operation. In most cases requiring choice, structural design changes are apt to be more beneficial than mere technical changes.

Most systems design problems concern themselves with outputs wanted by management, inputs and files needed, and the necessary processing procedures to link input and output. Equipment selection requires consideration of the processing specifications of the system, the special requirements of the system, and the problems of installing and operating the equipment.

A major problem of obtaining data processing equipment is deciding on whether to rent or buy. The choice of a wise course of action is complicated by the variety of rental and purchase schemes offered by manufacturers.

The audit function also is in for some major changes as a result of automation. In the audit of the future, the computer and the auditor will be partners. There will never be any reason for the auditor to become subservient to non-human equipment, although he may become subservient to or even be replaced by another auditor who understands computers.

If internal reporting follows the principle of exceptions, there is no need to ask the computer for a complete listing of anything. Under these circumstances, any traditional auditing document is a special item with special costs.

Computer operating personnel balk at creating additional paperwork purely for purposes of audit. But certain concessions to management will need to be made in the next few years. Members of any management group who know next to nothing about a computer tend to react negatively. Therefore, a good system will need to defend itself by creating lookup records to help reconstruct past events and show how the computer acted and reacted.

Planning is a major function of automated accounting. Even though the planner is removed from operations, he can be quite sure that data processing operations will proceed according to his design. In a partly or completely manual system, complete acceptance of the planner's ideas usually is not obtained.

It is only natural that operators of partially or completely manual systems will interpret new ideas according to what they already know. Modifications of original systems designs may be produced quite accidentally in this manner, although such modifications also may be intentional. The planner is often disturbed by such changes, but they do tend to ensure that control will be spread over the entire operating group, and this is a desirable side-effect.

Control of an automated system tends to coincide with the planning and implementation of the system. This is quite different from a conventional system in which there are after-the-fact evaluation techniques. It is an involved, tedious task to develop an effective computer program of conventional methods. The conscientious planner is apt to resent after-the-fact requests for changes in a program that he has designed for the purpose of improving control. This sort of change will not be easy to make, and a "hindsight review" of internal control will become more difficult. Control problems should be reviewed carefully as soon as system planning starts.

Early thinking about auditing automated systems limited consideration of changes in auditing procedures to the influences of vastly increased speed and accuracy. There generally was failure to recognize the importance of organizational factors to the auditor's function. Machine decision-making was viewed as a simple series of "yes-no" comparisons. Complete honesty forces us to admit that much of what middle management calls "decision making" is just a complex network of "yes-no" decisions made in serial fashion. The fact that such a network is complicated tends to throw up a screen which easily is mistaken for judgment or analysis.

The primary purpose of training for automated accounting should be to increase the number of persons qualified to judge the output of such systems. Such training should not be undertaken simply to increase the number of qualified machine operators. An auditor trained in EDP can use the computer as a mechanized assistant to improve his auditing procedures and increase the size and descriptiveness of his samples.

The old saying that "a little bit of knowledge is a dangerous thing" is quite appropriate in terms of computer understanding. There is a great variety of physical pieces of computer equipment, and it is not easy to understand "hardware" utilization, the design of the related "software," and the proper use of "computerese" in communications.

Most automated accounting systems measurably reduce the amount of data necessary to make the system function. Since this is the case, requests for print-outs impose special demands on the system and will have to be properly scheduled in order to avoid delaying the regular work. Indirect methods of lookup for information will also have to be employed.

We have considered together just a few of the ways in which accounting practice will change in the near future. Many more ways could be mentioned. The next few years are truly promising ones for the accountant.

QUESTIONS

1. What is the distinction between data and information?

2. With automation, which accounting records will become less necessary? Why?

3. Under what circumstances could accounting information be made available too soon?

4. In an automated system, how will end-of-period adjustments be prepared? Trial balances? Financial statements? Subsidiary ledgers proved?

5. What are the effects of automation on control?

6. A professor of finance has stated that "with the advent of computers, accountants are rapidly becoming the dinosaurs of the business world." Do you agree? Why?

35

Future of the
Accounting Profession

David F. Linowes

GENERAL ENVIRONMENT. . . . Unquestionably we are in
a stage of great change, a turning point has been reached
in world history. This turning point is evidenced by two
signs . . . : international (trade and cultural) movements
and technological progress which so affect our changing
environment, at the same time are affecting and will continue to severely affect the accounting profession of the
future.

CHANGE NECESSARY. In its May 1964 issue, *Fortune*

From *The Accounting Review*, vol. XL, no. 1 (January, 1965), pp.
97–104. Reprinted by permission of the editor. Mr. Linowes is a
Partner of S. D. Leidesdorf & Co. He has been a Vice President of
the American Institute of Certified Public Accountants and Associate
Professor of Accounting in Southeastern University. EDITORS' NOTE:
Although this article focuses on the public accounting profession, it
seems applicable to all accountants and accounting generally.

Magazine said in effect: Today the human race is at the threshold of a new epoch in world history. The accelerating rate of change that man has achieved through science and technology has ushered in an era of unprecedented problems and opportunities. Fear of change holds danger for individual freedom. Fear of change holds danger for the democratic constitutional state. Fear of change holds danger for the business system.

The accounting profession today does not fear change. It welcomes it with optimism and deliberate enthusiasm.

Because of the developments of operations research and electronic data processing on the one hand, and of global business expansion on the other, all accounting mores are being challenged and attacked. Change—deep and basic change—is on its way.

PROFESSION'S RESPONSE TO CHANGE. Our profession's early approach to keep up with the developing changes in our environment during the past two decades was to attempt to relieve the problem by sponsoring and encouraging professional training courses—both indirectly through the various types of accounting schools, and directly by occasional technical programs of the American Institute of CPAs and various state societies.

When it was realized that this was hardly adequate, attempts were made to help force a higher level of education and preparation by increasing the educational requirements as a prerequisite to sit for the CPA exams, as well as to improve and make uniform the quality of the CPA examinations in all the states. By so doing it was felt that persons unqualified either by ability or by education would be screened out before entering the accounting profession.

Experience showed that society and technology were changing too rapidly, more was needed. Positive steps were then taken to upgrade and substantially revise the courses at universities; and to formalize and improve professional training programs for CPAs already in practice. The breeding grounds of CPAs were subjected to rigorous re-examination.

A couple years ago our profession realized that this was still inadequate. The headwaters of the streams of men entering the profession had to be reviewed. We began asking ourselves questions such as what background should a young man have in order to be able to successfully practice accountancy in this cosmic age. What kinds of abilities should he have? What subjects should he study in college? What common body of knowledge would best qualify a man to enter this dynamic profession? In an attempt to answer these questions, a Common Body of Knowledge Committee was established about a year ago. This committee is a research group jointly sponsored by the Carnegie Foundation and the AICPA. It is made up of 13 men— including CPA practitioners, business executives, bankers and educators. Dean Robert Roy, Dean of the Engineering Science School of Johns Hopkins University, not an accountant, is directing this committee and we are all looking forward to the committee's findings.*

LRO COMMITTEE. The inciting element in back of the more recent self-evaluating and self-advancing programs is a small group known as the Long Range Objectives Committee. To my knowledge, never before in the history of any profession has there ever been the kind of forward-looking, long range planning represented by the Long Range Objectives Committee of the AICPA. The accounting profession is doing today, what no other profession has ever attempted to do. We are charting our course over the next decade or more. We hope to help guide our own destiny, and not wait for destiny to mold us. In this effort we hope to apply to our profession a basic Aristotelian concept. As you know, Aristotle gave to the world the concept that we should view a thing in light of the best it can become—not from the standpoint of the position it may have come to by reason of the doings of the lowest effort.

Now how are we going about it?

About three years ago the Long Range Objectives Committee, which is made up of four members of the AICPA plus John Carey, its Executive Director, who is ex-officio member, undertook a series of conferences with consultants of many different callings. We interviewed two corporation executives, three bankers, a behavioral scientist, a public relations man, a corporate lawyer, an economist, a sociologist, a psychologist, three accounting educators, a dean of a graduate school, the Commissioner of Internal Revenue, the Chairman of the Securities and Exchange Commission and others.**

The object of our efforts is to try to predict where the profession

* EDITORS' NOTE: This report was scheduled to be released by the AICPA in the fall of 1966. It stresses the significance of communication skills, the continuing shift in emphasis from accounting that is essentially retrospective to accounting that is essentially prospective and the emergence in accounting of applications of some of the newer mathematical techniques and disciplines. The chapters dealing directly with the statements of the common body of knowledge concern the following subjects in order: Written and Oral Communications; Accounting; Economics, Finance and Law; Mathematics, Statistics, Probability; Marketing, Production, Personnel; and Behavioral Science.

** EDITORS' NOTE: The substance and conclusion of these studies appear in the book "The CPA plans for the future" by John L. Carey. This book was published by the AICPA in 1965.

of accounting will be in 1975. In so doing, it was inevitable that we should identify directions and movements which will substantially mold our profession in the period well beyond 1975, into the next generation of accountants.

ACCOUNTING DEFINED. One of the first things we asked ourselves is, what is "accounting"? In the past it has been described as the language of business. Definitions were all rather fuzzy, but essentially accounting has been understood to be that body of principles underlying the keeping and the explanation of *business* records.

Later the definition was expanded to cover all *financial* data, not just business records. More recently the definition has been enlarged and somewhat formalized, describing accounting as the measurement and communication of *financial* and *economic* data.

Now we find important leaders of academia equating accounting with the entire measurement concept. Some even suggest that consideration should be given for accounting to be established in a separate school of measurement, thereby divorcing accounting from the business environment. Men such as Dr. Paul Lazarsfeld, internationally renowned sociologist, and Dr. John Gardner, president of the Carnegie Foundation,* believe that there exists a bed of knowledge common to the accountant as distinct from that which is common to the businessman. The deeper one goes in accounting, the more he gets into basic measurement; and the deeper he goes into measurement, the farther out he reaches. The unusually capable, vital individuals in accounting must go in the direction of broad measurement. Qualified practitioners could be called upon to measure anything for which standards exist. They would cross disciplines in applying objective standards for evaluation.

This is exciting, and opens unlimited horizons for the coming generation of accountants.

ATTEST FUNCTION. The extension of the attest function in the future holds great promise for our profession, as well as for all society.

The independent opinion giving credibility to financial statements has made a major contribution towards facilitating accumulations of great quantities of capital for major business undertakings, and for the orderly conduct of the financial markets. Basically the independent opinion or so-called "certified statement" has been the primary expression of the attest function in the past. There have been others, but they have been incidental. For example, not too long

* EDITORS' NOTE: Dr. Gardner has since become Secretary of Health, Education and Welfare under President Johnson.

ago, a promotion man wanted to determine the odds of having a professional golfer hit a hole in one. To study the odds, he engaged a pro, two caddies, two cameramen, and a CPA. The job of the CPA was to count the strokes, and attest to the number. Incidentally, it came to 442 to 1. Another incidental application of the attest function, as we all know, is with the Academy Awards. Each year a CPA controls the ballots and presents the results of the Academy Awards voting —thereby lending credibility to the honesty of the selections, and secrecy of the results.

For the accounting profession as a whole in the future, however, these extensions of the attest function are not important. Not because we would not like to take part in such painstaking verifications, but because most of us cannot qualify as experts in golf, nor do we have the attractive physical features to make us TV idols.

There are several significant applications of the attest function which the future could very well demand.

LABOR-MANAGEMENT RELATIONS. The single greatest problem in our business economy today for which there does not appear to be any formula for solution is in the area of labor-management relations. As each union contract expires, in practically every industry there begins a round of talks, negotiations, demands, threats, and badgerings until finally new higher rates and terms are agreed upon. These new rates have no relationship to the productivity of labor, nor to the operating results of the business. This is so largely because labor does not believe the figures management presents; and management does not believe the statements, claims, and cost-of-living needs presented by the union. After each cycle of forced wage increases, our country goes off on another inflation cycle.

Labor basically claims it only seeks its share of increased productivity. Management basically indicates a willingness to pay out a portion of this increased productivity, if the business as a whole can continue to operate profitably by so doing.

Is there any reason why in the future, labor and management cannot agree on a formula for wage increases, tied into the increased productivity of labor, and the profitability of the business, all of which would be attested to by an independent certified public accountant? If all financial data and statistics admitted as bases for union negotiations were required to be examined and verified by a qualified CPA, much of the suspicion and distrust which now so frequently fills the conference room would be dispelled.

An extension of our attest function into this area alone could have a major impact on our society. To achieve this will require the dedicated efforts of capable, well-educated men who have imagination, resourcefulness, courage and patience. The rewards, however, will be great.

GOVERNMENT REPORTS. Our Federal, state and local governments produce mountains of statistical and financial data. World-wide decisions are frequently based on the statistics developed by the agencies of our Federal Government. Actions significantly affecting our personal daily lives in areas of education, welfare, sanitation, and safety are taken by our state and local governments on the basis of statistical reports, the accuracy of which is sometimes questionable. Here is another area in which it has been suggested for us to extend our attest function. The CPA could verify and give credibility to economic data in this area of government reports—these same reports which are the bases for major decisions affecting our personal lives.

INCOME TAX RETURNS. In the income tax area, the Federal Government has already begun to look into the practicality of having CPAs attest to tax returns they prepare, thereby relieving the Internal Revenue Service from auditing those returns. How desirable such an extension of the attest function might be is open to question. Nevertheless it was suggested by Commissioner Caplin of the Internal Revenue Service, and discussions have been undertaken with representatives of the American Institute.

PROSPECTIVE ACCOUNTING. Our profession has always identified itself with historical data—looking back. In more recent years, as an aspect of our management services function, prospective accounting services have been rather generally performed.

Now, there appears to have developed a need for someone qualified in accounting and budgetary matters to examine business projections and plans and to express an opinion. This aspect of verifying the fairness of presentation of prospective business plans could very well be an important constructive contribution to business management of the future.

MANAGEMENT PERFORMANCE. As accounting increasingly becomes recognized as the profession of measurement, we may expect society to look to us to extend our attest function to cover management performance. As quantitative standards continue to be developed which may be used to indicate the effectiveness of management, the CPA will be called upon to apply these standards to management's performance. We will become evaluators of management itself.

This pattern is already evident in some auditing practices followed abroad. And even in this country, a number of companies have begun adopting the procedure of having the CPA appear before the Audit Committee, with management executives excluded, for a frank discussion of overall company business affairs.

INTERNATIONAL AREA. One of the most far-reaching opportunities of the future is in the international field. In the past our profession developed by responding to demands made of it by outside influences. The industrial revolution required extensive costs and record keeping to control newly amassed capital and productive facilities. The income tax laws required exacting profit and loss computations. The Securities and Exchange Regulations required extensive refinements in record keeping to facilitate full disclosures. In each instance, we responded to the extent our clients requested. Now a new demand is being thrust upon us.

Business is becoming world oriented. Many businesses no longer think and plan in national terms, but in global terms. The word "multinational" has been coined to identify such companies. Their needs are for world-wide thinking. Their posture must transcend national habits, different languages, strange monies, and all the flesh colors: white, black, brown, red, yellow. Business must be flexible and adaptable to equatorial heat and Alaskan cold; high culture and savage tribes. Accounting usage and business practices throughout the world are anything but uniform. Standards vary greatly, currencies fluctuate, governments topple, yet business goes on.

Businessmen desperately need help in this international area. They need creditable financial statements, which are meaningful, timely, and comparable. They need to know about business practices in the foreign countries, about social mores, about government regulations and taxes, and they need to know it in language and terms they understand.

In this area they sorely require not only historical professional accounting help, but also planning guidance.

We as the profession which serves business have the responsibility to fill this global need, and some progress is being made. The AICPA has a Committee on International Relations studying the entire field. A number of larger accounting firms have set up International Departments. Broadly-educated, well-trained CPAs whose interests lie in international affairs may very well become the future statesmen of multinational business, being called upon to evaluate political, economic and social influences throughout the world.

ELECTRONIC DATA PROCESSING. Electronic data processing is

just beginning, yet its impact has been overpowering. The changes effected in the information system of business are so great, that we must actually experience them to believe them. A tabulation and verification job in our own office which required 3,125 hours, or about seventy-eight 40-hour weeks before EDP now takes 2¼ hours.

An RCA expert estimates that two minutes on a computer—using its full capacity today—equal 50 years of pencil work, based on a 40-hour week.

The internal information system in a business includes the recording, accumulation, classification, analysis and transmission of financial data. Traditionally the accountant has been an integral part of that system. With the advent of EDP, engineers, statisticians, and other scientists have also become essential to the overall functioning of the information system.

The person in charge of this system will be the most important man in an organization, next to the president.

Through this system will flow the projections of proposed alternative courses of action as well as current operating data. These projections will be communicated to the top executive for his final decision by the man in charge.

For the accountant to qualify as the man-in-charge here, he must have a general understanding of the statistical, and engineering aspects of computer operation. He must know what the computer can do and how it is programmed; as well as what needs of management may be furnished by this fantastic machine. As never before, the accountant must understand the client's organizational structure, its policies, and its objectives.

Especially in the EDP age the CPA must appreciate the need for effective communication. No amount of comprehensive data can serve an operational purpose unless it is expressed in meaningful terms and placed in the proper hands within an organization.

The need for guidance is so great in this fast-moving field, that CPAs in every level of public practice will increasingly be called upon to perform services related to the computerized internal information system.

PROFESSION INTERNALLY. All of what I have said thus far about our profession in the future relates it as an entity to business and society. That is, I have dealt with the external aspects of certified public accounting. But what about the profession internally? What does the LRO crystal ball indicate will be the nature of the CPA in 1975; what will the accounting firm be like; in what direction will our professional societies devote their major efforts; will educators be an integral part of our profession, or will they tend to sit on the periphery, as they have done all too frequently in the past?

MORE LEARNING. The CPA of 1975 and beyond will have to understand much broader and deeper concepts of business, of economics, of politics, of all society. He must recognize fully that learning is a lifetime effort, and that education does not end with the college degree or CPA certificate. The degree and certificate even today are only licenses to qualify one for further learning. To some extent such learning should be in specialized areas, such as operations research, electronic data processing, merger evaluations. To some extent such learning must provide for a personal continuing interest in literature, economics, politics, and other cultural areas. This emphasis on intellectual activity must include the important function of research in our own field.

RESEARCH AND EDUCATORS. To intelligently explore our constantly changing needs requires vital basic research not only of technical accounting subjects but of the profession itself. For this research we need people of high intellect and of academic inclination. Most often such qualifications are found in institutions of higher learning.

The academic world will be cultivated and made an integral part of the practicing accounting profession. Not in the sense that professors will serve on accounting staffs, or practicing CPAs will serve as part-time professors (although this is helpful), but in the sense that AICPA will take the initiative for establishing the mechanism so that a continuing dialogue will take place between researchers and standard setters on the one hand; and practitioners and standard appliers on the other. . . .

MORE EXECUTIVES, FEWER TECHNICIANS. It is obvious from my remarks that the CPA of the future must and will be a "learned" professional man, with executive capacity and training, and able to deal comfortably and effectively with well-rounded, highly educated future officers of industry.

But, what of the Indians? What of the accounting technicians, those who are now performing the routine, the mechanical, the repetitive detail? These are being replaced even today by the computer, the man-made brain. The day of full mechanization of all administrative operations is rapidly approaching. Accounting firms of the next decade will have many chiefs, and very few Indians, and most of those will be computers, not humans.

CONCLUSION. In conclusion what I have been trying to say is

that imagination and dynamism have seized our profession and its leaders. The spirit of renewal is alive. The cumulative effect of space age technology; world oneness; and social re-awakening has placed its mark indelibly on the direction and path of the accounting profession. . . .

QUESTIONS

1. The following is an actual accountant's report or opinion which appears in the annual report.

We have examined the balance sheet of Donaldson Company, Inc. as of July 31, 1965 and the related statements of income and retained earnings and changes in working capital for the year then ended. Our examination was made in accordance with generally accepted auditing standards, and accordingly included such tests of the accounting records and such other auditing procedures as we consider necessary in the circumstances.

In our opinion, the accompanying balance sheet and statement of income and retained earnings present fairly the financial statement of Donaldson, Inc. at July 31, 1965 and the results of its operations for the year then ended, in conformity with generally accepted accounting principles applied on a basis consistent with that of the preceding year. Further, it is our opinion that the accompanying statement of changes in working capital for the year ended July 31, 1965 presents fairly the information shown therein.

Ernst & Ernst

Minneapolis, Minnesota
September 29, 1965

    a To what have the accountants attested?
    b To what else do you think accountants should attest?
    c With reference to (b), explain how the accountant would be able to attest?